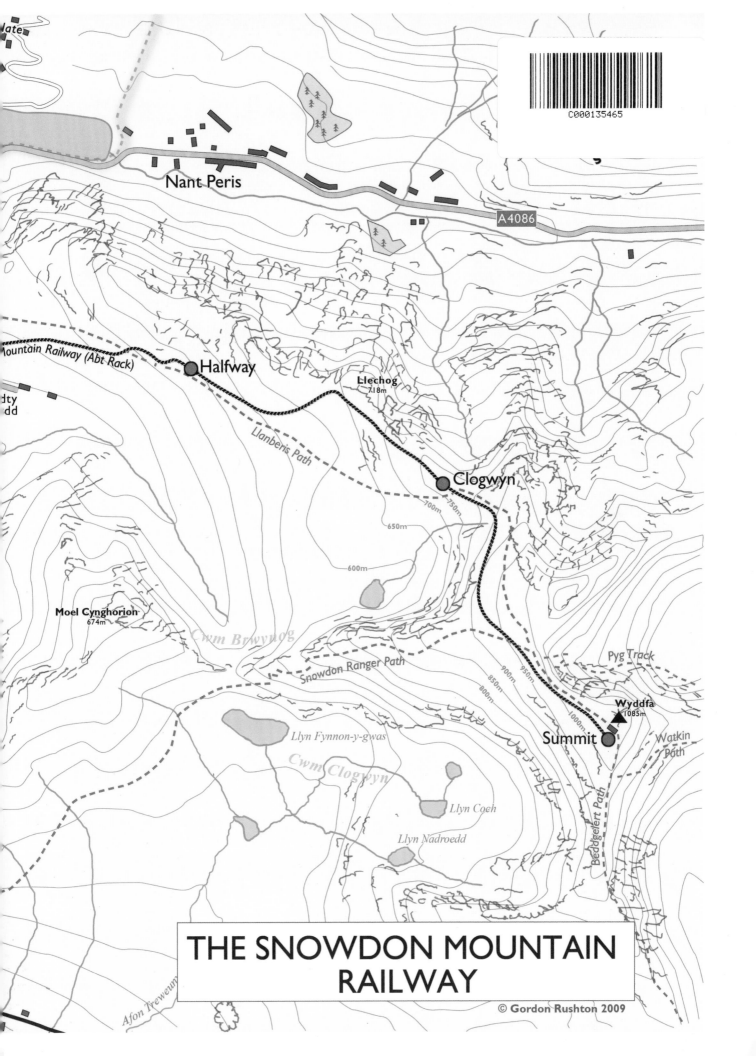

Nant Peris

A4086

Mountain Railway (Abt Rack) ●Halfway

Llechog
718m

Llanberis Path

dty
dd

●Clogwyn

700m 750m

650m

600m

Moel Cynghorion
674m

Cwm Brwynog

Snowdon Ranger Path

Pyg Track

900m
950m
850m
800m

Wyddfa
1085m

1000m

Summit ●

Watkin
Path

Llyn Fynnon-y-gwas

Cwm Clogwyn

Beddgelert Path

Llyn Coch

Llyn Nadroedd

Afon Treweum

THE SNOWDON MOUNTAIN
RAILWAY

THE SNOWDON
MOUNTAIN RAILWAY

THE SNOWDON MOUNTAIN RAILWAY

PETER JOHNSON

PEN & SWORD
TRANSPORT

AN IMPRINT OF PEN & SWORD BOOKS LTD.
YORKSHIRE – PHILADELPHIA

Front cover: No 6 *Padarn* with the heritage steam service above Clogwyn on 6 June 2019. (Mike Spencer)

Back cover:
Top: No 3 *Wyddfa* at Llanberis soon after delivery in 1895. (Photochrom)
Bottom: No 14, one of the railway's ulta-modern hybrid locomotives on test in 2020. (SMR)

Half-title page: Passengers poses for a photograph as they wait for their train to leave Llanberis.

Title page: The grandeur of Snowdon - No 2 *Enid* propels the first heritage carriage towards the summit. (Mike Spencer)

First published in Great Britain in 2021 by
Pen and Sword Transport
An imprint of
Pen & Sword Books Ltd.
Yorkshire - Philadelphia

Copyright © Peter Johnson, 2021

ISBN 978 1 52677 609 9

A CIP catalogue record for this book is available from the British Library.

Typeset in Palatino 11/13 by SJmagic DESIGN SERVICES, India.

Printed and bound by Printworks Global Ltd, London/Hong Kong.

Pen & Sword Books Ltd incorporates the imprints of Pen & Sword Books Archaeology, Atlas, Aviation, Battleground, Discovery, Family History, History, Maritime, Military, Naval, Politics, Railways, Select, Transport, True Crime, Fiction, Frontline Books, Leo Cooper, Praetorian Press, Seaforth Publishing, Wharncliffe and White Owl.

For a complete list of Pen & Sword titles please contact

PEN & SWORD BOOKS LIMITED
47 Church Street, Barnsley, South Yorkshire, S70 2AS, England
E-mail: enquiries@pen-and-sword.co.uk
Website: www.pen-and-sword.co.uk

or

PEN AND SWORD BOOKS
1950 Lawrence Rd, Havertown, PA 19083, USA
E-mail: Uspen-and-sword@casematepublishers.com
Website: www.penandswordbooks.com

CONTENTS

ACKNOWLEDGEMENTS

Writing about the Snowdon Mountain Railway since the 1980s, I have been assisted by several people who had different roles in running the railway. Ninian Rhys Davies, company chairman and director, whose father, Evan Robert Davies, had been one of the trio that took over the railway in 1921, and his daughter Gillian Davies, who had been a director for several years. The Davies family retained its connection as shareholders until 1998.

David Edward Aubrey Crowe, son of director Norman Ronald Aubrey Crowe who had worked for E.R. Davies; he had been a shareholder on his own account thanks to a bequest from Charlotte Pauline Macinnes, widow of Henry Jack Macinnes, originally Henry Joseph Jack, one of E.R. Davies's friends.

Nigel Ross, company chairman, who took control of the company in 1984 and arranged the financing required to fund the modernisation of the railway with diesel locomotives.

Managers were Derek Rogerson, Tony Hopkins, Alan Kendall and senior managers were Vince Hughes and Mike Robertshaw.

Former employees were Nigel Day and Tony Ellis. Tony's father and grandfather had both worked for the railway.

Clayton Equipment's managing director, Clive Hannaford, provided information about the company's SMR hybrid locomotives and Mark Hambly shared his notes on them.

Paul Abell and family analysed the Snaefell Mountain Railway photograph, and the railway's marketing manager, Carrie Probin, dealt with my queries.

Photographs were kindly made available by Chris Parry, Ralph Berry, Mike Spencer and Dave Waldren (Cutting Edge Images). Photographers are named where known. Photographs not credited were either taken by me or are from my collection. A few photographs have been included for their historic interest despite being technically imperfect.

Many thanks, once again, to Gordon Rushton for creating the plan used on the front endpaper.

Public collections consulted were the Parliamentary Archives, the National Archives, Gwynedd Archives, the Hunslet Archive (Statfold Barn Railway), the City of London Corporation's Guildhall Library, Companies House and the University of Leicester's David Wilson Library.

I have also made use of the company's minute books (1894-1959, unfortunately the volume covering the years 1925-40 is missing) and a small collection of papers dealing with the Cadogan takeover that came to light after my previous book on the railway (*An Illustrated History of the Snowdon Mountain Railway*; Oxford Publishing Co, 2010) had gone to press.

The timeline was constructed by combining the minutes and other historical documents with newspaper reports found at Welsh Newspapers Online (newspapers. library.wales), the British Newspaper Archive (britishnewspaperarchive.co.uk), the digital archives of *The Times* and the *Manchester Guardian*, and my reports for *Railway World* (1991-5) and *Steam Railway* (1995-2019) magazines. Genealogical information was obtained from ancestry. co.uk, findmypast.co.uk and the General Register Office.

The information contained in Appendix 8 and Appendix 9 was obtained by making Freedom of Information requests of the Office of Rail and Road and the

Rail Accident Investigation Board. The information contained in Appendix 10 was extracted from the Snowdonia National Park Authority planning department's website.

Some material was first published in the earlier book. The availability of more historical material and many more photographs have revealed many insights into the railway's history than could have been envisaged ten years ago.

Any opinions are mine and not those of the Snowdon Mountain Railway. I am, of course, responsible for any errors.

Peter Johnson
Leicester
April 2021

Crown copyright is reserved for illustrations sourced from the National Archives and the Ordnance Survey.

Welsh Place Names
In the eighteenth and nineteenth centuries many Welsh places frequented by English tourists had their names anglicised. In the 1970s the Welsh forms were restored although the archaic forms are used here where appropriate. For clarification, the places concerned here are: Carnarvon / Caernarvon = Caernarfon; Portmadoc = Porthmadog; Quellyn = Cwellyn.

No 8 with its cab-roof oil tank and carriage No 6 approach Clogwyn, the terraces and tips of the Dinorwic slate quarries dominating the background. 6 July 1975.

INTRODUCTION

Set in north-west Wales, Snowdon is a mountain like no other in the British Isles. It is not the highest, Ben Nevis and other Scottish peaks are higher, but it is the only one with a rack railway and a visitor centre on its summit.

The mountain, known for its snow covering in winter, which gave rise to its name, was created from Ordovician rocks and was once covered by an ancient sea. Granite and slate brought industrial activity to the area.

Most of the land between the north face of the mountain and the Menai Strait at Bangor was part of the Assheton-Smith family's Vaynol estate, which gave it considerable control or influence over developments. The estate included the Dinorwic slate quarries just outside Llanberis, the village growing as the quarries expanded. Both the slate and tourists were essential to the economic well-being of the locality.

The opening of the Rigibahn in Switzerland in 1871 appears to have triggered the first attempts to promote a railway to Snowdon's summit, but by 1875 Vaynol opposition had seen off two Bills deposited in Parliament to obtain powers.

Twenty years later the estate's response to the idea of a railway on the mountain was very different. Over the intervening years there had been a big increase in the number of visitors to Llanberis and Snowdon, many of them conveyed from the mill towns of the English north west by train. Since 1881, the North Wales Narrow Gauge Railways, running from Dinas, three miles from Carnarvon, to Rhyd Ddu, on the far side of Snowdon, had taken a little of this market, but not enough to cause anyone sleepless nights.

But when the NWNGR renamed its terminal station Snowdon in 1893, and instantly attracted hundreds of passengers who would previously have reached the mountain via Llanberis, the effect on the village's economy was dramatic, enough to persuade the Vaynol estate that a railway on the mountain would safeguard its tenants' wellbeing.

A company was formed, and despite opposition from the newly formed National Trust for the Preservation of Sites of Historical Interest and Natural Beauty, in December 1894 the first sod of the Snowdon Mountain Tramroad was dug. The directors and engineers had looked to Switzerland for inspiration, adopting the Abt rack design, embracing a metric (800mm / 2ft 7½in) track gauge and ordering equipment from Swiss makers.

However, the effort that went into building and equipping the railway was overshadowed by the accidents and the tragic death of a passenger that occurred on the first day in April 1896. The setback was overcome, and after a year the railway was reopened, to become an essential part of Snowdon, of Llanberis, of Wales.

The summit visitor centre originally comprised a range of timber huts that provided refreshments and basic overnight accommodation. The railway company took powers to own and run hotels too, starting with the Royal Victoria in Llanberis and one of the summit outlets. Its stated ambition to provide 'proper' facilities at the summit was not fulfilled until the 1930s, with the construction of a building designed by Clough Williams-Ellis. No longer owned by the railway but managed by it, it was replaced by the award-winning *Hafod Eryri* in 2009.

Although the railway's traditional steam locomotives still play a major role in its operations, it has been an early adopter of new technology, in the form of wind turbines and solar panels to power the passing loops, and in 2019 it placed an order for advanced hybrid diesel-electric locomotives to replace the diesel locomotives acquired in the 1980s.

These few words encapsulate the Snowdon Mountain Railway's story. Research in many sources combine to explain how it developed and became one of Wales's major tourist attractions. Sadly, the book has to end with an account of the effect of the Covid 19 virus on its 2020 traffic.

The grandeur of Snowdon. On 13 September 2019 a train arrives at the summit with Cwellyn visible on the left and the Menai Strait and Anglesey in the distance. (Chris Parry)

CHAPTER 1

SETTING THE SCENE

In January 2020, the Welsh Government reported that in 2018 Snowdon was the third most popular tourist attraction in Wales, attracting 650,000 walking visits and 140,000 on the Snowdon Mountain Railway.

Set in the heart of Gwynedd, originally Carnarvonshire, in north-west Wales, the mountain is 3,560 feet (1,085 metres) above sea level, the highest in Wales. In Welsh it is Yr Wyddfa or Eryri, the former meaning tomb or monument in reference to a mythological tomb, and the latter, Snowdonia, a reference to the snow that caps the peak in winter.

There are six main paths to the summit, the easiest being from Llanberis, a village on the northern flank that developed to serve the nearby Dinorwic slate quarries, 348 feet above sea level. In the early nineteenth century the village had a population of fewer than 500. It is located at the south-eastern end of Llyn Padarn, or Llanberis Lake, a natural feature some two miles long.

Some 250 years ago, visitors were rarely seen in the area, which was considered to be remote. The development of tourism is usually attributed to Thomas Pennant, whose account of his visit was published in 1781. Access was improved with the construction of Thomas Telford's Holyhead road in 1815 and the opening of the railway from England to Bangor in 1848 and Carnarvon in 1852.

Summit of Snowden, Caernarvonshire.

An imaginative early 19th Century engraving of Snowdon, with a good procession of visitors heading for the summit. (Newman & Company)

Llanberis Village from Nor[th]

46735.

7050 SNOWDON. C.N & CO.

Llanberis looking west at the turn of the 20th Century. (James Valentine)

Looking east along Llanberis Lake, Llyn Padarn. G.W.D. Assheton-Smith's private 4ft gauge railway ran along the far shore. The Gilfach Ddu quarry workshop is visible at the head of the lake. (Carl Norman & Co)

Accommodating visitors and guiding them to the summit, either on foot or on horseback, became occupations that also contributed to the village's prosperity, alongside the work in the quarries.

Most of the land between the north face of Snowdon and the Menai Strait at Bangor, 36,000 acres at the end of the nineteenth century, was part of the Assheton-Smith family's Faenol, Vaynol in English, estate, which gave it considerable control or influence over developments. Dating from

the sixteenth century, since 1859 the estate had been owned by George William Duff Assheton-Smith. Born George William Duff in 1848, he had changed his name when he inherited on the death of an aunt.

In Llanberis the estate owned 9,100 acres of the parish's 10,400 acres. By the time of the 1891 census the village's population was 2,818, having peaked at 3,033 in 1881, most of the growth undoubtedly due to expansion at the Dinorwic slate quarries, which not only made the family

Vaynol Hall from S.E., Port Dinorwic

George William Duff Assheton-Smith

extraordinarily rich but contributed to the expansion of the village to house the quarrymen and to provide accommodation for visitors.

Sir Richard Moon, chairman of the London & North Western Railway, is often attributed with inspiring attempts to make a railway on Snowdon, Frank Oswell, the resident engineer in 1895/6, claiming that he proposed the idea during the speeches made after the lunch held in Llanberis to commemorate the opening of the Carnarvon & Llanberis Railway in 1869.

The lunch was held at the Royal Victoria Hotel on 5 July 1870, the day that the town line through Carnarvon was opened, the branch having previously operated in isolation from a temporary station in Carnarvon. However, according to the

Vaynol, the Assheton-Smith family home, located close to the banks of the Menai straits. G.W.D. Assheton-Smith kept a menagerie that included bears, kangaroos, monkeys, llamas, angora goats, and exotic birds and permitted visits from Sunday schools and the like. (James Valentine)

This 1886-dated photograph hints at the enormity of the Dinorwic slate quarries and shows slate waste tipped into the upper lake, Llyn Peris. Tipping slate waste into Llyn Padarn at Glynrhonwy was said to be one of the reasons that tourism declined in Llanberis in the 1890s. A pumped storage power station was opened in the mountain here in 1984. (James Valentine)

The terminus of the Carnarvon & Llanberis Railway, a branch of the LNWR opened in 1869. Beyond the station, to the right, are the Royal Victoria Hotel, the Snowdon Mountain Railway's station buildings and Ty Clŵb, the building that pre-dates the railway and used as offices. (Pictorial Stationery Company)

VICTORIA HOTEL, LLANBERIS, IN THE OLD COACHING DAYS.

verbatim report of the event published in the *Carnarvon & Denbigh Herald* on 9 July, although Sir Richard chaired the affair and proposed toasts to the Queen and the Houses of Parliament, neither he nor any other speaker mentioned Snowdon.

Before any railway could be built there the approval of the Vaynol estate would be required, as it owned the requisite land. Nevertheless, Bills were deposited in Parliament in 1871 and 1874 without its approval, and it was not forthcoming. The promoters of both schemes were probably inspired by the opening of the Swiss Rigi rack line in May 1871 which, by 1874 was demonstrably making good profits.

Both schemes were entitled The Snowdon Railway, the first being described as 'a railway four miles one furlong six chains or thereabouts in length commencing … in

Llanberis … and terminating … near the crossing of the roadway from Llanberis to the summit of Snowdon at its crossing over the parish boundary between the parishes of Llanberis and Bettws Garmon.' Its gauge was unspecified. The £20,837 16s construction estimate was signed by Eugene Buclin on 27 December 1871. The capital was to be £30,000, the promoters John McMillan and John Wilkinson. Just who they, or Buclin, were is unknown. Their Bill passed standing orders on 9 February 1872, was read for the first time on 13 February and for the second time a week later, but on 14 March they informed the Parliamentary authorities that they did not wish to proceed.

The second Bill was deposited in December 1874. *The Times* (30 December 1874) said that it was being promoted by unnamed

An impression of the Royal Victoria Hotel when first opened in 1832. It was built by Thomas Assheton-Smith to take advantage of a tourist boom anticipated after the track over the Llanberis pass from Nant Peris to Pen y Gwyryd, and thence to Capel Curig, had been made fit for wheeled vehicles in 1831.

Using Niklaus Riggenbach's rack system, the Rigibahn was an immediate success when it was opened in 1871, inspiring the first attempts to build a railway to the summit of Snowdon. Seen here on 14 August 1876, its first locomotives were vertical boiler designs.

The deposited plan for the 1871 Snowdon Railway proposal. (Parliamentary Archives)

capitalists because of the immediate financial success that followed the opening of the Rigibahn. The route was similar to the 1871 proposal, the Parliamentary notice saying that it terminated near a spring called Fynnon Dwfr Oer, about 900 yards from the public house at the summit, a point above the present Clogwyn station. Again, the gauge was unspecified, but the Bill was withdrawn on 29 January 1875.

Another scheme was probably little more than a desktop exercise. In 1896 John Sylvester Hughes, the Festiniog Railway's general manager, claimed, in the *North Wales Chronicle* (17 April), that circa 1880 he and Charles Easton Spooner, then the FR's secretary and engineer, had planned a route from what was to be the North Wales Narrow Gauge Railway's Rhyd Ddu terminus to Llanberis via the summit. He said that afterwards he had also drawn up schemes for railways to the summits of Snaefell, on the Isle of Man, Skiddaw, Cumberland, and Ben Lomond, Scotland,

The deposited plan for the 1874 Snowdon Railway proposal. (Parliamentary Archives)

but that the landowners would not agree and that 'as such lines could not be put on the same footing as to public utility or necessity like railways in general, an Act of Parliament with compulsory powers could not be got.'

This last point would probably have seen off the 1870s schemes even without Assheton-Smith's objection. It was another 100 years before railways, and their role in the development of tourism, were deemed to be in the public interest.

Much speculation accompanied the news in July 1889 that the railway magnate Sir Edward Watkin had bought the 1,500-acre Hafod y Llan estate on the Beddgelert side of Snowdon at auction for £5,750. With the estate including land extending to the summit, newspapers were quick to suggest, erroneously as it turned out, that he would be sure to build a railway there. They were not deterred from the notion when in 1893 Watkin acquired the adjacent Fridd estate, which included Rhyd Ddu and its North Wales Narrow Gauge Railways terminus in its 500 acres.

Watkin himself said that he intended to offer a site at the summit to the Royal Observatory for an observatory like the one on Ben Nevis (1883-1904) and to improve the track to the summit (*Flintshire Observer*, 18 July 1889). The eponymous Watkin Path adapted a former miners' track to create an eight-mile walk, said to be the toughest of the summit routes but with the best views. In September 1892 Watkin's friend, the prime minister W.E. Gladstone, visited to inaugurate it.

Attracting large crowds wherever he stopped, Gladstone's route to Beddgelert included travelling on the North Wales Narrow Gauge Railways' line between Dinas and Rhyd Ddu. It might be no coincidence that in 1893 Rhyd Ddu station, already promoted as 'closest to the summit of Snowdon' was renamed Snowdon, a gesture that immediately led to a big increase in passenger numbers on the NWNGR and a serious loss of business for the hotels, guest houses, catering establishments and guides in Llanberis. *Railway News* (22 December 1894) also attributed both the tipping of slate waste from Glynrhonwy into the lake and Watkin's path to the decline. Nothing came of the observatory proposal.

When Assheton-Smith's agent, Captain Neil Patrick Stewart, attended a meeting

906. SNOWDON AND WATERFALL FROM WATKIN PATH (ABRAHAMS' SERIES)

Snowdon seen from the lower section of Watkin's path. On the left is the formation of the South Snowdon slate quarry incline. (G.P. Abraham)

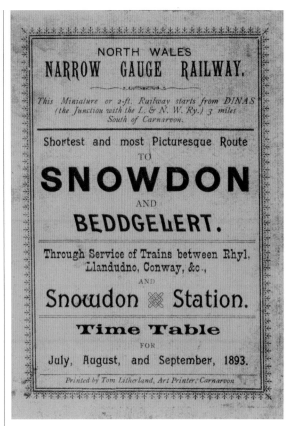

Sir Douglas Fox

of the village's 'improvement committee' during the first half of 1894, and told villagers that Assheton-Smith was minded to support the railway proposal, the notion was greeted with enthusiasm and a resolution offering support was immediately passed.

Events moved quickly. On 2 June 1894 the *North Wales Chronicle* was able to report that a party of three surveyors had made a survey for an electric railway between the LNWR station and the summit. Led by Frank Oswell, they were employed by Douglas Fox & Partners. Sir Douglas had received his knighthood in 1886, in recognition of his work on the Mersey Railway between Liverpool and Birkenhead and its tunnel under the river. Stewart must have been very persuasive, for at this stage no company existed and there were no funds from which to pay the engineers.

News of the railway proposal reached the metropolis before the end of the month, a Llanberis visitor writing to the *Daily News* (quoted in the *Carnarvon & Denbigh Herald*)

Francis Fox

to complain that it was 'widely reported' that within twelve months a railway would be built to the summit and a large hotel erected. As, he wrote, the originator of the scheme is said to be also the proprietor of the land there will be no need for an Act of Parliament, so that there seems but little chance of preventing the disfigurement of the most beautiful and grandest of all the Welsh mountains. But, perhaps if lovers of nature would make their voice heard the scheme might yet be reconsidered, and the monarch of the Cambrian Hills saved from the vandalism of the contractor.

This prompted Canon Hardwicke Drummond Rawnsley (1851-1920), the secretary of the newly formed National Trust for the Preservation of Sites of Historical Interest and National Beauty, to go into battle, writing to Stewart to ask if there was any truth in the rumours, claiming that 'a large number of people in all parts of the United Kingdom are alarmed ... They fear that if once the interest of the railway engineer or hotel proprietor are allowed on such a mountain as Snowdon to outweigh the best interests of the lovers of our native land undisfigured and undestroyed there will be an end to all real enjoyment of mountain scenery throughout the country. The deplorable example set on Snowdon will touch every mountain height…' What was acceptable in Italy and Switzerland, where the heat of the plains and valleys encouraged development in the mountains, 'would seem to be hardly necessary or practicable in our own climate.'

Stewart replied that although a line had been surveyed, he could not say 'to a certainty' that it would be built and pointed out that Assheton-Smith was not promoting the scheme but was merely granting facilities to others. He continued: 'But, assuming that a railway is made, I do not see that this need deprive mountain climbers of their climb. They can have their climb all the same, if they prefer it to be being whisked to the summit by steam or electricity. Don't you think on reflection, however, that the view you take of the matter is rather selfish? Why should Mr Assheton-Smith

be debarred from promoting the interests and prosperity of the people amongst whom he dwells? Why should Snowdon be reserved exclusively for the enjoyment of mountain climbers? Why should they have the entire monopoly of the mountain? Are there not thousands and tens of thousands of people, some too young and some too old and others who from various causes find themselves unable to make the ascent who would like to inhale the exhilarating air of the mountain and from the highest summit in England or Wales look down on the glorious panorama that lies beneath? Is not the greatest happiness of the greatest number the true end to be achieved? And is not he who lends a hand in this direction a benefactor of this country?'

On 23 October, Rawnsley acknowledged that Stewart's reply was courteous before attacking Assheton-Smith for agreeing 'to this objectionable scheme of vulgarising one of our grandest natural possessions.' He was still hoping that Assheton-Smith would see that 'Snowdon, unvulgarised and uncommercialised, is, after all, the best investment for "a declining Llanberis," and may believe that it is no selfish spirit but a real love of our country and a real belief in the growth of the appreciation of nature among the people that would urge him at the eleventh hour to refuse to others the "reasonable facilities" to which he is really opposed and of which he has refused to avail himself' before concluding: 'It seems to me, though, of course, it is only my opinion, that anyone who will deprive the people of the chief joy of such an ascent by taking away all the association with mountain solitude, as will be done the moment a railway and its accompaniments are imported to the scene, is directly taking away the greatest happiness of the greatest number for the sake of the profit to the few, and he who lends a hand in this direction can surely in no sense claim to be a benefactor of his country.'

To which Stewart replied (1 November) 'I am glad you acknowledge my letter to have been a courteous one, and regret to discover so little of that quality in yours. When you find yourself defeated in argument you indulge in sentiment, and I can only regard your epistles as the sulky, sentimental dribble (canonised) of a dreamer and faddist. I must ask you not to trouble me with further communications.'

In fact, Rawnsley had already gone over Stewart's head by writing to Assheton-Smith on 23 October: 'If it could be shown you that the preponderant sense of the nation were against such innovation, you would take firm steps to prevent so sacred an inheritance as Snowdon being thus robbed of its chief charm for future generations, and vulgarised for ever.' Suggesting that developments on Snowdon would set a precedent for other mountains in the UK, he went on to appeal to Assheton-Smith's sense of patriotism, concluding: 'It is in very few places in our crowded country that man can be alone with nature, and with their God – and Snowdon is one of them. To rob Snowdon, so easily accessible as it is both by night and by day, of its grand natural solitude and super eminent charm will be to inflict a loss upon the whole world.'

Assheton-Smith answered: 'I regret to say that I cannot take the same view of the matter as your association appears to do. You are right in saying that I was in former years opposed to the scheme; but times have changed, and if in many ways one does not advance with them, one is left alone. In trying to direct the tourists to Llanberis, and making things easy for them, I am consulting the interest of the estate and the neighbourhood in which I live, and I cannot recognise any outside interference in the matter.'

Ratcheting up the pressure, Rawnsley responded on 27 October: 'I felt from what I had heard that you had at last, in your kindness, given way to certain local representations, and that probably in heart you were opposed as ever to the scheme. Knowing that many of my fellow-countrymen, from no selfish spirit, are strongly opposed to the introduction into our land of the Swiss mountain-railway craze, with its utter destruction of one of the chief charms of mountain scenery for all future time, and feeling that the interest in preserving Snowdon from such harm was more than local, I venture to approach you. I hope you will have no objection to our correspondence being made public.'

Not satisfied with the answers he had received, Rawnsley put part of this fine example of Victorian gentlemen politely sniping at each other in the public domain by sending his correspondence with Assheton-Smith to *The Times*, which published it in full on 6 November. In his covering letter Rawnsley concluded by claiming that there was no need for the railway. The mountain was already accessible to all but the infirm, and the 'little refreshment house on the summit, with its four beds probably satisfies the needs of those who wish to see the sun rise.' He agreed that the railway would be good for Llanberis but at the expense of the existing guides and the other villages used to make the ascent. They – he cited Beddgelert and Capel Curig – might then promote their own railways to the summit. Swiss mountain railways demonstrated that there would be no cheap fares, so the railway would only benefit the 'well to do'. As the tourist season was so short the only way that the railway could cover its operating costs would be by exploiting the mountain for mineral traffic. 'Those who remember what Llanberis was before the quarries existed, are naturally not anxious to see the Llanberis experiment repeated.'

His greatest objection, however, remained what he called the '"commercialising" of scenery'. 'Snowdon unrailwayed, unvulgarised, and unexploited,' he said, 'is a better investment for Wales, for Llanberis ... than Snowdon turned into a mixture of tea-garden and switchback.' 'The love of natural scenery –' he continued, 'hardly more than a century old in Great Britain – is working gradually downward into the mass of the people; and the inevitable crowding into the cities, with all the accompaniment of train and tram, as inevitably makes men desire more and more something that is without these accompaniments for their rest and enjoyment.' He closed by referring to the Lake District, where 'within the past few years the claims of natural scenery have been held by Parliament to be superior to the claims of the railway promoter's pocket.'

What he did not say, but what he surely meant, was that the railway would attract the working classes and detract from the solitary pleasure enjoyed by professional and/or moneyed people like himself, although there is no evidence that he had ever visited the mountain himself. The *Liverpool Mercury* (8 November) said that excursionists would visit Llanberis and Snowdon regardless of whether the railway was built or not and it was for the Welsh to decide which type they preferred.

Stewart's final shot on Vaynol's behalf was published in *The Times* on 9 November where he pointed out that Rawnsley had also been in correspondence with him and had only released half of the correspondence with the estate, saying, 'The rev gentleman considered it necessary to supplement the letters by a lengthy disquisition setting forth his own particular views. I refrain from following his lead in this respect, and content myself with merely supplying you with copies of the correspondence, and leave it to your readers to form their own conclusions.'

In his covering letter he disputed Rawnsley's claim that if Llanberis, with the railway, became more prosperous, it would be at the expense of Capel Curig and Beddgelert, predicting that half of the

A guide with his pony and client en route to the summit. (Francis Bedford)

railway's passengers would only travel one-way, descending to one of those places. In a postscript he added that Rawnsley was ill-informed about the mountain, saying that it was not uncommon for 500 people to ascend in a day and that on one day earlier in the year more than 1,000 had reached the summit.

The exchange was repeated in other newspapers. In *The Times* it attracted support for the railway proposal from Robert St John Corbet of Shrewsbury, saying, 'only one side of the giant hill would be disfigured' and 'a cultured man like Canon Rawnsley ... need [not] fear anything from the multiplication of excursionists, male and female, learned and ignorant, serious and frivolous.'

The *Manchester Guardian*'s Welsh correspondent (13 November 1894) was critical of the railway, saying, 'If Welshmen have a spark of genuine patriotism in them they will rise as one man against this "desecration" as it may well be called, of the grandest natural feature of their country... I shall be much disappointed if Welshmen will allow a commercial enterprise to ruin the charms of the most glorious of all their mountains,' which prompted Llanberis GP W.O. Lloyd Williams (15 November) to defend the averagely-fit: 'It is absurd to say, as Canon Rawnsley does, that none but the absolutely infirm need fear the ascent of Snowdon; the journey up and down is very exhausting except to the strong and healthy, and most of those who cannot walk are either unfit or too timid to ride.' Suggesting that the objection was to the working classes, he wrote that they were sometimes tempted by cheap fares to enjoy a day in the fresh mountain air but his limited experience of mountain railways' fares did not encourage him 'to expect much of that class of traffic'.

A few days later the editor of the *North Wales Chronicle* (17 November) added, 'The action of Mr Assheton-Smith in granting facilities ... has called forth the indignant protest of the secretary ... and the usual aesthetic persons always ready to join a newspaper correspondence, which may serve to exhibit their "superiority"... the secretary had all the facts before him when he first lifted up his voice against the so-called desecration of Snowdon, but those facts seemed to have no effect whatever upon the reverend gentleman, whose sense of beauty is apparently out of all proportion to what ordinary folks would call common sense. It is always an easy matter to pose as a champion of the preservation of natural beauty, but the fact that the sympathy of unthinking people is enlisted with ease should be a caution to plain men to be quite sure that there is really a good case before any question of desecration or vandalism is publicly raised. We venture to think that if Canon Rawnsley had tempered his platitudes with a little respect for common sense and a regard for facts, he would not have failed to appreciate the kindness which prompted Mr Assheton-Smith and his advisers to grant facilities for the construction of the proposed Snowdon Railway ... Had Mr Assheton-Smith turned a deaf ear to the petitions of his people, the radical and socialist press, which is now filled with shrieking denunciations of the desecration of Snowdon, would not have ceased from holding up to obloquy the landlord who preferred his own sentimental fancy to the prosperity of the thousands who inhabit Llanberis. The people who live in the Snowdon district have no need to be told that it is no unusual sight in summer to see long trains crowded with tourists going in the direction of Snowdon, but it is equally well known that, by a clever device of the promoters of the narrow gauge railway, the stream of visitors has been almost entirely diverted from Llanberis. The re-christening of the Rhyd Ddu terminus and calling it Snowdon attracts thousands of tourists annually, with loss to the lodging house keepers, hotel keepers, and the general population of Llanberis. As Captain Stewart pointed out ... it is absurd folly to speak of the solitudes of Snowdon during the summer months, and it is equally silly to describe the people who make the ascent as 'bun and whisky' tourists. As a matter of fact the crowds that visit Snowdon are ordinary and decent people ... It is therefore under a sense of what he owes to the people of Llanberis, Mr Assheton Smith withdraws his opposition to the scheme, from which he derives no benefit whatever.'

Naturally the editor of a North Wales newspaper was not going to criticise the Vaynol estate. A council member of the National Society for Checking the Abuses of Public Advertising (*The Times* 19 November) took a different stance, saying that the real issue was not with the railway itself but with 'the perfectly gratuitous disfigurements which it is generally allowed to bring in its train.' 'Let, then, 'he continued, 'those who would if they could keep Snowdon as it is reserve some part of their energy for securing that the intrusion of the locomotive shall do the least possible harm to the amenities. They can, if they choose to concentrate their energies, make it a condition that neither the stations nor the line shall be used for puffing disfigurements; that the buildings and all else shall be modest, and not unnecessarily out of keeping with the scene… There is really no reason why places where meat and drink are dispensed should cause offence. I admit that they generally do, but that is because people take it for granted that they must. But, if need were, I could mention instances where much-frequented hostelries have been not merely useful, but perfectly harmless, additions to fine scenery.' The society, which sounds like a very modern concept, had been formed in 1893 and played a part in securing the 1907 Advertisements Regulation Act; the designer and socialist William Morris was a member.

The president of the Board of Trade, James Bryce MP, addressing members of the recently-formed Norwegian Club in London on 11 December, declared that he hoped that access to Norwegian mountains would not be carried out as in Switzerland, by means of railways, and wished that he had the power to 'check the attempt to make a railway to the top of Snowdon'. As the railway would be on private land, he was powerless to act against it. Switzerland, he added, 'was a general resort of the holiday maker, but nobody went to Norway except those who were thoroughly capable of appreciating the country.'

During the autumn of 1894 two companies were registered. The first was The Hotels & Railway Company of North Wales Ltd, registered on 20 September. With a capital of £6,000 in £10 shares, its objectives were to construct a railway to a point near the summit and to erect and operate a hotel nearby. The subscribers were Francis Usher Holme (1842-1913), architect; R.E.L. Naylor, banker; Wallace William Cragg, agent; Francis Wynne Turner (known as Frank), quarry agent; J.W. Hebblewaite, banker; G. Nicholson, accountant; Arthur Hill Holme, contractor.

F.U. and A.H. Holme were brothers, based in Liverpool, as was Nicholson. Naylor was based in New Brighton, Hebblewaite in Chester and Turner in Carnarvon. In theory Indian-born Cragg was based in Kent although in practice he lived at Glyn Padarn, on the edge of Llanberis, and ran the Glynrhonwy slate quarry nearby.

The second company, the Snowdon Mountain Tramroad & Hotels Company, was registered on 16 November. Its objects were quite wide ranging but principally 'to construct a tramroad from Llanberis ... to a point at or near the summit of Snowdon, in the parish of Beddgelert ... and to erect an [sic] hotel at or near the summit; to enter into agreements; to construct extensions to the tramroad, and other tramroads, tramways or railways in Great Britain, and lines of telegraph or telephone wires and other works; to maintain and work and carry on the tramroads, tramways or railways and to carry on the business of carriers of passengers and goods by land or water; to carry on the Victoria Hotel ... and the hotel proposed ... and any other hotels in Great Britain ...'
The share capital was £70,000 in £10 shares. The registered office was at the hotel.

The original subscribers were W.W. Cragg, Lieutenant Colonel; George Holme, architect; Frederick Morton Radcliffe, solicitor; Henry Cottingham Nicholson, stock and share broker; J.H. Welsford, shipowner; Harry Clegg, esquire; Frank Turner, gentleman. Only the last two had local connections, Cragg, as noted, was from Kent, the others were from, or based in, Liverpool. George Holme (1822-1915) was the contractor's uncle.

Two agreements were specified in the company's articles, the first with the Hotels & Railway Company, the second with Arthur Hill Holme and Charles Wilden King, the contractors. They were an established partnership experienced in railway work and seem to have had the resources to undertake more than one contract at a time. They had just completed widening the LNWR between Euxton and Standish in Lancashire and in 1889/90 they had built the Hastings West Hill cliff lift, which gave them experience in working on steep gradients, albeit only over a distance of 500 feet. Holme also undertook contracts with other partners.

The Railway & Hotels company appears to have been a device to transfer Assheton-Smith/Vaynol property to the Tramroad company. A preliminary agreement made on 15 October 1894 provided for the sale of the land required for the railway by the trustees of the Vaynol Estate to Cragg, or to a company to be formed by him, for £1,500, for the lease to him of the Royal Victoria Hotel and for a plot of land at the summit for a hotel to be built there by Assheton-Smith personally. A second agreement on 16 October 1894 required Cragg to transfer the land and leases to the Railway & Hotels company.

Incorporation of the company on 16 November 1894 triggered two agreements made on the same date. Firstly, the Railway & Hotels Company agreed to transfer the property to the Tramroad company in exchange for 600 fully paid £10 Tramroad company shares to be issued when the property transfers had been completed. Railway & Hotels company shareholders included John Sutherland

Harmood Banner, a chartered accountant from Liverpool, R.E.L. Naylor, Turner, Stewart and Cragg. Its function served, the Railway & Hotels company was wound up in February 1896, when Banner was appointed liquidator.

Secondly, the Tramroad company appointed the contractors, Holmes & King, to 'construct, complete and equip' to the 'reasonable' satisfaction of the company's engineers and to the satisfaction of the Board of Trade to 'deliver over the tramroad and works to the company fit to be opened for public traffic for passengers and goods' by 1 July 1895. Plans, drawings, sections and specifications had been prepared by Sir Douglas Fox, now appointed, with his brother, the company's engineer, for the tramroad, stations 'and works necessary or incidental', also for 'the rolling stock, plant and articles necessary for the equipment and working of the said tramroad'. The contract price was £64,000.

The contractors were to pay for any additional works or equipment required to meet the inspecting officer's requirements, even if they had not been specified. They were to start work as soon as the company had given possession of the land or not later than two months after signing the contract. They were to pay all expenses of and incidental to the company's and HRCNW's incorporation and the land purchase. They were to take the risk that £64,000 was sufficient to complete the works as required and would be paid £64,000 in fully-paid £10 shares. While any shares remained unissued the contractors could require the company to issue a prospectus for the unissued shares on terms to be agreed by them, the net proceeds of any money received for such shares being paid to the contractors in lieu of shares.

The 'specification of works and equipment' that accompanied the contract emphasised that the latter was for 'a fixed amount without extras' and required 'the entire completion ready for public traffic of a single line of tramroad (with passing places) of the gauge 2ft 7½in'. Although

not mentioned specifically in the contract, it was to be an Abt rack railway, and having Continental origins the gauge converts to a very precise 0.8 metres. After opening to public traffic the contractors were to maintain the works, equipment and permanent way for three months. The company would not be liable to compensate them if there was any delay in making the land available.

Concerning the contractors' labour force, wages were to be paid in 'current coin of the realm'. The contractors were responsible for preventing riotous and unlawful conduct by their men and were to provide suitable housing for them within reasonable distance. The designs of huts or other dwellings were to be approved by the engineers who could specify 'such sanitary arrangements and precautions as they may think necessary for the health of the men ... Each man shall be provided with a separate bed which shall not be occupied during his absence.'

The company put the onus of establishing 'the strata to be passed through, the character of the excavations, the water or snow to be expected and the nature of the soil ...' on the contractors. The formation in cuttings was to be 12ft wide, 10ft wide on embankments. Three miles, presumably half that amount of route, of 'substantial dry fence walls' were to be topped with 'two seven-strand wires fixed thereon upon iron standards let into large stones with sheep netting between'. The remainder of the route was to be substantially fenced with wire netting. There were to be fourteen level crossings 8ft wide with iron gates and padlocks. Gradient and mileposts 'of

approved pattern' were to be provided and installed.

Station buildings at the termini and two intermediate stations were to be of 'neat but plain' design with rubble walls, slate roofs and 'well seasoned' timber floors, doors and windows. Each was to have five rooms, including WC accommodation for men and women. Platforms of sufficient length for three cars were to be 15ft wide. The station specification was not adopted at Llanberis, and was only partially adopted at Hebron.

The running shed, to accommodate four locomotives and three carriages, was to be 130ft long and 40ft wide and built of stone with a slate roof. A water crane, coal stage and ashpit were to be constructed at the entrance.

A General Post Office-specification two-wire telephone system was to be installed with 'speaking and receiving instruments' at each station and both of the hotels.

In summary, the contractors were told that the 'tramroad and equipment shall be equal in detail and quality to the Brünig railway of Switzerland except where otherwise specified.' Opened between Alpnachstad and Brienze, 28 miles, in 1888,

The metre gauge Brunigbahn, which has two rack sections, was opened between Brienz and Alpnachstad in 1888. Brunig station is its highest point. The railway's contractors were instructed to make a line that was comparable. (Wagner)

the metre-gauge Brünigbahn remains a part of Swiss Federal Railways.

Compliance with the condition to satisfy the requirements of the Board of Trade, while well-intentioned, would be difficult to meet. As a railway built without parliamentary powers the Board of Trade had no status on it. We shall never know just how serious any of the parties were about the expectation that a mountain railway could be built in a little over seven months.

The Abt rack system was devised by Carl Roman Abt (1850-1933) to overcome the problems inherent in the Riggenbach ladder rack system first used on the Rigibahn in 1871. Abt's system used two or three rack bars offset to each other to ensure that the locomotive's pinions were permanently engaged. Because the rack used less steel and the turnouts were less complex it was also cheaper to build. Introduced in Germany in the 1880s, it is the most widely used of the rack systems.

The date of the company's registration, 16 November 1894, was also the date of the first board meeting, held in Chester. Of the promoters, Clegg, Stewart and Cragg were present. They confirmed an agreement made on 8 November to appoint themselves together with J.S. Harmood Banner, R.E.L. Naylor and Frank W. Turner as directors. Lord Alexander Paget, scion of the Marquess of Anglesey, was also appointed a director, and Turner was appointed secretary. The loan of £5,000 from the Hotels & Railway company was approved to be repaid from the proceeds of the issue of the debentures. £2,756 was used to purchase the hotel's furniture and effects.

Opened in 1832, the hotel had been built by Thomas Assheton-Smith, who had hoped to host a visit by 13-year-old HRH Princess Victoria, the later queen, during her visit to Wales that year. However, on 25 August, the day scheduled for the visit, she was indisposed, and he had to settle for her mother, the Duchess of Kent. Assheton-Smith's willingness to dispose of the hotel suggests that either it was not as profitable

as he would have liked or that it took more management effort from him than he felt it warranted.

With the legal structure in place, the survey to produce working plans and sections was started on 2 December 1894. An article about the line and its construction in *Engineering* (3 April 1896) says that the route as built did not match Frank Oswell's preliminary survey at all, partly because Assheton-Smith had made objections requiring a considerable deviation to the first half of it. Other alterations were made to equalise gradients, reduce earthworks and improve views, which had the effect of taking the line 60ft closer to the summit.

All the directors were present when the board met on 15 December 1894, the day of the sod cutting ceremony. Banner was appointed chairman. The construction contract, awarded to Arthur Hill Holme and Charles Wilden King, a partnership, of Liverpool, and signed on 16 November, was approved and the conveyance of the Vaynol estate land was sealed. The directors with an interest in the Hotels & Railway Company agreement abstained when it was confirmed.

In 1895 Fox bound copies of documents relating to the contract together for the company's use, from which the data reproduced in Appendix 2 has been extracted.

With a share capital of £70,000 the company needed to borrow up to £20,000 to fulfil its ambitions. Fox calculated that if 300 passengers paying 3s each were carried on 130 days per year the railway would earn £5,850 annually, an amount that would be increased to £11,700 if two locos were used and the passenger numbers doubled to 600 per day. The probable revenue, however, was more likely to be in the region of £8,775. The engineers calculated that two locos could operate an hourly service from Llanberis, making the return journey in two hours; they made no provision for taking fuel and water, or for cleaning the fires. Likely working expenses were calculated as shown Appendix 3.

Rinecker, Abt & Company, holders of the Abt patent, provided a technical specification of the materials to be used in the rack and an exposition on the relationship between the rack and the carrying, adhesion, rail; they were dated 15 and 13 January 1895 respectively. Rack bars and chairs were to be steel, bolts, fish plates and couplings of wrought iron. The specification of the rack bars was particularly detailed, requiring them to be rolled with the Abt trademark and stamped with a batch number. The rack bars on steeper gradients would also be 25mm thick, compared with 20mm on shallower gradients and switches. Rinecker, Abt's inspector was to be present during manufacture and his requirements for testing were to be accommodated. Before delivery all rack components except chairs were to be cleaned and dipped in hot boiled linseed oil. The chairs were to be painted with the Maritime & General Improvement Company's black varnish. The components required to make 1,800mm of rack are shown below.

Rack bars	2
Chairs	2
Top bolts with nuts	4
Base bolts with nuts	4
Spring washers	8
Fish plates	2
Couplings of base bolts	2

Fox specified, on 19 February 1895, the adhesion rail to weigh 41¼lb per yard and to be manufactured to the Indian State Railway specification. All track materials were to be stamped 'S.M.T.' and have the year and name of the manufacturer rolled into them.

There are no drawings surviving of the route as intended. The specification describes the Llanberis terminus as being near the Royal Victoria Hotel and about 200 yards from the LNWR station. The land was a part of the hotel estate and the examination of an Ordnance Survey explains its choice, a narrow strip between a rock outcrop and the river, unsuitable for any other purpose.

No deviations from the plans were to be allowed without the engineers' approval, although the specification reveals that a deviation at Ceunant Mawr waterfalls had already been surveyed. The falls have a total fall of 100ft in two stages, and judging by the number of picture postcards that illustrate them they were once much more popular attractions than they are now.

The *Engineering* article already referred to says that the surveyors had difficulty keeping in advance of construction. The most difficult part to lay out was a 30-chain section near Clogwyn, where the first 1 in 5½ gradient was encountered. The segment was on a continuous curve, mostly 10 chains, and the end of it had to reach a specified altitude to meet firm ground.

In this view of the Dinorwic quarries the location of the strip of land alongside the river that became the railway's terminus is indicated. Also visible are the quarries' Gilfach Ddu works, the Royal Victoria Hotel and Victoria Terrace.

The Ty Clŵb premises and the hotel are highlighted in this map of the railway terminus.

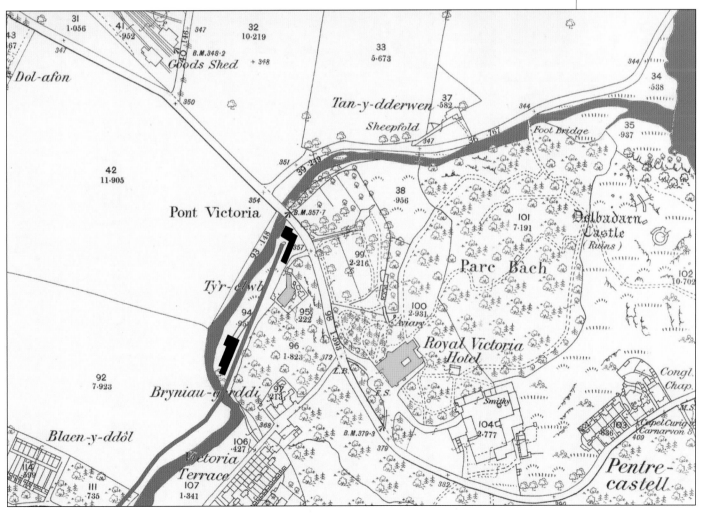

Every Victorian visitor had to visit the Llanberis falls and there was much concern lest the tramroad construction would damage them.

It is unfortunate that, apart from Abt's general specifications of the rack system, locomotives, track and turnouts, which would have been issued to any intending purchaser, no user specifications for the locomotives and rolling stock have survived, for compliance with them turned out to be an issue before too long.

The *Manchester Guardian* (15 December 1894) added some detail of the intended railway: it would have maximum gradients of 1 in 5½, 264ft (4 chains) maximum radius, tramcar-type carriages to accommodate at least 50 passengers with seats facing fore and aft and tilted to suit the gradient, two cars to form a train, it would be nearly five miles long and the journey time would be less than an hour.' To begin with, powerful steam locomotives will be employed ... but eventually it is intended to adopt electricity as the chief motive power, the steam locomotives being supplementary in case of a stress of traffic. ... The route has been carefully chosen to afford the best view of the surrounding district during the journey,

including the Ceunant Mawr waterfall, which will in no way be interfered with; and care has been taken not to spoil the appearance of the mountain itself.'

Had it been possible to use the waterfall to generate electricity then the railway might well have been electrified from the start, but no other suitable water sources were identified. A lake could have been enlarged to make a reservoir, but the directors wanted to open the railway as soon as possible.

The 'first sod' ceremony had been set for 5 December and Assheton-Smith's wife, Laura Alice, invited to perform the ceremony. When she became unwell it was deferred to 15 December. As it became apparent that she would still not be well enough to attend the second date, the duty was deferred to their daughter, Enid.

The ceremony, which took place in front of Ty Clŵb, an existing building on the proposed station site, was a grand affair, opening with a procession led by the Llanberis Subscription brass band. Comprising friendly societies and tradesmen, the procession met the Assheton-Smiths at the entrance to the village and led them to the site. The *North Wales Chronicle* estimated crowds in the order of 3,000 and some 200 invited guests. While they were assembling, a strong wind had blown a photographer's cape away, causing much amusement, especially as his assistant got his feet wet recovering it from the river; unfortunately none of the photographs appear to have been published or to have survived. The sound of some 2,000 rock cannon made for the 1832 royal visit signalled the start of proceedings.

Introduced by Sir Douglas Fox, Assheton-Smith gave his daughter, 9-year-old Enid, a miniature spade with which she dug and placed the first sod into a miniature wheelbarrow. The spade had a silver blade and a silver plate engraved 'First sod of the Snowdon Tramroad cut 15th December, by Miss Assheton-Smith' attached; the barrow was mahogany. Miniature replicas of the barrow and spade, together with a pick axe, decorated in sterling silver and gold and mounted on an ebony base which had a silver shield engraved were presented to Enid. The late Hon Sir William McAlpine Bt told the author that the barrow and spade had once been in his collection, but that he sold them.

Among the speeches delivered before the guests adjourned for lunch, Assheton-Smith made what must have been an unexpected comment about 'the hotel keepers and others who catered for ... visitors'. If the railway brought the tourists back to Llanberis he hoped that they 'would not make the mistake of imposing extortionate charges and so drive people away again', saying that Llanberis had a reputation for extortionate charges and unsatisfactory accommodation.

Lunch, prepared by a Liverpool caterer and served at the Royal Victoria Hotel, was followed by more speeches. Assheton-Smith took the opportunity to say something about Canon Rawnsley, who had thought it unreasonable that he, Assheton-Smith, should change his mind about the railway. A friend had told him that Rawnsley could also change his mind, that when Manchester Corporation had wanted to make use of Thirlmere to improve the town's water supply, Rawnsley had objected, but that when the scheme was complete he was among the first to congratulate the authority.

Reporting on the event was generally supportive, the *Manchester Courier* (22 December) saying that it had little sympathy with the critics. Sooner or later a railway was going to be built on Snowdon, either on one side or the other. It was Assheton-Smith's duty to support his tenants.

In contrast, the *Manchester Guardian's* Welsh correspondent complained (26 December) that the 'promoters of the enterprise have chosen to figure as the friends of humanity, inspired by a consuming anxiety to benefit the weak and infirm,' before continuing, 'What has afforded many not a little amusement has been the spectacle of several estimable Welsh public men posing as philanthropists in this carnival of unmitigated Philistinism.' After targeting the Bishop of Bangor, he went on, 'But the two most facetious statements of the day were made by Mr D.P. Williams and Sir Douglas Fox, the engineer. Mr Williams expressed his opinion that "the railway would mark an era in the history of Wales." There are few gentlemen who are usually more measured and sober in their utterances than the respected ex-chairman of the Carnarvonshire County Council, and one scarcely expected that the [railway] would have led him to lose so grievously his sense of proportion. Sir Douglas Fox, however, eclipsed both the bishop and Mr Williams when he declared that "every care has been taken to deal in the most tender way with all the beautiful scenery."'

Rawnsley (*Carnarvon & Denbigh Herald* 28 December) denied that he had opposed the Thirlmere scheme and claimed, in brief, that his words had been taken out of context.

The *North Wales Chronicle* (22 December) had, incidentally, reported that the company's motto was 'sic itur ad astra', a quote from Virgil's Aeneid, 'thus you shall go to the stars'. The newspaper thought it was rather a joke and, joke or not, that seems to have been the first and last time it was mentioned. Within eighteen months the company's star had fallen to the ground with a resounding crash.

CHAPTER 2

CONSTRUCTION

Despite the letting of the construction contract and the first sod having been cut there was still a great deal of work to be done before trains could run.

Among the business carried out by the board on 29 January 1895 was the allotment of £6,000 of shares to the Hotels & Railways Company. It also resolved to invite applications for the post of manager and secretary.

Shares were issued to the signatories of the company's articles on 16 February, one each. On the same date transfers from the Hotels & Railway company were approved in favour of Holme, George Nicholson, J.W. Hebblethwaite, Stewart, Naylor, Banner, J. Marke Wood, John Ernest Greaves, Cecil Webb Cragg, W.W. Cragg (brothers) and Turner. Hebblethwaite and Naylor had 75 shares each, the rest had 50 each. John Ernest Greaves was the owner of the Llechwedd slate quarry at Blaenau Ffestiniog; his shares were transferred to Edward Seymour Greaves, his brother, on 31 May.

Following a decision to issue £35,000 of first mortgage debentures the board resolved to accept the offer by the company's bankers, Leyland & Bullins, Liverpool, to cash a £1,500 4% debenture payable on 31 July 1895. Presumably the purpose of this arrangement was to provide the company with working capital.

Details of the early works are sparse. The first report hinting at any activity did not appear until March 1895, when the lake froze over, an unusual occurrence apparently, and Thomas William Rigby (1856-1924) and Clinton James Wilson Holme (1863-1931) were noted among those seen skating on it. The former was Holme & King's agent, who had managed the Euxton-Standish widening and had transferred to the Snowdon contract in

December 1894, the latter was Holme's nephew, a civil engineer who had trained at Stothert & Pitt's Bath ironworks and worked for the Great Eastern Railway in Essex and at Liverpool Street station.

Fox had submitted a letter reporting progress to the 16 February meeting and on 28 March the board resolved to inform him that he was not to authorise any extras without the directors' approval. His attempts to obtain payment were rebuffed by the directors in March and May; on the second occasion they offered half of the £600 requested, to be paid after shares had been allotted.

The *Carnarvon & Denbigh Herald* (22 March 1895) published an interview with Frank Oswell, Sir Douglas Fox's resident engineer. He said that although cold weather had slowed work on the viaducts and had stopped them working on the upper reaches, they had completed two miles of earthworks. Masonry work had been subcontracted to Owen Morris of Carnarvon and a Mr Chambers of Manchester. The workforce of 150, mostly local and Welsh, was expected to be increased to 3-400; the men refused to work on higher ground until huts had been provided for their accommodation.

The first rail, rolled by Messrs Cammell at Workington, Cumberland, was delivered via Carnarvon, arriving on board the steamship *Solway King*, an iron vessel built on the Ribble in 1883, on 27 March. When the unloading took 50 hours instead of the scheduled 24 due to the lack of labour to clear the wharf, the ship's owners sued the contractors for 7s 6d an hour demurrage, £9 15s. In court in May, the contractors' barrister successfully argued that the contract was with the consignors, Richard White & Son, iron merchants of Widnes, not the consignees. At the resumed hearing

The contractors'
temporary
construction railway
on the viaduct
site, April 1895.
(*Black & White*)

A site hut and
temporary tracks
near the foot of the
viaduct, April 1895.
(*Black & White*)

in June, when the consignors were heard, the judge ruled that the delay had not been as much as claimed and awarded only £5 5s to the plaintiffs.

Three candidates for the post of secretary and manager had appeared before the board on 10 April 1895 and Gowrie Colquhoun Aitchison was appointed on a two-year contract that could be terminated by the directors at three months' notice. In post by 21 May, when the prospectus was issued, his salary was £300, without a house, for the first year, and he would be responsible for working the tramroad, the hotels and refreshment rooms, for making all returns, keeping accounts, conducting correspondence and 'generally organise traffic'.

Born in 1863 in Poona, India, Aitchison had been educated at Clifton College, Bristol, and Queen's College, Cambridge. Leaving university, he joined one of the limestone quarrying and processing companies in north Derbyshire, all of which used railways internally and to transfer produce to main-line railway companies. In the 1891 census he gave his occupation as assistant manager. In November 1891, twelve of the quarry companies and their agents amalgamated to form Buxton Lime Firms Company Ltd, and he was sufficiently well thought of to make and sign the contracts governing the amalgamation, which raises the question about why he gave up an apparently promising career for an untested venture in Llanberis.

To raise capital, a prospectus offering £20,000 in £100 4½% debentures and 6,343 £10 shares was issued on 21 May 1895. It stated that the share capital would fund the railway's construction while the debentures, redeemable at par after ten years, would fund the hotels, land required, and other expenses not included in the construction contract. Half of the formation had been constructed and partially ballasted and it was anticipated that the tramroad could be completed and ready for passenger traffic 'during the present season'.

Would-be investors were informed that Assheton-Smith and the trustees of the will of the late Mrs Assheton-Smith had conveyed all of the land required for the tramroad and stations. The Royal Victoria Hotel had been in the company's possession since the previous November, held on a 50-year lease from Assheton-Smith for £220 a year. The hotel estate comprised the hotel and 32 acres of land, including Dolbadarn Castle and fishing rights. Extensive improvements had been made and the 'sanitary arrangements remodelled on the most improved principles'. A refreshment room was to be erected at the lower terminus.

Estimating that profits should not be less than 8% of capital, the directors likened the undertaking to the Swiss Rigibahn and noted that that line had been paying 8% on £50,000 capital after paying interest on £38,000 debentures and without any hotel revenue. By 31 May, the issue had closed two days before, the company had received thirteen applications for shares and ten for debentures.

Douglas Fox's 17 May report, included in the prospectus, informed the directors that the centre line had been set out and levelled for 3½ miles from Llanberis and earthworks were in progress over three miles, 1¾ miles was ready for track and half a mile was ready for bottom ballast. Good progress had been made with the abutments and piers of the lower viaduct and those for the upper viaduct were nearly ready for the arches to be formed. Four bridges were ready for concreting.

Stone was being used for the piers and abutments of the viaducts, culverts and bridges and brick arches adopted where possible. Ornamental timber would be used for the Llanberis station building while the other station buildings would be 'simple buildings, of local stone'. A locomotive and carriage shed would be provided to house and repair the rolling stock. There would be four locomotives and three trains of two carriages, each train accommodating 112 passengers.

The Societé Suisse pour la Construction de Locomotives et de Machines (in German Schweizerische Locomotiv &

Maschinenfabrik, the Swiss Locomotive Company - SLM) had despatched the first locomotive from its Winterthur works on 10 June 1895. Shipped on the SS *Ptarmigan* from Antwerp to Liverpool, it arrived at Llanberis during the week ending 6 July. J.H. Welsford & Company invoiced the contractors £46 15s 11d for the charges incurred in dealing with its import.

Unloading took 54 man-hours at 6d per hour and the LNWR charged £14 15s 9d for delivery to Llanberis. The second locomotive was delivered on 3 August, the *North Wales Chronicle* (10 August) describing how it was transported between the two stations using temporary rails laid along the road, a method that was presumably used for the other rolling stock. Costing £1,525 each, inclusive of the Abt royalty, the locomotives were named *L.A.D.A.S* and *Enid* after Assheton-Smith's wife and daughter.

The contractors were sufficiently confident about progress to suggest, on 9 July, that as soon as the railway was finished they would operate it until the end of the season at their own expense, using the company's locomotives and carriages and taking the revenue. In return for this they would pay the shareholders 5% interest on the issued share capital 'as soon as possible after 1 January next'. The offer was accepted by the board the next day. At the same time approval was given to the loco shed being built of timber with a stone foundation and slate roof instead of the rubble walls specified in the contract.

The offer was probably designed to distract the directors, because the Cardiff-based *Western Mail* (27 May) had already forecast that the railway was not likely to be ready for a July opening. According to the paper, the track had reached Halfway but the work had progressed more slowly than anticipated. The *North Wales Express* (28 June) had noted that the trackbed was close to the summit and the viaducts remained incomplete. The account of the second locomotive's delivery forecast an opening at the end of September.

Just a few days after the first of the locomotives had arrived at Llanberis in July 1895 the Liverpool Engineers' Society visited the Dinorwic quarries and the railway construction site, where some of them posed for a photograph. The remotely worked chimney covers do not appear to have lasted very long. (R.C. Symons)

Snowdon Train

No 2 seen outside the shed with two carriages soon after delivery. The colours are probably quite a good representation of how the trains were when the railway was new. (James Valentine)

After the arches of the lower viaduct had been sprung the locomotive was worked onto it for photographs. (R.C. Symons)

There are fifty-six foremen, labourers, and boys, and two loco crew in this photograph of No 1 on the incomplete viaduct. The shed on the right partially conceals a stone crusher, probably the source of the troublesome ballast. This photograph illustrates how the angle of the adjacent arches changes. (R.C. Symons)

Fox told the directors that he had certified work valued £25,044 on 10 July 1895 and they issued 2,100 shares in part payment. When the shares were reallocated on 25 September, the contractors kept 743 for the partnership, 286 for Holme and his wife, and 236 for King and his daughter, effectively putting Holme in control of the company. On 21 June the contractors had submitted a statement of their current position and a breakdown of the track materials already obtained.

Earthworks	Contract total	£26,200	
	Still to do	£8,664	£17,536
Permanent way	Materials on ground		£4,929
			£22,465
		Less 10%	£2,246
			£20,219
Provisions	Law and other expenses		£750
	Locos on account		£1,500
	Advertising		£1,152
	Underwriting		£2,000
			£25,621

23 March	307 tons 18 cwt 2 qtr – rails	£7 per ton	£2,155 9s 6d
	37 tons 16 cwt 3 qtr – fishplates	£10 per ton	£378 7s 6d
11 April/10 May	47,300 Grover spring washers	£4 per 1,000	£188 14s
2 May	7,200 fish bolts, 2 tons, 12 cwt, 1 qtr 4 lb	£12 10s per ton	£32 17s
1 June	2,000 yard – rack rail with fastenings	£1,760 per mile	£2,000
7 June	5½ steel sleepers	£7 10s per ton	£41 5s
19 June	3,300 fish bolts, 1 ton 3 qtr 7 lb	£12 10s per ton	£13
20 June	3 tons, - rail clips and bolts	£40 per ton	£120
			£4,929 13s

Steel track components for the rack had been supplied by Charles Cammell & Co Ltd of Sheffield; a delivery note for components to make up two miles was dated 29 June 1895. They had been despatched via the Manchester, Sheffield & Lincolnshire Railway in four wagons, Nos 15524, 5588, 213 and 13100. Bolts supplied by Richard White & Sons of Widnes had been despatched on the same date; according to the contemporary technical press White was the main sub-contractor for the track materials. While Cammell rolled the bars at its Sheffield plant, the Yorkshire Engine Company cut the teeth into them. Rail, as noted, and fishplates were made at Cammell's Workington plant and sleepers by the Ebbw Vale Steel, Iron & Coal Ltd. In 1899 Yorkshire Engine had surplus rack bars in stock and Aitchison was authorised to offer scrap price for them.

The Lancaster Carriage & Wagon Company submitted carriage doors for inspection on 10 July. The board approved them and instructed that they be painted in the (unspecified) colours shown.

Aitchison was well entrenched in his position by 6 August, for the board instructed him to 'visit the Swiss mountain railways' as soon as possible. What he learned during his 28-day visit was not recorded. Fox had, incidentally, made a three-week tour of European rack railways in November 1894 and his 16-page handwritten report is contained in the specification volume.

In anticipation of opening, Aitchison was instructed to recruit a station master and superintendent and fares were set at: return - 5s maximum/4s minimum; up - 3s 6d/2s 6d; down 2s 6d/2s. George William North was subsequently appointed at

£1 5s per week with effect from 1 January 1896; Aitchison was given authority to increase the rate of pay when the railway started operating. North (born 1855) was a Yorkshireman who had recently moved to Wales from Shipley, his birthplace, where he had been a station inspector.

As the summit hotel was obviously expected to make a substantial contribution to the company's income an attempt was made to take control of the existing summit property. The land was in the ownership of Assheton-Smith, Sir Edward Watkin and Sir Richard Bulkeley, a situation that caused problems for the company. The existing outlets were known as 'the old original', run by Thomas Roberts, and 'the Snowdon Summit hotel', run by Robert Owen. The former appears to have been quite basic, the latter slightly less basic. Both were partially on Assheton-Smith land in Beddgelert parish. He had given the tenants six months' notice to quit on 12 May 1894, but on 31 May 1895 it was reported that they refused to give up possession. Legal action against them was concluded on 13 August by an out-of-court settlement to leave them in place for the remainder of the season.

In anticipation of the railway bringing more customers, Owen had been enlarging and improving his property, building a south-facing veranda with storage rooms beneath. His application to renew his license was heard in Portmadoc on 30 August 1895. Assheton-Smith's solicitor opposed, on the basis that the premises had been altered and were not the same as those licensed.

A farmer resident at the appropriately named *Snowdon View* in Nant Gwynant, Robert Owen (1854-1927) claimed to have been trading on the summit for 30 years, to have held a license for 15 years, and there had been no complaints. The second and third claims might have been true but 30 years before he was only 11 years old. The coffee room, he said, held about 120 people, the bar-parlour, twelve. There were four bedrooms and accommodation for ladies. Sanitary arrangements were being made. When the clerk pointed out that it was customary to renew licenses to publicans of properties built on the sites of previous licensed premises, he got his license.

Most 19th Century views of the summit were taken from this angle. The 'old original' hut is on the left. The sign above the door of the summit hotel promotes it as a bazaar, offering refreshments, including beer.

4384 SNOWDON The Summit

Summit layout with
the railway.

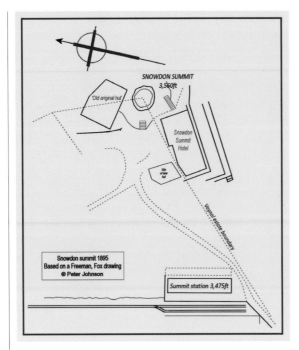

SNOWDON SUMMIT
3,560ft

'Old original hut'

Snowdon
Summit
Hotel

Site
of later
hut

Vaynol estate boundary

Snowdon summit 1895
Based on a Freeman, Fox drawing
© Peter Johnson

Summit station 3,475ft

At the same hearing Aitchison applied
for a license for the hotel the company
proposed to build on an acre of Assheton-
Smith's land it had secured on a 50-year
lease. It intended to spend £5,000 to build
it. A barrister had been appointed to object
on behalf of Beddgelert residents; apart
from Owen and one of the guides, the
other five witnesses called in support of
the objection were visitors. None were
from Beddgelert. The application was
refused.

Learning this, the directors resolved to
ask Assheton-Smith if he would be willing
to forego the requirement to spend £5,000
on the hotel. In July they had asked the
architect to reduce the number of rooms to
seventeen and to include a drying room.

'Vigorous' progress was reported
by the *Carnarvon & Denbigh Herald* on
13 September. The formation was complete
to the summit and track was laid for the
first 1½ miles; the locos were being used
to take up the track materials. Visitors had
taken to walking up the railway route in
preference to the old path.

The board appeared to be unhappy
with Fox and work carried out by the
contractors when it met on 13 November,
resolving to refer the size of the engine

and carriage shed to him and asking if he
had authorised it. Aitchison was told to
inform Fox that the directors wished to
be consulted about any plans before the
work was undertaken. Fox was also to be
informed that if there were any savings
made on any work he should ensure that
they were credited to the company.

Having received three locomotives the
directors decided, also on 13 November,
to order a fourth and to get prices from
English builders to compare with SLM.
On 7 December Aitchison was instructed
to request Fox to order the locomotive and
two more carriages, delivery to be before
the end of May 1896.

By the time of a report published in the
North Wales Chronicle on 30 November,
work had been sufficiently advanced for
Oswell to issue permits for 'trial trips'.
Track had been laid within ¾ mile of the
summit, workmen were working on the
'steepest and most dangerous portion' of
the railway and, although the 'nipping
cold and short days' prevented much
work from being carried out, track laying
would be completed within a few weeks;
this despite the *Liverpool Mercury* having
already, on 12 November, announced
the suspension of work due to severe
weather.

Based on a site visit, the report's author
was clearly impressed that despite poor
weather conditions on the upper sections
of the mountain there had been no serious
accidents involving the workmen. In fact,
unlike other construction projects familiar
to the author, no reports have been found
of any of the workers being summonsed
for drunkenness or other misbehaviour
either.

There were 10 gangs of 10 to 25 men
according to *Engineering*. Hourly rates
varied according to the height being
worked at: labourers, 5d/6½d; masons,
8½d/10½d. They lived in huts erected
by the contractors, one at each 'half-way
house', and stayed there from Sunday
evening until Saturday. The contractors
supplied soup every day when it was cold.
Iron-shod sleighs hauled by three horses

carried materials up the mountain before the rails were laid. It took half a day to drag 7cwt to the second half-way house, a distance of three miles. To maintain continuity of access during construction temporary bridges were erected on the sites of the bridges crossing the bridle path below Hebron and above Clogwyn.

Engineering (3 April 1896) explained that the best results were obtained by laying the sleepers and the rack before the rails. The 4mm play in positioning the rack was tested by using a stepping gauge across four teeth in the adjacent bars before they were tightened up. On the inside of curves the rails were shorter than on the outside; there were five combinations for the five radii used. Fourteen men started tracklaying above the viaducts on 2 September and finished on 6 January 1896, 72 working days. The average length laid per day was 122 yards; the best day's work was 350 yards, and the best week, nearly 1,500 yards. Track on the section below the viaducts had been laid before 2 September.

By the end of the year, Fox had issued five construction certificates. No 3, approved on 30 October, was for £12,218; the contractors were paid £14,872 by cheque and £1,390 in fully-paid shares. On the figures given the company had overpaid by £10 at this stage. The company's bankers were asked to loan the company £14,172 at 4% against future income on its share allotment and first-call accounts. Fox was paid £750 on account of his commission. Certificates Nos 4 and 5 were issued on 7 December 1895, for £5,070, and a cheque was issued for the full amount. There is no indication available about how much of this money was for construction and how much was for equipment, but expenditure of some £43,000 compared to the construction and equipment budget of £64,000 suggests that there was still a good proportion of work to be carried out.

No explanation for the contractors' failure to meet the 1 July target has been uncovered. It must always have been over-optimistic, but they must have thought

This works photograph of No 3 represents the first batch of locomotives as delivered.

Tracklaying
just above the
viaduct, with the
locomotive following
close behind.
(C.J.W. Holme)

they stood some chance of running the railway before the season ended, even if the offer to do so was to distract the directors from the lack of progress.

Nor was any explanation offered for the resignations of N.P. Stewart and Lord Alexander Paget from the board during the autumn. Perhaps it was the lack of progress, but in Stewart's case there could well have been a conflict of interest with his position as Assheton-Smith's agent, and Paget could have been ill, although his death aged 57 on 26 October 1896 was reported (*Cheshire Observer*, 31 October 1896) to be sudden.

The *Carnarvon & Denbigh Herald* (10 January 1896) reported that the first complete train had reached the summit the day before. Carrying 'a few passengers connected with the project', it comprised a locomotive and two carriages and the journey took about an hour. After twenty minutes at the summit the descent took the same time. The line was complete except for fencing and signalling, it said, concluding its report by saying, 'The line will not be opened to the public at present, but several trains will run, it

is thought, to accommodate the Easter excursion traffic.'

There was no mention of that first trip to the summit when the board met on 16 January 1896 but Fox was asked to arrange for a Board of Trade inspection. Construction certificates Nos 6 and 7 were mentioned but their value was not recorded; payment would be made when the contractors had met the calls on their shares which were in arrears; a balance cheque for £6,543 was to be issued to the contractors on 12 February. Regarding the boundaries, the board agreed to walling above the river bridge being replaced by fencing subject to Assheton-Smith agreeing. Neither of the English companies that had quoted to supply a locomotive could deliver before August, and SLM, which had quoted £1,575, could not guarantee delivery before the end of July. Holme agreed to the company dealing with SLM direct, using the equipment budget, and waived his claim on commission on the order.

An accident involving 'No 2 engine' was reported to the directors by Fox when they met on 12 February 1896, but no other details were recorded; a report into the 6 April accident gave 31 January for this one. It was subsequently reported that it had become the practice to run trains carrying workmen up and down the line and that there were several occasions when the loco mounted the rack during the construction; no importance was attached to these incidents, presumably, it was suggested, because the works were unfinished.

The company's negotiations with SLM had borne fruit to the extent that two locomotives were ordered – perhaps SLM was prepared to give a better delivery, and price, for two. In March it was agreed that the cost of locomotive spares and 'two more carriages' should be taken from the £12,000 equipment budget even if ordered by the company direct.

No answer was recorded to the request for Assheton-Smith to consider foregoing the commitment to build the summit hotel, but the directors were informed that he intended to install his own refreshment room at the summit so they decided to arrange for building a portion of the hotel's foundation to enable the platform to be completed. At the same time Robert Owen had repeated his previously unrecorded offer to the company, his summit hut and its license for £3,000. It was refused, the price being considered prohibitive.

Dealings with Assheton-Smith were handled, via Stewart, with kid gloves. He was the landowner, he was wealthy, he had ultimate control. The prospect of him setting up in competition for summit revenues must have horrified the directors for they must have known that a trading monopoly on the summit would be as profitable as running trains. Earlier they had sought to establish his position if additional land was required for a second track; he had told them that the company could buy what they needed at any time at the same price per acre as the land already taken.

At Llanberis the situation regarding public facilities was more easily dealt with. The plans were approved on 10 July 1895, after they had been altered to incorporate Aitchison's requirements, to give extra WC accommodation for both sexes, a manager's room and office. Owen Morris's £595 tender for its erection was accepted on 11 December.

Llanberis station early in 1896. Before April another building had been built in the foreground to serve as a refreshment room. (C.J.W. Holme)

As the line approached completion so did the fund raising. The position by 30 November 1895 was that 6,111 £10 shares had been issued, of which £12,954 had not been called and £5,575 was in arrears. £18,200 debentures had been subscribed, of which £11,050 was uncalled. In addition to the 600 shares allocated to the Hotels & Railway company to purchase the land, £39,422 had been spent on construction, engineering charges, land purchase and legal expenses.

On 30 October 1895 Aitchison had also been instructed to collect payment in full on the six, out of seven, subscriber shares that had not been paid for; perhaps their recipients thought they were a gift. By January 1896 two shareholders were in arrears with their calls and the company placed the matter with its solicitor. The final calls on the shares were made on 12 February, by which time one of the errant shareholders had paid up. To give the shares credence an application for listing on the Liverpool Stock Exchange had been made in October 1895.

To promote the railway, an unsolicited offer to supply a manuscript guide to the line was accepted and Aitchison arranged printing in October 1895. A meeting held with the LNWR at Euston in December resulted in an agreement to advertise in the LNWR's North Wales guide if the price was agreeable. Others saw the railway as an opportunity and in February 1896 W.H. Smith's tender for advertising at stations for three years was accepted.

The company's first annual report, published on 9 March 1896, gives a small insight into the state of construction just before the railway was due to carry its first fare-paying passengers. 'The work of constructing the tramroad has progressed satisfactorily towards completion, although it has taken considerably longer to carry out than originally expected,' Banner and Aitchison wrote. They also noted that three locomotives and six carriages, 'being three complete trains,' had been delivered. Fox's report is more revealing and was written on 28 February, the day after another trip to the summit according to *The Times*. 'The viaducts and bridges are nearly completed, as also the fence walling,' said Fox, 'The ballast is now in a forward state, and the signalling is

Ballasted track just above Waterfall station. The stone does not appear to be properly graded and there are sleepers visible that are not fully supported. (C.J.W. Holme)

nearly ready for work. There are several minor works, including drainage, yet to be completed, and the mountain stations have not yet been commenced. We do not see any reason why passenger traffic should not be run at Easter and we have given first notice to the Board of Trade with this view.' No comment was made, here or anywhere else, about Aitchison taking over from Turner as secretary.

When the directors met on 18 March Fox advised them to get a letter from the contractors making it clear that if the company did run trains at Easter the line was not to be considered as complete.

Fox's first notice to the Board of Trade had been submitted on 1 May 1895. Although one officer was prepared to find a way to permit an inspection, another noted that the president had already objected to the railway in public and he was also opposed to voluntary inspections. Fox was seen on 20 May and a file note records that he was told the position and had agreed to inform the directors. 'It is fully clear that he is anxious that the line should be inspected to relieve himself from responsibility.'

It appears that the directors did consider applying for Parliamentary powers; a letter from the solicitor on the subject was mentioned in the minutes in October 1895. At this stage, with the railway partially constructed, an application would be a high-risk and expensive strategy. Not only would it have given Rawnsley and others a fresh opportunity to object, but it might have failed.

Fox's second request to the Board of Trade for an inspection had been made on 21 January 1896, when one of the officers minuted, 'I am still of opinion that we should not impose on the inspecting officers the responsibility of inspecting and approving a speculative and technical undertaking of this character. No Parliamentary powers have been obtained.

'The argument the other way is this. The directors ask for a government inspection. It is refused. There is an accident subsequently and the public will not understand why we did not use the opportunity given us to do what we could to insure public safety.'

This paragraph was prophetic. Another officer said that he would like to send Major Marindin. It is intriguing that, whatever the president's views, the Board of Trade was still reluctant, given that on 16 August 1895 Colonel J.H. Rich and Major P. Cardew had inspected the 3ft 6in gauge Snaefell Mountain Railway on the Isle of Man, which was completely outside its jurisdiction.

In London, on 16 March 1896, Fox caught the Board of Trade out by serving a second notice on the prescribed form which cited section 4 of the 1842 Regulation of Railways Act, 'That no railway ... shall be opened for the public conveyance of passengers until ... after notice in writing of the intention of opening the same shall have been given.' 'The promoters ... have given notice of their intention to open their line under an act ... which appears to leave the Board of Trade no option in the circumstances but to inspect it in the interests of public safety.' Major Francis Arthur Marindin (1839-1900) received his orders.

The Isle of Man's double track 3 feet 6 inch gauge Snaefell Mountain Tramway was opened on 21 August 1895, while Holme & King were still trying to complete their Snowdon contract. This photograph was taken before the end of the 1896 season. (R.C. Symons)

CHAPTER 3

THE INSPECTION

Before moving on to Marindin's report, a few words about the technical description that accompanied Fox's notice are required. Compiled by Frank Oswell, Fox's resident engineer, on 13 March, much of it covers the same ground as Aitchison's later description (Appendix 4) but there are some additional items. Facilities along the line were given in the table:

Chainage M Ch	Height above sea level	Intervals	Rise in feet	Rate of rise (mean)	Comment
0·00	352. 06				Water, main siding, three running shed sidings
1·07	924. 72	87ch	572. 66	1:10	Water, main siding, dead end siding (goods)
2·00	1,635. 79	93ch	711. 07	1:8. 6	Water, main siding
3·30	2,526. 29	90ch	890. 50	1:6. 7	Water, main siding
4·53	3,490. 55	103ch	964. 26	1:7. 0	No water, main siding (dead end)

The aggregate length of 35 curves along the line amounted to 42½% of the whole, their radii being 3.90, 4, 5, 10, 12 and 20 chains. Eight bridges and viaducts were as listed:

Structure	Chainage M Ch	Type	Material	Span	Crossing	Height
Bridge	0 7½	Girder	Steel	30ft	Stream	
Viaduct	0 15	Viaduct	Masonry, 14 30ft semi-circular brick arches	500ft		43ft
Viaduct	0 32	Viaduct	Masonry, 4 30ft semi-circular brick arches	190ft		37ft
Bridge	0 53	Masonry	Brick segmental arch	50ft	Stream	10ft
Bridge	0 75	Masonry	Brick semi-arch	15ft	Occupation road	
Bridge	2 0	Concrete/girders			Bridle path	
Bridge	3 40	Concrete/girders			Bridle path	
Bridge	4 18	Girder	Light steel		Tramroad	

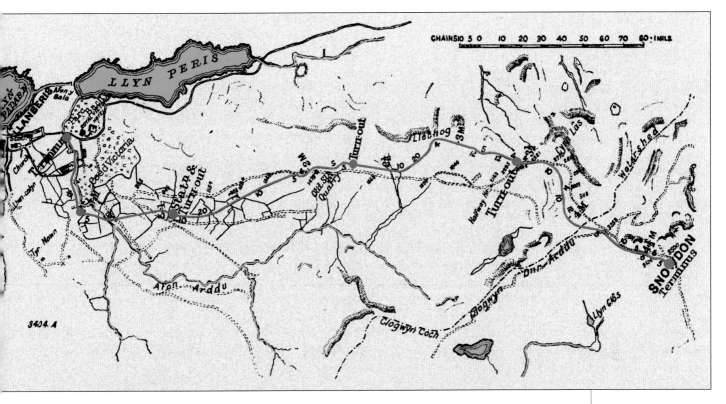

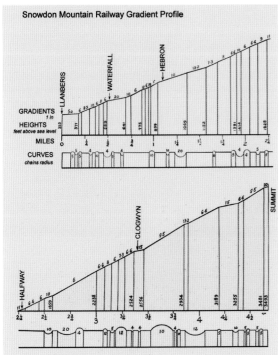

Gradient profile and curvature.

The last, intended to carry the bridle path over the railway, was not built. There were also six culverts with spans ranging from 3ft to 6ft. The first bridge, by the end of the loco shed, had no handrails.

The carriages were 38ft long overall, 6ft 6in wide and 9ft 4in high. They weighed 5 tons 13 cwt empty, about 9 tons laden, and had seven eight-seat compartments with a coupé at the front for the guard. The latter operated the brake which was connected to a double pinion carried on its own axle mounted in the centre of the down-hill bogie frame. The bogie centres were 28ft apart and the carriages were unglazed with canvas curtains provided to keep out the weather. The length of a complete train was 91ft.

Marindin made his inspection on 27 March and submitted his report on 3 April, Good Friday. A detailed description of the railway, presumably supplied by Fox – it is very fulsome – was published in *Engineering* in instalments from 3 April and contains details of the inspection not mentioned by Marindin. His train, two carriages was implied, was loaded with cement to represent the passenger load. On the descent the locomotive's automatic brake was allowed 'to run full speed on a 1 in 6 gradient, and when 5mph was attained the brake automatically stopped the locomotive.' The carriages were

Douglas Fox & Company's plan of the route.

S.M.T. Viaduct—near Half Way, Llanberis

The route near Halfway, showing one of the cuttings and an underbridge. (James Valentine)

A Snowdon train on the upper viaduct. Only this photograph of a train of two full-sized carriages is known to exist, and that probably because it was chosen by the LNWR for its popular postcard series. The image also shows the copings and railings on the completed viaduct.

SNOWDON MOUNTAIN RAILWAY TRAIN, LLANBERIS.

allowed to 'run downhill separately and stopped on their own handbrakes.'

The line was 4m 53.75ch long, wrote Marindin. Of the passing places, at Hebron, Halfway and Clogwyn, only the first had a building. Waterfall had a building but no loop. For most of its length the railway was a surface line but there were several small embankments and cuttings, some of the latter through rock. The biggest embankment was 12.25ch long and 13.76ft high; two other embankments were 16.50ft and 16.20ft high. The biggest cutting was 34.15ch long and 16.79ft deep, the others were 14.90ch long/10.68ft deep and 9.10ch long/20.15ft deep. The only works of any large dimensions were, he said, the viaducts. 'These works have been well constructed and appear to be quite sound. The girders of the underbridges have sufficient strength and were satisfactorily tested. The brakes on the train are thoroughly efficient, the train being under perfect control, both on the ascending and descending journey, and when detached from the engine each carriage can be stopped, or let down slowly as may be desired, on the steepest gradients, by means of the brake attached to it.'

He thought that it would be 'desirable to devise some method of preventing a driver from tampering in any way with the automatic brake, which, when set to come into action when the regulated speed is exceeded, should not be able to be altered at the discretion of the driver.'

Semaphore signals were worked from ground frames at Llanberis (six levers), Hebron (seven), Halfway (six), Clogwyn (six) and Summit (four). The points at Waterfall were locked by the train staff. The slow speed and ability to stop trains very quickly rendered distant signals unnecessary, Marindin said. He thought that disc signals indicating the position of points would have been sufficient for the same reason.

A cutting higher up the mountain awaits the arrival of the track gang. (C.J.W. Holme)

One of the lower viaduct arches crosses a minor road, on the right in this photograph. The man on the left in No 1's cab is smoking a pipe of distinctly continental appearance, which could indicate that he is Amadelo Taechella, the Italian engineer sent by SLM to train the Snowdon drivers. There's a woman standing with the group under the second arch. (R.C. Symons)

A view of the lower viaduct as completed. The bridge over the river was replaced by a larger structure in the 20th Century and the riverside footpath closed off. (A.P. Francis)

Concerning the fencing, he said, 'As there are only a few mountain sheep on the high ground I see no objection to the proposal to dispense with fences above 2m 70ch provided a grid is placed across the line at the termination of the fencing.'

There was still a good deal of work to be done on the station buildings, but he did not think that that should hinder the line being opened. He did require, however, a 'substantial' buffer stop at the end of the platform line at the summit. At Hebron

he thought that a second platform should be provided. Concerning the trains, he thought that lifeguards fitted to the leading ends of the carriages would be a benefit.

Marindin foresaw that high winds would render the carriages 'liable to upset' and listed six combinations, ranging from trains being full to empty and with the curtains being open or half closed, that would cause concern at different wind speeds. He identified the line above Clogwyn as a location of particular concern and recommended that one or more wind gauges should be erected, and train operation suspended 'whenever a dangerous pressure is recorded'.

The Board of Trade sent a copy of the report to the company on 4 April, the draft covering letter being altered to make Marindin's recommendations advisory instead of mandatory. The board had instructed Aitchison to buy a wind gauge on 18 March.

A sign that the railway was expected to boost both visitor numbers to the summit and profits came with the launch of the Snowdon Summit Hotel Company in March. Its abbreviated prospectus was published in the *Llandudno Advertiser* on 2 April. With a capital of £4,000 it sought to place 440 £5 shares. The directors were Robert Owen, two Llandudno businessmen and a Portmadoc ironmonger.

The venture was to acquire Owen's Snowdon Summit hotel, its goodwill and its license. The business comprised a luncheon room, bar, kitchen, pantry, four bedrooms and lavatory and was held on a lease with 30 years outstanding, £25 annual rent payable for the next 13 years, followed by £30 a year for the remainder. Owen wanted £2,300 for the business and intended taking £400 in shares. £300 of improvements were envisaged.

Justification for the floatation was that 'Until last September the business was conducted in small miserable huts in a somewhat rough-and-ready way; and the vendor who held the license in respect of the premises for 16 years, although a thoroughly respectable man, has had but little experience in good-class catering, for which reason it is felt that in order to cope with the expected great influx of tourists, and to meet the public demands in a satisfactory manner, the hotel should be under the control of a thorough business man, or a board of businessmen, and managed by a trained caterer. If this

The three signals at the summit are prominent in this view that also shows a pony still being used on the mountain after the railway had been opened. (British Mirror)

The summit station in relation to the summit buildings. The Snowdon Summit Hotel, with its veranda and basement, is on the right. Two signs promoting Wrexham lager beer have been mounted by the entrance to the station building, which is already showing signs of weathering.

Cog Railway Station Snowdon 3570 feet above the Sea-level. August 21st 1899.

Although it is undated, Aitchison probably produced only one rule book during his period in office and it would have been compiled before train services started.

General Rules & Regulations

FOR THE GUIDANCE AND INSTRUCTION OF THE

OFFICERS AND MEN

IN THE SERVICE OF

THE SNOWDON MOUNTAIN

TRAMROAD.

Subject to any alteration which may at any time hereafter be made.

By Order,

G. C. AITCHISON,

Manager.

PRINTED AT THE CAMBRIAN PRINTING AND BOOKBINDING WORKS, CARNARVON, BY TOM LITHERLAND.

was done, it is confidently believed the concern will prove an exceptional opening for making money, and the property will greatly enhance in value in the future.' Rather a back-handed compliment of Owen there.

Amongst the pre-opening visitors was a party of engineers from the LNW, the Midland and the Manchester, Sheffield & Lincolnshire Railways who travelled on 24 March, leaving Llanberis at 10.00pm. The group included F.W. Webb, the LNWR's locomotive engineer, and Sir Edward Leader Williams, the Manchester Ship Canal's engineer. They went over the line twice, during the day and at night; no explanation was offered for the latter.

Residents paid reduced fares to travel on a special train on 4 April. They had to make the last few feet of their journey on foot after a stone rolled out of a cutting near to the summit and derailed the leading carriage bogie. It took fifteen minutes to get the train under way again, Aitchison told the inquest later in the month.

CHAPTER 4

THE ACCIDENT AND THE INQUEST

I n preparation for the opening, the *Manchester Guardian* published an article about the railway on 4 April 1896. The Snowdon Mountain Railway was, it said, outclassed by the Pilatus line and would seem a small thing beside the daring Jungfraubahn in the Bernese Oberland. It was, nevertheless, a work of magnitude and originality, an entirely new step in British railway enterprise, designed to incorporate the best of these lines, not to copy any of them. It was, however, an experiment pure and simple and its failure or success would determine whether a system that flourished in Switzerland was capable of success in Britain.

A trial trip operated for the press earlier in the week had been accompanied by Aitchison, Oswell, the resident engineer, and Rigby, the contractors' foreman. 'Looking back on the journey,' wrote the journalist, 'one is struck by the entire absence of anything that could make it sensational. The ascent is safe, gradual, uneventful. There are no dangerous-looking stages to attract the adventurous and to frighten the timid – no chasms crossed by slender bridges, no overhanging crags that threaten to crush you. It is all plain sailing... It is, as already intimated, a pure experiment, but when it has become better known and the dread of a possible accident has passed away, it is expected to attract a sufficient stream of tourists into the district to reward the enterprise and outlay of the promoters.' The suggestion that a new venture might be accompanied by danger is clearly not a recent one. (A much shorter report published in *The Times* on 6 April, which included the comment about the railway

being an experiment, said that there had been several trial trips.)

On 6 April, Easter Monday, the weather started fine. A pilot train was run to the summit at 7.30am and left personnel at their stations as it returned. Seven permanent way gangers were left along the line to keep an eye on it and to look out for stones falling out of the sides of cuttings.

Without ceremony, No 1 *L.A.D.A.S.* propelled the first public train of two carriages, conveying 83 passengers, up the mountain at 10.50am, 20 minutes late because the LNWR connection was late; a second train of a single carriage propelled by No 2 *Enid* left some 20 minutes later. It was what today would be called a 'soft opening'. There were no dignitaries, no directors, no invited press. It the circumstances, this was probably a good thing.

After the second train arrived at the summit, the first started its return journey, between 12.30 and 12.45pm, Aitchison told the inquest. Cloud had come down and the curtains were drawn on one side of the carriages. After about half a mile, the automatic brake activated, stopping the train and indicating that its speed had exceeded 5½-6mph. The brake reset, the journey resumed. The driver, William Pickles, told the inquest that about half-a-mile further on the loco lurched to one side; telling the fireman to jump off, he applied the brakes and, as the loco's speed increased, jumped off himself. Without the loco to control its descent, the train also increased speed. Aitchison and Frank Oswell, in the uphill carriage, and the guard, in the carriage next to the loco, applied the brakes, bringing the train to a stand.

With a crowd of more than thirty and including women and children, this image is quite unlike any other Victorian photograph taken at the summit seen by the author, which gives credence to the notion that it was taken on 6 April 1896, the first day of services on the Snowdon Mountain Railway. (R.C. Symons)

Two men ignored Aitchison's shouted order to remain seated and jumped off, one of them falling onto a boulder before rolling back and getting caught up by a carriage running board. The *Manchester Guardian* (8 April) said that the female passengers behaved with greater coolness. No explanation was offered for other men sustaining minor injuries.

The loco meanwhile continued downhill, hitting a telegraph pole and literally flying over the Llanberis path, avoiding several walkers, and falling several hundred feet down Cwm Glas, the boiler separating from the frames as it did so. The *Guardian* report, and others, said that breaking the telegraph post 'disarranged the block signal system' and made a bell ring at the summit, which the second train crew took to be the signal to start. However, at the inquest, Aitchison said that the telegraph had been broken by a storm; they had got it working to Clogwyn but between Clogwyn and the summit they worked by telephone.

He sent someone to Clogwyn to telephone the summit to stop the second train but, he said, the message was not delivered. At the summit, the station master, waiting for a 'line clear' message that he expected to receive fifteen minutes after the first train left, waited 45 minutes before instructing the second train to leave, telling the driver to proceed slowly and to keep a good look out. Why he did not telephone Clogwyn to seek agreement was not explored.

The wrecked chassis of No 1. (R.C. Symons)

No 1's boiler.

With visibility hampered by the cloud, the second train collided with the carriages of the first. This loco also mounted the rack but the impact made its pinion re-engage with it and it stopped safely. Fortunately the first train's carriages had been evacuated, for the collision sent them off towards Clogwyn. There the quick-thinking pointsman set the points midway, derailing the carriages; they came to a stand at the downhill end of the station without causing further injury. The passengers from both trains were directed to continue their journey on foot.

The Dinorwic quarry doctor was summoned to treat the injured passenger, Ellis Griffith Roberts. Another passenger, Benjamin Blower (1849-1921) of Shrewsbury, gave him brandy and first aid, staunching the blood. Blower said he was not a member of an 'ambulance class' but his wife and her friend were,

and they told him what to do. A carriage seat was broken and used as a make-shift stretcher. Dr Robert Herbert Mills Roberts (1863-1935), the Dinorwic quarry doctor, arrived nearly three hours after the incident and supervised Roberts' removal to his home, the Padarn Villa Hotel, using the Clogwyn cabin door as a stretcher and taking another three hours. There Roberts's leg was amputated, but he had probably lost too much blood for he died in the early hours of the following day. Later, the company paid Blower £1 9s for expenses incurred in attending the inquest.

The company put out a statement that briefly described the accident and the Press Association circulated it, adding that Harry Jackson (born 1867), an Oswestry solicitor who had sustained head wounds when he had also jumped off the train, had returned home after receiving attention at the Dinorwic quarry hospital. It said

Queueing for refunds at Llanberis on 6 April 1896. (T.W. Rigby)

that hundreds of people visited the site the next day, 200 yards of track had been damaged, that traffic had been suspended and that it understood that no trains would be run until 1 May. The *Manchester Guardian* report already mentioned said that notwithstanding the destroyed loco and the fatality, 'a large number of people presented themselves' to make the ascent by train over the next two days.

Aitchison's report of the accident and the fatality, submitted to the Board of Trade on 7 April, generated a flurry of telegrams. There would be no inquiry and Marindin could attend the inquest voluntarily, at the coroner's request, to provide technical assistance. He, Marindin, reached Llanberis on 8 April, in time to walk up to the incident site, to return via the site of the destroyed locomotive, attend the inquest, and write an informal report to a Board

of Trade colleague that was posted the same day. The locomotive's boiler was some 250ft below the point where the loco left the line and the remainder was 250ft further down, 1,500ft above the Llanberis Pass.

At the accident site the path of the loco from the point where it became separated from the rack to the point where it went over the edge, about a ¼ mile, could be clearly seen, Marindin wrote. The pinions, he said, 'seem to have mounted the rack, and to have run along the top of the rack for nearly the whole distance, the carrying wheels keeping on the rails in an extraordinary way until shortly before the final leap, when the speed must have been very high.'

He could confirm that the overspeed brake had activated because the pinions were still locked when he examined them.

Some of the curious at Clogwyn, with the location of No 2 *Enid* and its train indicated. (R.C. Symons)

A few more of the curious at Clogwyn. The signalman's cabin, which had its door removed to make a stretcher, appears to have been sealed. The groundframe for working the signals is located in front of it. (R.C. Symons)

Carriage No 2 with its end stoved in when locomotive No 2 collided with it. (R.C. Symons)

Four of the pinion cogs had been cut out nearly an inch deep by the rack cogs, 'as if by a chisel'. The other pinion cogs were unmarked, demonstrating the brake's grip on the axle.

He could not account for the pinion mounting the rack and speculated that 'the road at the point where this occurred had got a little rotten on the break up of the sharp touch of frost that prevailed at the time I went over the line; and that the engine must have given a bad lurch when on a sleeper which gave under the weight, but this ought not to have been sufficient to cause such a serious accident.'

'The road at that point,' he explained, 'is certainly not as solid as it was when I went over the line, but it was gauged last Thursday and thoroughly examined on Monday; and an engine and wagon were sent up and down again on Monday morning before the regular train was allowed to start.' Commenting that the efficiency of the carriage brake had been demonstrated, he went on to say that some means should be found to prevent the pinion mounting the rack and that 'some additional retarding power should be provided to come into action in case the three existing brakes are rendered useless.'

The inquest into E.G. Roberts's death was opened on 8 April. Before starting, the coroner and jury discussed, in Welsh, whether it should be conducted in that language or in English. One of the jurors said that some of them were not fully conversant in English and there had been cases where a decision had been reached only for some jurors to admit that they had not understood all the evidence. The coroner explained that he was required to conduct the inquest in English and that if any of the jurors did not understand what was being said they were to ask.

The coroner continued that he had asked the Board of Trade for assistance and had been told that despite the railway being built without statutory powers it would treat the situation as a special case. Marindin was there to act as an adviser; in reality he was there to protect the Board of Trade from criticism. After taking identification evidence, the inquest was adjourned until the following week.

Roberts was buried in a private ceremony at St Padarn's churchyard in Nant Peris the next day. *Y Genedl Gymreig* (14 April), the only local paper to report it said, in Welsh, that a crowd had gathered at the hotel to pay its respects. The sense of grief felt by his family must have been compounded when his father died on 5 May, aged 77, although his widow must have felt some relief when *Titbits* magazine paid her £100 from its readers' compensation scheme. *London Kelt* (9 May) explained that although Roberts did not have a copy of the magazine at the time of his death, the Carnarvon branch of W.H. Smith's newsagents had been able to confirm that he had been a regular purchaser.

Roberts had married Annie Margaret Elizabeth Lane (born 1870) in 1892. His death was the second family tragedy to

Ellis Griffith Roberts, owner of the Padarn Villa Hotel, who died after jumping off the first train when its loco ran away, was buried in St Peris's churchyard at Nant Peris. His infant son had died of croup the year before.

occur within twelve months, for their only child had been less than a year old when he died in February 1895, and it was not the last. She married the Rev Thomas August Jones, a curate, in 1907, but he died in 1910. By 1911 she was living with her mother, but she cannot be traced after that.

While the story of the accident and Roberts's death naturally received widespread coverage, some newspapers were able to add to it information provided by their readers who were on the train or on the mountain. A Mr Badger of Birmingham told the *Cambrian News* (10 April) that he and a friend were walking on the embankment above Cwm Glas when they heard a noise, looked up and saw the locomotive above their heads; they went to the crash site to render assistance.

The *Bradford Daily Telegraph* (10 April) had heard from two men who had seen the accident; they were unharmed but one of them spoke in most uncomplimentary terms of the railway, which he considered to be much inferior to those constructed on the Continent.

The *Kentish Mercury* (10 April) editorialised that the accident taught 'the oft-taught lesson that no matter how ingenious the appliances employed, no matter how safe they are in theory the structure and the mode of working, these daring flights of engineering are always liable to accident, accident more likely to be serious than trivial.' While the company claimed that the accident did not prove that it was unsafe, as none of the passengers would have been hurt if they had kept their seats, 'the fact remains that they did not all do so, and it is hardly to expected that in a trainload of passengers there should not be some who, like the unfortunate man who has lost his life, are unable to retain their presence of mind in such an alarming emergency.'

The *Leicester Journal* (10 April) thought that the accident could be explained by an unattributed remark that it had heard, 'It is the Swiss system without the Swiss engineers.'

Thomas George Hobbs (1854-1941) wrote to the *Luton Reporter* (10 April) to pay tribute to Roberts as a kind and genial hotel proprietor who in 1895 had told him that he was looking forward to the railway being an incentive to the area's tourist traffic.

Seeing an opportunity for self-promotion, the engineer G. Croydon Marks thought he should claim (*Sheffield Daily Telegraph* and others, 10 April) that the tramroad was being confused with the cliff railway he was building in Aberystwyth, although the author has seen no evidence to support this claim. He also took the opportunity to remind readers about the features of the other cliff railways, and the Matlock cable tram, that he had been responsible for.

A mountaineer signing himself A.W.P. told the *Westminster Gazette* (11 April) that during the 1895 season a mountain guide had forecast a mishap at the spot where the accident had occurred, reasoning that the railway there was on made-up ground that was naturally unstable, unreliable and 'always shifty'. During the winter, strong winds would blow snow into the embankment where it would freeze. On thawing the ground would be sodden and likely to sink. The Swiss engineers, he wrote, did not mind gradients or curves so long as they could found the railway on sound rock. On the day of the accident, the writer expounded, the weight of the two trains had caused the ground to sink, enabling the loco to lose contact with the rack and causing the accident.

George Grantham Collins of St Paul's vicarage, Alverthorpe, Yorkshire, told *Yorkshire Post* readers (10 April) that the Board of Trade should hold an inquiry into the accident even if there was no legislation requiring it to do so. Either, he continued, it was impossible for a locomotive to slip on a rack railway or the railway was unjustified. If he made a dangerous ascent on foot, he took the risk. If a company made a profit by 'conducting wholesale ascents' then the company took the risk. The public should have the protection of the Board of Trade, he declared.

For one passenger, her presence on the opening train proved to be her 'claim to fame'. When Elizabeth Hallows of Old Colwyn died of 'lung congestion' on 9 May, aged 65, it was the only significant thing that the *Liverpool Echo* (18 May) knew about her. All that can be added now is that she and her husband, James (born 1824), were born in Liverpool. Before moving to Old Colwyn, they had lived in Upton, Cheshire. He was a retired metal broker and lead smelter, who was unlikely to have seen much of her £23 17s 7d estate as two claims made against it had to be settled in court. He died in 1898.

Resumed at the Prince of Wales Hotel, Llanberis, on April 14, the double-spaced typescript of the inquest's verbatim proceedings, commissioned by the Board of Trade, runs to 69 pages. The first witnesses were passengers who confirmed that Aitchison had called out for them to keep their seats before Roberts jumped off.

In falling, Roberts had injured his leg before rolling back and colliding with the train, where it was crushed between the footboard and the ground. Afterwards he remained conscious, but his knee bled heavily. Asked why he had jumped, he told Aitchison that it was because he had seen the loco crew jumping.

Aitchison explained that the track at the accident site had been laid in December 1895, that there had been four or five trains a day during construction, which consolidated it, and that there had been one incident where a loco, No 2, had mounted the rack. In that case No 2 had stopped within 10 yards and got on to the rack again without intervention, the incident that Fox had reported to the board in February. He also described the derailment of the residents' train on 4 April.

Incidentally, Aitchison concealed the exact nature of his prior experience from the inquest, saying that that he had 'learned' his profession (as an engineer, he was not a member of the Institution of Civil Engineers),

Douglas Fox & Company's plan of the accident site produced for the Board of Trade. (National Archives)

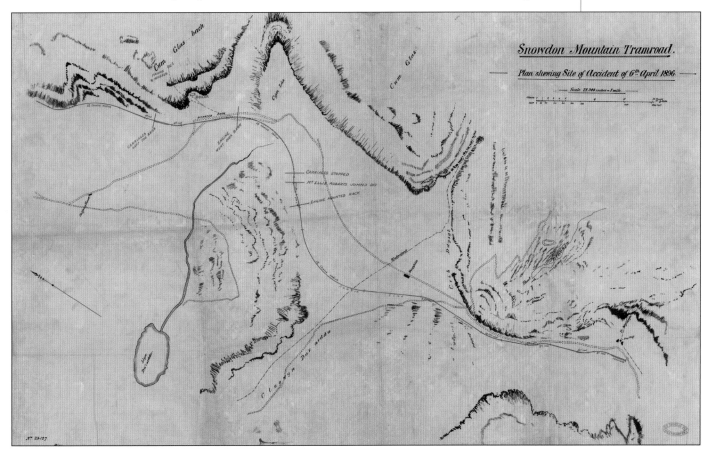

that he had been 'engineer on a line for the last ten years'. Replying to a question about his experience, he referred only to the 28-day tour that he had made of Swiss mountain railways since joining the company.

Amadelo Taechella, SLM's representative, an Italian, had accompanied the first locomotive in June 1895 and had remained for five weeks to train the drivers. Returning in March, he had travelled with Aitchison and Oswell on the first train. Admitting that he was a mechanical engineer, he thought the ground, which had been frozen, had settled, allowing the loco to mount the rack. Fox confirmed that there was a slight subsidence in the formation, a depression of about 2in that extended for some distance. Five or six sleepers had been disturbed but none fractured.

No 1's driver, William Pickles, born John William Thomas Pickles in Essex in 1852, was the son of a peripatetic railway construction site locomotive driver and had followed that career himself. With 20 years' experience as a driver he had joined the construction team when No 1 had been delivered in July 1895, making five or six journeys a day without incident.

His fireman, not named in the reports, was his nephew, William Dickinson, then 16 years old, the son of his wife's brother George. When the 1901 census was taken, William was lodging with a quarryman close to where Pickles lived, occupation: stoker on railway engine.

No 2's driver was John William Sellars, a Yorkshireman born in Whitby, who had had 17 years' locomotive experience when he moved to Llanberis in the summer of 1895. Pickles had trained him on the rack locomotives. He and his unnamed fireman had been on No 2 when it had left the rack on a ballast train working in February and on 6 April, both men jumping off the loco on each occasion. He stood his ground when pressured to give an opinion on the reason his locomotive had lurched, but perhaps he thought that it was not his position to have opinions.

Mills Roberts, the Dinorwic quarry doctor, had commandeered a pony and then a horse to reach Clogwyn at about three o'clock. Roberts was very cold and in a state of collapse. They heated old beer bottles and tins used by quarrymen to carry tea on the fire and used them to warm him until a pulse was restored. He injected four pints of saline solution. After an hour they started to carry him down the mountain, using the cabin door padded with coats as a stretcher. It took three hours to reach Llanberis. The treatment Roberts had received before he arrived could not be faulted; his leg had been tied up skilfully. (In 1900 Mills Roberts was one of several Welsh medical personnel who went to South Africa for several months to provide clinical support during the Boer war.)

Marindin asked several questions during the proceedings, particularly about the rack and the existence, or otherwise, of devices to prevent the rolling stock from parting company with it.

Summing up, the coroner said that no blame should be attached to Roberts for panicking and jumping off the train. He (the coroner) might have done the same in the same circumstances. There was no response when he addressed the jury in Welsh, saying that if there was anything that had been said in English that had not been understood a translation should be requested.

After deliberating for 40 minutes a verdict was returned that the loco had left the rack and the deceased had followed the loco crew's example and 'jumped out of the compartment and met his death,' with a rider that there was not sufficient evidence to show why the engine mounted the rack.

Calling the result of the inquest inconclusive, a writer to *Engineering* (24 April) asked if a slight settlement of the track was accepted as a cause of derailment why did it not affect the carriages? In the same issue another writer complained, in a letter submitted before the inquest, that the military engineers employed by the Board of Trade were unqualified to inspect civil engineering works. The case of the Snowdon accident illustrated his point, he said. An inspector had declared that the

railway was safe and fit for public use, yet the accident on the first day had shown his opinion to be worthless. Now 'another' inspector has gone to investigate the cause, the possible lapses of the Board of Trade and their inspectors are being judged by themselves. 'In such circumstances, can the public possibly have any confidence in the result of their verdict?'

There were others with theories about the accident's cause to share. On 10 April, John Ord, a customs examining officer at Nelson dock, Liverpool, informed the Board of Trade that he might be able to shed some light on it and what he saw as the company's attempt to conceal the cause of it. In the course of his work he had examined a packing case intended for the railway that contained '24 pieces of machinery apparently intended for brakes'. On enquiring, he established that the locomotives had 'not been furnished with these appliances ... and my suspicions were deepened by the eagerness of the person who applied for the case ... he stated that it was a matter of life and death ... I examined and counted the pieces and secretly

marked most of them ... The impression made on me is that these appliances may be attached to the engines ... and the cause of the disaster thus concealed.'

Writing on 12 April, Marindin said, 'I think I can explain ... The two [sic] engines which were in use on the Snowdon Railway are disabled, one having been broken up. The others which were used in construction work are in the shops for repair. One of them is all right except that the brake blocks are so much worn that the engineer declined to use the engine to take me up to the scene of the accident. The company can do nothing in the direction of clearing the line and bringing down the disabled engine and carriages until they have another engine in perfect order, and they are very anxious for the arrival of the new brake blocks, which they told me last Wednesday were on their way from Switzerland, where the engines were built. They told me at the same [time] they were trying to hasten the delivery, as they had no blocks in store.' So apart from Marindin losing track of the number of locomotives available to the company it was all perfectly innocent.

When this view of Clogwyn was published as a postcard in 1905 it seems unlikely that the publisher appreciated its significance, that it showed the two derailed carriages in 1896. (James Valentine)

CHAPTER 5

PREPARING FOR REOPENING

No 2 and its carriage loom out of the mist at the accident site. They were not recovered until No 3 had been made fit to operate.

I t was to be a year before the railway was fully opened to passenger traffic. Not only did it become obvious that a great deal of work needed to be done but it was necessary to ensure that there could be no repeat of the accident. There were compensation claims, the company's capitalisation, and other issues to deal with as well.

The first post-accident board meeting was held on 13 April, when the directors heard reports from Aitchison and Oswell. Aitchison had told the Lancaster Carriage & Wagon Company to postpone work on the carriages on order in case modifications were required, which implies that all six

had not been delivered. Approval had also been given to the contractors to use locomotive No 3. Before adjourning to visit the accident location, the directors resolved to express their condolences to Roberts's widow and relatives. Afterwards, the contractors had been instructed to retrieve the damaged rolling stock on the basis that the company would pay until the issue of liability was resolved.

Railway Times reported on 9 May 1896 that the track had been repaired and made safe, and that as a demonstration of confidence, Assheton-Smith had taken a party up the mountain in a special train. On 16 May the *Cheshire Observer* announced that reopening

would be delayed for six weeks and that a patent device to prevent the rack being mounted would be installed.

In the House of Commons (22 May) the MP for Central Finchley laid down a question, asking the president of the Board of Trade what information he had on the cause of the accident, who had certified that the line was safe for traffic, when any reports would be published and if, and by whom, the line would be tested before being used by holiday traffic. The brief reply ignored Marindin's involvement, saying that as the line was not constructed under any statutory authority the railways acts did not apply and no passengers would be carried until precautions had been taken to prevent another accident.

Before services could be resumed it was essential that the company and its engineers could demonstrate that there was no chance of another accident. Reputations were at stake. It would not be sufficient merely to say that the track had been re-ballasted because that would be

an admission that the work had not been done properly in the first place. Despite the Abt patentees saying that their system was perfectly safe, which it was if done properly, something needed to be done to prove it. The *Cheshire Observer* report alluded to this.

Fox offered a device that comprised an angle iron mounted on either side of the rack, with grippers mounted on the rolling stock that would hook onto it. His report was submitted to the directors before they met on 18 April but, while agreeing to adopt the device, the directors also wanted him to report on the accident's cause and to tell them how their line differed from the Swiss. They also sought his opinion on whether trains should be limited to a single carriage 'when the ballasting is properly completed to his satisfaction'. His further report was considered on 5 May and his proposal for adding 'safety angle irons' to the rack adopted. Approval was to be given to employing the Carnarvon iron founders, de Winton & Company, to 'fix the gripper

No 3 *Wyddfa* at Llanberis while the contractors were still on site. All the first locos had the recessed cut-outs for the smokebox door clamps but it was not a feature that survived. The single storey building behind No 3, part of Ty Clŵb complex, was demolished after the company purchased it from Assheton-Smith in 1897. (Photochrom)

arrangement on locomotives 2 and 3' on 26 August 1896.

Fox had investigated other mountain lines about the precautions taken to prevent 'rack mounting' and consulted several engineers, including SLM but not Rinecker, Abt, concerning the practicality of the angle irons and having received their approval, on 16 May the board agreed to tender for its supply, the order to be awarded on price but taking delivery time into consideration. The president of the Institution of Civil Engineers, Sir Benjamin Baker, who acted for the contractors, gave the angle irons his approval too. No details were recorded about the tenders received.

As news of the modification circulated, questions were asked of Rinecker, Abt & Co, the patentees, about the safety of existing Abt lines. Feeling its reputation slighted and faced with the lack of an inquiry into the accident and

its representations to both Fox and the Board of Trade ignored, the company submitted the correspondence to *The Engineer*, which published it on 17 April. Rinecker, Abt had been surprised, it said, when Marindin had approved the line for public operation, for on 19 March their own engineer, Frank Bailey Passmore, had inspected the line at Fox's request. He had written, 'The ends of the sleepers in many places project beyond the ballast. In other places the ends of the sleepers rest on boulders forming the bottom ballast. In some places where this occurs, and where the sleeper is not packed further along, the end of the sleeper is bent up. I drew attention to this on my last visit. I don't know if the damaged sleepers have been removed but I notice that some of them have not. As, however, many are now covered over with ballast, I cannot speak of those so covered. In many cases I could

There are no known photographs existing of the track works being carried out in 1896. This postcard shows the track with the safety rails in place at Clogwyn. The original timber building has been replaced by a brick structure that has taken the ground frame under its roof. (Peacock Series)

S.M.R. from below Hebron Station

The track with
safety rail between
Waterfall and Hebron
stations. (Frith)

put my arm halfway up to the elbow under the sleeper ends. In many places you can stand on a sleeper and shake two or three on either side of you. The ballast is far too large, and the sleepers can never be properly packed with it. The ballast in many places is very dirty, and should be taken off, as it will work into the mud to the detriment of the road. I saw one gang putting on soil from the sides to make up ballast. There are a great many places where the alignment is very bad ... where the road is low. There are many curves bad [sic]. The change of grade at the downhill side of the chapel bridge at 1m should be improved ... I found many of the [rack] bars wrongly spaced... The rack is very dirty. In places the dirt and stones have been pressed in hard by pinions, and if by accident a stone should get in at one of these places, it would very probably throw the engine off the line. Where anchors have been put in, the rack is left covered with cement. The rack should be thoroughly cleaned and cleared of all soil, dirt and ballast, so that if anything gets in it will fall through. The rack should

then be well greased, and the ballast should not reach to the bottom of the rack. The rack has been very inefficiently greased, and no oil has been used to lubricate the teeth of the pinions of the engine. The driver's excuse is that the oil freezes. This surely could be obviated by the use of kerosene mixed with the other oil. The result of the ill-usage the rack has received is that it shows more wear than would be represented by a year's proper use of the tramroad in full working [sic]. There are distinct hollows on the face of the teeth and burrs on the side in many places... in my opinion three-fourths of the line will require to be lifted, straightened and properly packed. Someone ... has taken it upon himself to alter the switches supplied by Messrs Cammell & Co and has, of course, spoilt them – in fact they are dangerous in their present state.'

Having the benefit of being written before the accident, this report must be accepted at face value. The track was quite clearly poorly laid, probably by labourers with no track laying experience. It was probably adequate for the standard gauge lines the contractors were used to but not for something where more technical knowledge and experience was required. If, as seems likely, the ballast was produced on site then it would probably have benefitted from being evenly graded.

Passmore's report raises the question of the nature of Marindin's inspection. He did not mention the track. The defects Passmore saw could not be fixed in a week, he estimated two months, and they would have been visible to a walking inspection or to anyone riding in the guard's coupé at the front of the train. One can only imagine then, that Marindin's inspection was by train and that he travelled in one of the passenger compartments. Whether this was a deliberate ploy by the contractors and/or Aitchison is open to speculation.

Passmore (1844-1915) had served an apprenticeship at the LNWR's Wolverton works and had since worked in India, Switzerland (on the Mont Cenis Railway),

Jamaica, Nicaragua and New Zealand. As a member of the Institutions of Civil Engineers and Mechanical Engineers he was suitably qualified to undertake Rinecker, Abt's commission.

Determined that a 'slight subsidence' in the rack would not cause a loco to mount it, Rinecker, Abt had addressed the specifics of the accident location in a letter to the Board of Trade dated 11 June. The company had established that there was a short section of 3.15ch (205ft) where the gradient was 1 in 13.2 between much longer sections of 1 in 6.6, above, and 1 in 5.5. The 1 in 13.2 section it called a step or bench, saying, 'It is so short that it is impossible to ease the corners with vertical curves of sufficiently long radii, and the velocity of a down train meets, therefore, with a rapid succession of changes, necessitating also rapid changes in the handling of the different parts of the air brake.

'Close to the lower end of the lower vertical curve, at 3m 66ch, where the line

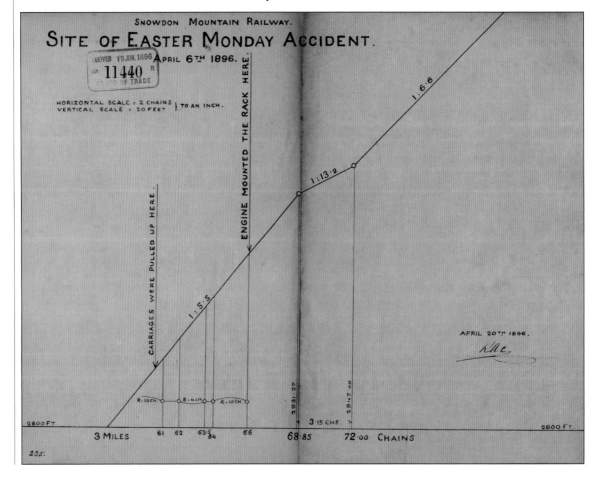

The plan showing the gradients at the accident site sent to the Board of Trade. (National Archives)

was badly packed, a short length of rail being quite loose, and where the super elevation was quite excessive, we hear that the engine gave a lurch and the pinions mounted the rack, not only of the first train, but also of the train following. It is quite immaterial whether the train descended at a speed of 3. 5 to four mph as it is asserted, or whether it was a little more, since the speed after passing that bench must have increased quite rapidly; and even if the driver did not lock the pinions by closing the handbrake rapidly, then certainly the automatic brake caused the pinions to become locked. The speed of the train was close to the limit of the automatic speed brake when that badly packed spot was passed, and it is therefore possible that by the sudden jerk the automatic brake dropped and locked the pinions ... There is no doubt whatever, but that a pinion can mount the rack only when the speed is checked suddenly by closing the brake too rapidly, and thereby locking the pinion... When all the facts are considered, it must not be overlooked: that the accident happened to the first regular train at the opening of the tramroad; that this first train was composed of two carriages with full load, which is the specified maximum; that the line was entirely new and still in an unfinished and unsettled condition; that the time of the year was rather early and the frost hardly yet out of the ground; that the drivers, able as they may be, could not be supposed to have already acquired sufficient experience at once with a full load.

'None of all these facts point to any defect of the Abt rack system, and it is entirely impossible, therefore, to improve the condition of the railway by the introduction of so-called safety rails, forming, in our opinion, a new element of danger. But all the evidence shows the necessity of removing all the existing causes of accidents, and it should be made a point, in the first instance, that the above-mentioned bench is entirely removed and a steep gradient of about 1 in 7.5 substituted therefore; that the vertical curves are overhauled and flattened as much as possible; that the automatic brake is arranged in such a way that it cannot lock the pinions, or, better still, that it is entirely removed; and that the various faults pointed out by Mr Passmore ... be made good.'

In a letter to Fox dated 16 May, Rinecker, Abt pointed out that guard rails like those proposed had been introduced on the Rigi Railway, which used a ladder rack, 25 years earlier and were quickly found to be ineffective. Despite the Rigi locomotives having only a single driving pinion and gradients as steep as 1 in 4 there had been no accidents. If the tramroad really must have an additional safeguard, Fox was told, then a brake pinion on the trailing axle worked from an independent handle on the footplate was the answer. It would be less costly and more quickly accomplished.

Rinecker, Abt also pointed out to Fox that only the rack bars had been made to Abt drawings and specifications and under their superintendence. The locomotives, on the other hand, were of an Abt type made for other lines and had been ordered without Abt, Rinecker being consulted. The company had been faced with considerable difficulty in getting the locomotives' heating surface and tank capacity increased to make them suitable for the Snowdon line.

These two letters surely provide the best explanation for the accident than any other. The track quality was poor, and the resident engineers had failed to understand that smooth vertical transitions between changing gradients were crucial. Given that it was April and the section of track concerned was sheltered from any sun it is unlikely that there would have been sufficient change in ground temperature to reduce track stability. Several witnesses agreed that the loco had lurched, indicating that the track had moved under it. The descent of the first fully laden two-carriage train almost certainly played a part in what happened, but whether greater experience would have helped the driver in this circumstance is open to question.

One further influence on the cause came from the report commissioned by the contractors from Charles Assheton Whately Pownall (1862-1920) and Lionel Bury Wells (1843-1931), dated 15 July 1896. Quoted by J.I.C. Boyd (see Bibliography) – the location of the original is unknown – Pownall and Wells suggest that the locomotive was 29% overloaded on the downhill journey. 'Having regard to the comparative weights of engines and trains on similar lines, we are of the opinion that, although the Snowdon engines are capable of taking a full load of 18.5 tons uphill, they should be limited when descending to a load not exceeding their own weight.' This remark was going to exercise Aitchison for the next three years. The report's authors had worked for the LNWR and were members of the Institution of Civil Engineers.

When an SLM representative visited the line to assess the impact of the angle-iron grippers on the locomotives in December 1896, he was concerned to notice the number of changes in gradient over short distances, saying, 'On these short lengths it is very difficult to adjust the brake resistance so as to obtain a uniform speed especially when they occur in conjunction with curves. If it had been possible to keep the gradients for a greater distance uniform, even at the expense of more earthwork [sic] it would doubtless be an improvement.' Rinecker, Abt's appeal to Fox to ease the vertical curves appeared not to have been put into effect.

Returning to matters at Llanberis, by 16 May 1896 the board had become dissatisfied with the contractors' performance. They had failed to carry out construction and maintenance in a proper and efficient manner and had ignored instructions concerning the use of the locomotive, 'the same having been run

Track with safety rail looking down the upper viaduct towards Llanberis from Waterfall. (British Mirror)

over dangerous parts of the line contrary to direct orders'. The blame was directed towards Rigby, the agent, and Fox was asked if he could be sacked. The company also withdrew its consent for the use of locomotives except under controlled conditions. No doubt the contractors were responsible for the incident involving 'No 4 truck' that occurred on 11 June.

A show-down took place between the board and contractor Holme at Fox's London office on 26 June. Holme declared that he intended giving up the contract on 6 July and would allow the company £600 to complete the works. Fox replied that this sum was inadequate 'as so much remained to be done'. Holme replied that only the 'top station', the bridge at 4m 20ch, some fencing and some side drains remained outstanding and refused to 'do anything towards remedying the tight joints to the rails' – had his men left no expansion gaps? Asked if he would complete the line to specification and defer the matter of liability for payment to arbitration he refused. After Holme had left the meeting, Fox was asked to take legal advice with a view of serving the contractors with 21 days' notice to complete the railway and to supply lists of the outstanding construction work and the outstanding maintenance.

The notice was served on 1 July and the contractors replied on 24 July. The letter was read out at a directors' meeting, and an extraordinary general meeting of shareholders that followed, the next day. Details of their proposal were not recorded but as they were acceptable to Fox they were approved. Holme had told the shareholders that he had the largest holding and was the 'one mainly responsible for the scheme'. At the directors' meeting Aitchison was 'instructed to consult with the engineers and report as to how the work of carrying on the contract should be done after 1 August.'

Tidying up after the contractors started, Rigby, their agent was still on-site and was not given any facilities. The company agreed to take a Whitworth rail cutting machine against the contract but did not want a shed as it had no use for it. Although Oswell was instructed to employ a man to carry out the outstanding work, completion of the construction was actually carried out under Aitchison's supervision.

Although at the time Fox claimed the track was undamaged by the accident, on 16 May the directors had ordered that it should be 'thoroughly repaired and all the damaged rack bars removed where injured.' Cammell's tender for 300 rack bars and bolts and sleepers was accepted on 13 June. As the rack bars were 1.8m long, allowing for the double rack this gives a length of up to 270m, 885ft, that had been damaged. The *Cambrian News* (1 May) had said that forty trains had been run to the summit with ballast and goods.

Fox did not escape the directors' criticism, being told after their 13 June meeting that 'the directors regretted not having Mr Rowlandson's report placed before them'. Rowlandson had presumably been consulted on the cause or solution to the accident; possibly he was Charles Arthur Rowlandson of the Manchester, Sheffield & Lincolnshire Railway.

On the subject of compensation and other expenses arising from the accident, the directors agreed, on 28 April, that Roberts's executor's claim 'should have careful and sympathetic consideration ... the company do not admit any liability, also to ask for a basis to work upon before making any offer [of compensation].' Roberts had been the proprietor of the Padarn Villa Hotel. Despite it being quite clear that he had sustained injury because he disobeyed Aitchison's instruction to remain seated, the board felt some obligation to compensate his widow, and on 16 May it agreed to buy the hotel for £2,547, a sum that included £550 compensation. The purchase was completed on 23 May.

Other claims were made by H. Jackson of Oswestry, claim repudiated, the company would pay his doctor's bill, and H.E. Smith of Bristol, claim refused outright. Trying for

The Padarn Villa Hotel. The building remains in use, with a supermarket on the ground floor and apartments above.

more, Jackson was told that the company's final offer was £20 inclusive of his medical expenses. In June Mills Roberts', the Dinorwic quarry doctor's, bill of £10 10s was accepted as he had been called by Aitchison. A £3 3s offer to a second doctor was eventually settled for £5 5s.

A claim for shock alleged to have been sustained by a Miss Ethel Kilshaw (1883-1956), lodged with the company on 21 August, was refused, the directors resolving that it could not be entertained due to the time that had elapsed. With the contractors introduced as third parties, it was settled for £170 and costs at Liverpool assizes on 17 March 1897, the claimant's ability to employ a QC evidently being to her advantage.

Among the matters dealt with on 28 April was Aitchison's salary, which was increased to £400, so the directors obviously thought that his performance had merit. They awarded him £30 in respect of his accommodation during the previous year too.

In the circumstances, the company escaped lightly, for it obviously had no public liability insurance. On 6 March 1897 the directors approved an agreement with the Railway Passengers Assurance Company 'for insuring the company against damage to passengers by accidents.' When Aitchison had been authorised to run a train for a party of Royal Engineer officers and instructors on 22 June 1896 it had been at the travellers' risk.

To complete the company's capitalisation, a call for £25 per debenture and the final call of £1 per share on the post-16 August issues were to be paid by 9 June 1896. Aitchison applied for a listing on the Manchester stock exchange as well as the Liverpool exchange. The listing at the latter was in place by 9 July, when a further £25 call on the debentures was agreed. By November 7,000 £10 shares had been allocated although £2,250 remained unpaid. £19,000 of debentures had been issued, of which £1,750 was unpaid. The balance sheet gave a figure of £71,946 7s 10d for construction, 'including estimated cost of accident'. The hotels and Llanberis refreshment room had cost £6,303 17s 4d.

Some minutia dealt with on 13 June 1896 included the station refreshment room, presumably at Llanberis, to be opened as soon as the building was completed, and the names of the two new locomotives: No 4 to be *Snowdon* and No 5 to be *Moel Siabod*. At the extraordinary shareholders' meeting held on 25 July Fox reported, 'the fourth locomotive has been passed, and the fifth will be ready for despatch by August.'

Tenders for building the summit hotel from Owen Morris (£6,992) and Younger of Birkenhead (£5,600) were also considered on 13 June. It is likely that Morris's bid was more realistic and took account of the extra costs of working on the mountain, or it might have been adjusted if he had made losses on his earlier work. Neither was accepted and Aitchison recruited a clerk of works to construct the building by piece work. On 9 July the hotel was deferred until the railway was completed and Fox was asked to design a timber building to occupy a site at the summit identified by the county surveyor. Morris's subsequent tender of £367 for this work was also considered excessive.

At the shareholders' meeting held in Liverpool on 25 July, Banner (*Y Werin*, 1 August) said that materials for the safety rail were expected 'in a week or so', the line as far as the waterfall would be opened as soon as possible and all work was expected to be completed by 1 September, which turned out to be rather optimistic.

The fourth steam locomotive, *Snowdon*, was delivered on 20 August (*Evening Express* 22 August). Once again, temporary rails were laid along the road between the LNWR and the railway station for the final part of its journey. The arrival of No 5 was not recorded, either by the local press or by the directors. If it was despatched in August as anticipated, then it most likely arrived in September.

No 4 *Snowdon* at Llanberis soon after delivery. There are some differences between the first and second batches of locomotives, among them the grab rail towards the front of the water tanks and the dome covers. The grab rails on the water tank were only fitted on this side and were replaced with a simpler type during the Hunslet rebuild.

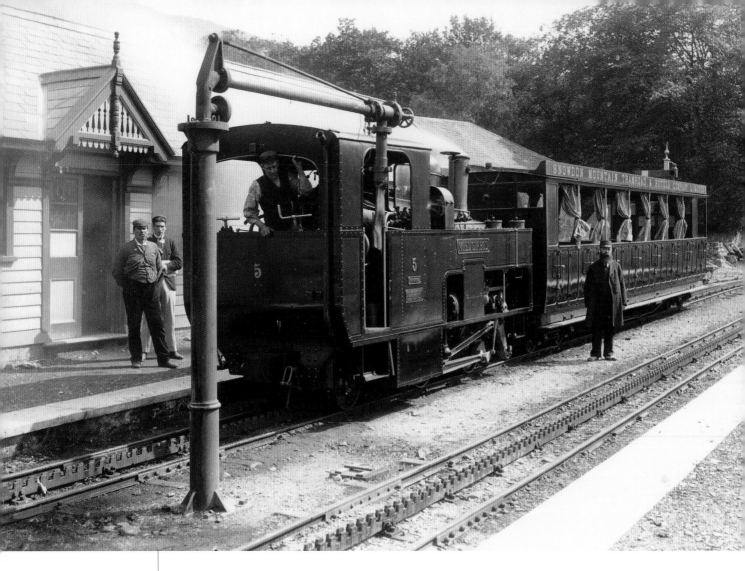

No 5 *Moel Siabod* waits at Llanberis for passengers to arrive. (Catherall & Pritchard)

A second license application made for the summit hotel was heard in Portmadoc on 3 September 1896 (*North Wales Observer*, 4 September). Aitchison said that the hotel would not be on the same site proposed previously and agreed that the existing accommodation had been improved. William George, opposing on behalf of the overseers and a large number of Beddgelert residents, argued that no case had been made 'last year' and nothing fresh had occurred to cause the bench to alter its decision. No more visitors had gone up this year but there was more accommodation for them. Deciding to hear no more evidence, the bench unanimously refused the application.

In an extensive editorial on licensing in the district, the paper supported the decision, saying that it was 'another attempt to fill the pockets of the Company, without any regard for the convenience or the requirements of the visitors.' The 'thirsty souls' were already satisfied by the existing arrangements, it said.

Progress in laying the 'safety rack' was slow, reported the *Carnarvon & Denbigh Herald* (11 September), saying that a large supply of the rack had been recently delivered and forecasting that the railway would not be reopened until 'next spring'. The company's loss, it thought, was made worse as the influx of visitors to Llanberis during the summer had been unprecedented, which was undoubtedly a consequence of the publicity that had followed the accident.

Rinecker, Abt clearly felt that its reputation still remained at risk and that its concerns were still being ignored when it returned to the pages of *Engineering* (11 September), regretting that there had been no independent investigation into the accident. The company noted that the accident happened to the first regular train, that it comprised two carriages, the specified maximum load, that the line was new and unsettled, that there was still frost in the ground, and that the drivers could

not have had sufficient experience to be entrusted with a full load. As the company had said in its letter to the Board of Trade (above) on 11 June, none of these defects could be attributed to the Abt system and it was therefore impossible to improve the line with so-called safety rails. It called for the irregular gradient at the accident site to be improved, for the vertical transitions to be flattened as much as possible and for the faults identified by Passmore to be made good. Doing so would bring the tramroad up to a first class standard, it concluded.

Services to Waterfall were started later in September although the exact date is unclear. The *Manchester Courier* (29 September) reported they had been announced 'on Saturday', 26 September, and 'frequent trips were run'. However, the *Carnarvon & Denbigh Herald* (25 September) had said, 'The Snowdon Railway is now open so far as the waterfall, frequent trips being run.' All that can be said for sure is that they started after Aitchison had received the Board of Trade's letter dated 23 September telling him that there would be no reinspection.

This letter was in response to one that Aitchison had sent on 16 September to

say that a section of 'safety angle irons' had been laid and grippers attached to the locomotives and that the company wished to start a service as far as the angle irons extended.

None of this was mentioned when the directors met on 1 October, although the operation of revenue-earning trains was considered and Aitchison was 'given discretion' to start a service as far as Waterfall, which he had already started, and to decide when the service should be discontinued for the winter.

Snow prevented the installation of the safety rail after mid-November, when it had reached a point about three-quarters of a mile from the summit, reported the *South Wales Echo* (19 November 1896). The paper also said that much agricultural produce had been conveyed up and down the mountain by rail during the year.

The lack of board meetings between 1 October 1896 and 6 March 1897 is indicative that there was little activity requiring the directors' attention. On the latter occasion they approved an agreement with the Snowdon Summit Hotel Company Ltd concerning the carriage of goods on the railway during 1897, resolved to offer the

Wind-beaten walkers near the end of their journey to the summit after landowner Assheton-Smith had erected his shed near the Snowdon Summit Hotel.

The rear of Waterfall station can be seen in this view of No 5 climbing the upper viaduct. The author knows of only two photographs of this station taken during the first sixty years of the railway's existence and very few have been taken since. Some sort of curtain to protect No 5's crew from the weather has been clamped to the loco's roof.

Ruthin Charities Trustees £100 per annum for the remaining 15 years of the Padarn Villa lease provided the trustees granted a new 99-year lease similar to the existing, whereby the company had power to deal with the property as it saw fit, rejected an offer to buy the Bulkeley estate's summit hut as the price, £1,500, was considered excessive, gave Aitchison permission to consult with Fox on his proposal to install a second independent brake on the carriages, and resolved that 'The line be opened for traffic for Easter if possible subject to Sir Douglas Fox's approval – the trains to run only as far as the state of the weather and line will permit.'

Regarding Aitchison, they decided to pay him £150 transferred from the share account as part-payment for his services in completing the contract work, increased his salary to £450 and ½% of gross takings,

and made his employment subject to six months' notice on either side, instead of three months.

Having heard that the Summit Hotel's Roberts was negotiating with Assheton-Smith and Sir Richard Bulkeley for assistance in erecting an enlarged hut on the summit, Aitchison was instructed to write to Assheton-Smith's agent drawing attention to the existing agreement and asking him to give no facilities that would prevent the company from obtaining a licence.

When the Snowdon Summit Hotel Company shareholders had attended their company's annual meeting on 12 December, they had been told that the hotel had been extended and improved, with new furniture installed and a substantial balcony overlooking Nant Gwynant erected. Despite poor weather in

August, trading results had been good and a dividend of 7½% was declared. Better results were anticipated when the railway opened.

Prepared for the company's annual meeting on 6 April 1897, surely not deliberately the anniversary of the accident, the annual report revealed that the company was in dispute with the contractors over the cost of completing the line. Fox's report stated that good progress had been made with completing the line under Aitchison's supervision and that the 'safeguard' was completed to within half a mile of the summit. The works, including the summit station, should be completed a short time after snow cleared, the shareholders were told.

The directors also met on 6 April and considered a letter from Francis Fox dated 1 April. He said that he had been as far as 4m 20ch in a train with Aitchison. He saw no reason why the railway should not be opened to Clogwyn at Easter, 'and to the summit as soon afterwards as the weather allows Mr Aitchison to do the necessary work.' Fox continued, 'I think he has made a great improvement in the line, especially looking to the manner in which Mr Rigby did the work originally. And not only has he done it very well but at a very reasonable cost.' The summit station, Fox explained, could not be recommenced until the snow had cleared; the weather had pulled the partially erected buildings into odd shapes as the roof had not been fixed before the winter.

The directors authorised Aitchison to open the railway for traffic as far as Clogwyn 'on or after Monday next' and

Finishing touches being put to Llanberis station in 1896. From the left are the café, station building and offices, Ty Clŵb and the loco shed with water tank. It seems remarkable that the station buildings and loco shed, all of timber construction, remain in use after more than one hundred years. The left wing of Ty Clŵb was subsequently demolished, as was the small building to the right of it. Between Ty Clŵb and the shed is No 1's boiler, awaiting a new owner. From this perspective the Royal Victoria Hotel overpowers the station buildings.

G.C. Aitchison and his staff around the time the railway opened. First and second from the left on the back row are probably William Dickinson and William Pickles, fireman and driver of No 1 *L.A.D.A.S.* on 6 April 1896. That being the case then J.W. Sellars, No 2 *Enid*'s driver, is one of those at the right-hand end of the back row. Standing behind Aitchison could be G.W. North, the station master and superintendent. Those on the front row left will include summit stationmaster H.J. Hayes and J.R. Owen, who later succeeded Aitchison as manager. Aitchison's chair remains in use in the railway's offices.

to the summit as soon as the line was complete. After a discussion with Holme, the directors decided that Fox should certify the amount, if any, due to the contractors and the amount to be deducted by the company for 'work omitted or done inefficiently by the contractor'. Aitchison was also instructed to draw up the company's statement of counterclaim.

No explanation was offered for the failure to complete the installation of the safety rail or the summit station building before the weather closed in at the end of 1896. The *Carnarvon & Denbigh Herald* (12 March 1897) said that two weeks of snow clearing had made it possible for work to resume 'this week'. On 16 April it said that a train had nearly reached the summit three days earlier. The amount of snow had been unprecedented and was 16ft deep in one of the cuttings.

CHAPTER 6

REGULAR OPERATIONS

aster Monday fell on 19 April in 1897. The *North Wales Chronicle* reported that Aitchison ran a pilot train to the summit at 8.00am and, finding everything satisfactory, the first of five trains left for Clogwyn at 10.45, the last leaving at 2.00pm and returning to Llanberis at 5.00pm, when it rained heavily. Each train consisted of just a locomotive and one carriage: 'It is intended to adhere to this arrangement for some weeks to come, if not permanently.' A longer report on the day's activities in the *Carnarvon & Denbigh Herald* said that large crowds watched the trains at Llanberis, while others ascended the mountain to watch them – some took 'snapshots' of the trains in motion.

The paper claimed that £9,000 had been spent on the safety rail and that it had been adapted by several Swiss railways, the latter almost certainly wishful thinking, for it remains unique to Snowdon. Reporters were shown No 1's boiler, where the only visible damage, they said, was a slight dent; it would be surprising if some of its stays had not broken.

The pilot train had carried what the *Shrewsbury Chronicle* (23 April) called a heavy load of provisions, furniture and coal

A trainload of Edwardian passengers waits to leave Llanberis. One of the four-wheel wagons is stabled in the arrival platform and supplies for the summit are stacked on the departure platform. The rope hanging from the carriage roof over the guard's position was connected to the loco's whistle, enabling the alarm to be sounded in the event of an obstruction being observed. (Francis Frith)

MOUNTAIN RAILWAY STATION & VICTORIA HOTEL LLANBERIS. 633-5

The visitors' entrance to Llanberis station. It can be seen that all road transport is still horse powered. (Doncaster Rotophoto)

for the hotel. The paper praised the view from Clogwyn, saying that the summit was enveloped in mist, with snow falling at intervals. Notwithstanding this, many of the passengers walked to the summit. The paper also commented that 'the road is far more solid than twelve months ago … there was no oscillation.'

John Partington, of the LNWR audit office, visited during the summer of 1897 and his account was published in the *Railway Magazine*. The train comprised a locomotive and carriage; the seats were not upholstered; the Webb-Thompson electric staff controlled the single line; at Clogwyn it was intended to build walls or an arched way to protect the trains from storms; the summit station building was unfinished; a GPO post box was located at the summit and the train that carried the mail ran non-stop to Llanberis. One of his fellow travellers had been Sir Edward Watkin, then aged 78; not for the first time apparently, he was carried to the summit hotel by the driver and guard in a sedan chair. No walls were ever built at Clogwyn.

Now that the railway was operating, the main issue facing the directors was settling the dispute with the contractors. On 8 May they offered to separate the Kilshaw claim from the construction dispute by suggesting that each party should pay half of the settlement. They refused to accept the contractors' suggestion, and were understandably cross about it, that Fox should act as arbitrator, and on 15 May proposed that a Mr Burrell QC should undertake the duty.

It is not known just how the arbitration was handled, but a preliminary agreement made on 6 July was signed six days later. Under its terms the contractors accepted £5,029 12s 4d less £744 16s 4d in settlement of the contract and £281 16s 9d in discharge of all accounts against the company; the Kilshaw claim offer had been accepted and the contractors were to pay their calls on debentures and shares.

This seems like a poor deal for the company, with the contractors paying only £744 16s 4d for the poor workmanship, if that is the correct interpretation, and nothing at all in respect of the accident. When the company's balance sheet was prepared for the annual report in November 1897, £76,430 18s 8d had been spent on construction and £1,942 2s 2d had been spent on preliminary expenses and the 'cost of reconstructing line after accident'. Even if the construction expenditure included Fox's payment, which might have been 10% of expenditure, the contractors appeared to have done well out of their £64,000 fixed-price contract. By 1899, incidentally, the cost of construction and reconstruction had been settled at £75,952 11s 7d and £2,292 2s 2d, figures that were repeated in each year's annual report.

Fox, too, should not have escaped without criticism, although he seems to have done. He and Oswell, his resident engineer, certainly should have done something about the sloppy trackwork. When he sought payment for extra work in July 1897 the board would only sanction £200, the balance due to him under the contract.

Having been critical of the original trackwork, it should be noticed that the contractors' structures have lasted well. The most substantial, the viaducts, have required very little consideration over years and stand as memorials to their work. Elsewhere, only the bridge abutments have received attention and at Llanberis the loco shed and the station buildings remain in use.

On 8 May 1897 Aitchison was told to investigate having an open carriage built. The cost must have been too much, and would not have been much different from the cost of the open vehicles already in the fleet, for in November a carriage was *sent* to Lancaster Carriage & Wagon Company for evaluation. On 18 January 1898 a payment of £50 10s was authorised to have it altered. It was returned without its roof and reduced in length, having only five compartments. The alteration might have been a consequence of the remark made by Pownall and Wells that the locomotives were overloaded on the downhill journey; having a lighter vehicle would help address both the weight and capacity issues. It is likely that the carriage chosen had been that damaged in the collision with No 2 on 6 April 1896.

The 1897 annual report stated that between 11,000 and 12,000 passengers were carried during the railway's first full year of operation, producing a profit of £499 4s 3d after the payment of £342 0s 5d debenture interest.

With the best part of a full season's traffic under its belt, the company decided to make a fresh application for a license, its third. It was heard at Portmadoc 3 September 1897, when Aitchison said (*North Wales Chronicle* 4 September) that 9,700 tickets had been issued between Easter and 'last week'. He explained that the proposed hotel would have 14 bedrooms and accommodate 200 diners. The hotel company's barrister called the application speculative because no witnesses were produced to claim that the existing provision was inadequate. Fourteen people had stayed at the summit on 20 June, the night of Queen Victoria's golden jubilee. After the barrister representing Beddgelert Parish Council and the Watkin estate got into an argument with the chairman of the bench when he thought his case was not being properly considered, the license was refused after a 10-minute adjournment.

Y Tyst (22 September) said, in Welsh, that the decision was in accordance with local opinion and congratulated the bench for its common sense. While Sir Edward Watkin's objection can be understood in terms of protecting his tenant, no explanation was given for Beddgelert Parish Council's objection.

However, on 25 September the company told the licensing bench that it had decided not to appeal against the decision as notified, effectively withdrawing its application. At the same session, the magistrates dealt with the Hotel company's application to renew its license, also seeking approval to enlarge the premises in expectation of increased business being brought by the railway.

The architect, Edward John Muspratt (1858-1928), explained that the coffee room would be enlarged from 24 x 16 feet to 54 x 25 feet 6 inches, sufficient to accommodate 120 persons.

RAILWAY

The four-compartment open carriage being propelled up the mountain. The station is visible behind the loco and the loco shed roof to the right of the telegraph post. The scar on the hillside in the centre of the picture is the Vivian quarry, part of the Dinorwic complex.

Seven bedrooms, increased from four, would accommodate two persons in each. The bar, including servery, would be 15 feet 6 inches x 8 feet 6 inches. The kitchen and scullery and rooms for the servants would be under the balcony.

Both the applicants and the magistrates appear to have overlooked the irony that a few weeks before, one party had argued, and the other had accepted, that there was no need for additional accommodation at the summit. The license was granted.

In consequence, Assheton-Smith put in hand his plan, notified to the directors as long ago as 10 March 1895, to build a wall along his boundary, cutting off access to the Summit hotel. A letter on the subject published in *The Times* (25 October 1897) caused a stir and was copied widely.

Signing himself 'Mountaineer', the writer said that he was 'sadly astounded' to find a brick wall being built across the summit, extending about 60 yards towards the station, blocking the hotel's door and obscuring it from the Llanberis path. Although its builders told him they were working for Assheton-Smith they could not explain the wall's purpose.

The magazine *Truth* (4 November 1897) thought that while the hotel's owners would take up the question of their access, it was incumbent on the authorities to stop any interference with public rights of way. Most comments on the issue referred to the 'desecration' of the summit. The *Carnarvon & Denbigh Herald* (12 November) copied a letter from the contractor A.H. Holme that put the company's point of view.

He said that it was the directors' wish to build a two-storey hotel of stone or concrete close to but not on the summit. It would have sixteen to twenty bedrooms, a large room for excursionists and a smaller and better furnished room for tourists; readers would understand the distinction, he wrote. Then the summit would be cleared of all the existing structures, except perhaps for a cairn on the summit. Seats would be positioned from which the best views could be admired, and a rock garden constructed around the hotel. The directors still intended to build the hotel and hoped that the land not owned by Assheton-Smith would gradually fall into their hands.

On 2 December 1897 the *Llandudno Advertiser* said the trains had run 2,000 miles without incident. The railway was now closed for the winter, except that special trains would be run when required. The LNWR had seen a significant increase in traffic on its Llanberis branch during the year, the paper added.

Minor issues remained outstanding from the line's construction. In January 1898 Assheton-Smith complained that the tramroad had taken more land than agreed and wanted a survey to be made. The directors agreed to support the survey and said that if the tramroad had taken more land then the boundaries should be relocated to reduce the amount concerned, but still sounding aggrieved, the directors told Aitchison to point out that they were not to blame if more land had been taken. Revised boundaries were agreed in March 1899.

The situation regarding the wall and the existing summit premises was resolved on 16 February 1898 when the company reached agreement to acquire the Snowdon Summit Hotel Company's property on a repairing lease of £160 per annum. The Summit Hotel company had offered to lease or sell its premises in November, but before accepting, the directors obtained Assheton-Smith's approval for 'a small building on the existing site in front of the hut and allow the wall to be demolished.' The ground rent, £20 for all Assheton-Smith's

The summit hotel building after it had been refurbished by the railway company makes a suitable backdrop for a photograph. The gent on the right also has a camera.

rights on the summit, including Roberts's portion, had been agreed in January, the arrangement releasing the company from the obligation to spend £5,000 on a new hotel. Sir Richard Bulkeley also agreed a lease for 'his portion of the original summit hut and surrounding land' for 21 years at £7 annually. The £160 lease charge was intended to return 4% interest to the Snowdon Summit Hotel Company shareholders.

To pay for the summit and other works Aitchison had obtained a £1,200 overdraft from Lloyds Bank, the directors signing the guarantee and £1,500 debentures being deposited as surety in February. The arrangement was terminated in March 1900. The need for an overdraft indicates a shortage of funds. When Aitchison had sought to commission an illustrated poster to promote the railway, the 'financial position' had been given as the reason for refusing permission.

On 12 March 1898, the directors had approved a £588 tender for a new building to be erected on the site of 'Roberts' hut'. The license was transferred to Aitchison on 27 May and the building was completed by July, when it and its contents were insured for £700.

Another property transaction had been completed in October 1897, when Ty Clŵb, the Club House, the chapel-like building used as offices at Llanberis, was purchased from Assheton-Smith.

The directors were faced with an almost existential quandary in March 1898. Was the tramroad a railway or not. The Inland

Revenue Board had levied 5% passenger duty on the gross passenger receipts, in compliance with the 1842 Passenger Duty &c Act, which they had not budgeted for. Unfortunately for the company, the Act merely specified that the duty was payable in respect of all passengers carried on 'any' railway so there was no obvious room for manoeuvre.

A.H. Holme, the contractor and since 12 March a director, replacing Paget, failed to use his influence with unidentified MPs to resolve the issue as promised in May. In November the company's solicitor was instructed to say that it was not liable for the duty and to compromise by offering to pay duty on 3d per mile, the same rate as the LNWR. Counsel's opinion was obtained and in January 1899 the directors resolved to issue a cheque for 5% on 3d per mile for the solicitor to pass on, saying that the remainder of the fare was to be treated as payment for use of the company's grounds and shelters and for access to the mountain, which seems a clever compromise. No other details of the settlement were recorded except that in November 1899 the directors signed a bond in favour of the board to guarantee that the duty would be paid in future, which was a requirement of the Act.

A small improvement to finances was made in March, when the sale of the boiler of 'No 1 engine' for £190 was approved. In May, when there would have been some revenue, a coloured poster and £10 of advertising in a Birmingham newspaper were authorised. In May 1899 1,000 more coloured posters were ordered at a cost of £19 5s.

Aitchison's involvement with other Welsh railways started in March 1898 when he told the directors that he had 'unexpectedly and without any wish on his part received the offer of the managership of the North Wales Narrow Gauge Railways'. The directors gave their approval provided that he made an undertaking that 'the interests of the company are not injuriously affected' and made arrangements for the supervision of operations in his absence.

After the shareholders' meeting on 17 May, held at Royal Victoria Hotel, the shareholders enjoyed a trip to the summit by special train and took lunch at the summit hotel, afterwards inspecting the improvements and alterations being made.

Arising from the reconstruction of the track, Oswell had obtained a patent for the angle iron. When Fox asked for £50 on Oswell's behalf in May 1898, the directors deferred responding until November. Then they told Fox that 'as commission has been paid on the angle iron there is no reason ... to make any payment to Mr Oswell and that Mr Oswell applied to the board before patenting the angle iron which was designed for their use and was informed that they had no objection as far as its use by other lines was concerned.' Fox had been paid £132 8s 5d for his part in supplying the angle iron in September. It is unlikely that Oswell made any money from his patent.

Another financial matter was discussed on 9 July 1898, when Aitchison reported on 'irregularities of abstracting small monies that had occurred'; G.W. North was given the option of retiring in one week, which suggests that he was guilty of theft, but, unless there is an error in the minutes, he remained in charge of the refreshment room. J.R. Owen, who had worked for the contractors and then joined the company later in 1895, was promoted from the summit station to Llanberis station and H.J. Hayes was transferred to the summit.

North subsequently became the North Wales Narrow Gauge Railways' traffic superintendent and succeeded Aitchison as manager there, so his offence, whatever it was, must have been quite minor. Llanberis-born John Richard Owen (1875-1934) also succeeded Aitchison as manager, but on the railway.

Summit stationmaster Henry John Hayes (1873-1943), a police sergeant's son from Bridgnorth, lived at Waterfall station with his wife in the one room allocated for accommodation. Conditions could not have been that pleasant, especially after children were born there in 1900, 1902,

1905 and 1907. The last one died there too, aged 16 months. After Hayes left the railway his domestic arrangements must have improved somewhat, as by 1911 the family was occupying three rooms in the Royal Victoria Hotel's yard. A 1936 list of employees included Hayes, identifying him as the Royal Victoria Hotel's farm bailiff; he was paid £2 14s per week.

On 17 August 1898 the GPO informed its staff that telegrams could be sent from the summit when the telegraph was working. During Aitchison's tour of Swiss mountain railways he had noticed that passengers would send telegrams and postcards from the summit and saw an opportunity for profit. His 1896 proposal to the GPO seems to have been overlooked until the Summit Hotel company made a similar request a

year later. Refusing the latter on 28 August 1897, the GPO accepted Aitchison's proposal on the same date, offering to pay 2d commission on each telegram accepted and providing a 'handing over' circuit

John Hayes, the first summit stationmaster who lived at Waterfall station, was buried in St Peris's churchyard, Nant Peris.

between railway premises and Llanberis post office.

The railway's telegraph was subject to an agreement made with Saunders & Company for maintenance made in September 1898. It required a special clause that might have been unique to the railway and which recognised its special circumstances; the railway was to provide the labour to re-erect 'any posts blown down'. The 14-year contract cost £25 per annum. In May 1900 Saunders proposed replacing the overhead wires on 'the top section' with a cable at a cost of £67, an idea that the directors accepted. In June 1901 a return earth wire was installed between the summit and Clogwyn at a cost of £4 10s.

There are no records relating to the number of telegrams sent from the summit or how long the arrangement lasted but it was perhaps a reflection of changing preferences that in 1901 the company made arrangements for the sale of postage stamps there. Thereafter many thousands of picture postcards were sold stamped with a 'Summit of Snowdon' cachet. The price of the ½d postage stamp was included in the cost of postcards sold at the summit from February 1906.

Passengers' experience was often likely to be influenced by the weather. Reverend

One of the first summit postcards, used in 1900. Thousands were sold but few survive.

H. Adler, of Craven Hill, Hyde Park, travelled on the 12.10pm from Llanberis on 29 August 1898. At Halfway the wind was 'somewhat strong' so the guard drew back the curtains, explaining that it would otherwise be too dangerous to proceed further. 'When we arrived at the spot the carriage oscillated violently and there seemed an imminent risk of the train being hurled down.' The train was immediately reversed, and the passenger's imaginings came to nought. 'But,' he wrote to the Board of Trade from his accommodation at Llanfairfechan, 'there must be a terrible liability to accidents on a line on which the safety of a train is dependent on the drawing back of curtains, and where a not excessive gust of wind can exercise the effect I experienced today. There were over 30 passengers on the train, many of them being greatly alarmed.'

Aitchison's response to the Board of Trade added more to the story. Previous trains that day had left Llanberis at 7.30am (8 passengers), 10.15am (11) and 11.09am (88) and had completed their journeys satisfactorily. After the 12.10pm departure, on which Adler travelled with 41 others, the weather 'became boisterous' and the train returned to Halfway where it met the 12.45pm departure. As the wind was easing, passengers were given the choice of continuing to the summit on the 12.45pm or returning to Llanberis on the 12.10pm. As it was raining, only five chose to continue to the summit. Finding Aitchison at Llanberis, Adler, 'in a very excited state', demanded a full refund. Being offered the difference between the journey he had paid for and the journey he had taken, he refused, saying that he would sue the company. A copy of Aitchison's reply was sent to Adler and nothing more was heard from him.

For 88 passengers to have travelled on the 11.09am would have required a train of two carriages, one of which could have been the vehicle altered by Lancaster earlier in the year.

Seeking to modernise his written communications, in January 1899 Aitchison

The Snowdon Mountain Railway.

Snowdon Summit Hotels

Via Llanberis.

❖

THE HIGHEST IN THE

❖

received approval to purchase a typewriter 'for the office'. He thought a Yost was the most suitable model.

A private visit by HRH Prince George, the Duke of York, later King George V, with his wife, to the Dinorwic quarries on 27 April 1899 gave Llanberis the chance to dress up. Thousands lined the road between the station and the quarry offices (*Carnarvon & Denbigh Herald*, 28 April) and the train was decorated with flags. In the quarry, the royal party saw demonstrations of slate splitting and dressing, travelled in a train of specially built carriages, and was hauled up inclines, where the Duchess triggered an explosion in the galleries. Returning to Port Dinorwic, the party travelled on Assheton-Smith's private 4ft gauge railway, known to enthusiasts as the Padarn Railway.

In September 1899 Aitchison reported that 'various renewals of parts' of the locomotives would be required during the winter but that they would need to be lifted before the parts could be identified.

This is the only reference to the locomotives in the minutes at this time, but Aitchison had been trying to resolve the issue of their capability raised in 1896. Although the entirety of his researches have not survived, a letter to him from Holme dated 3 August 1897 on the subject is indicative of continuing interest; concluding, 'I trust my notes are legible', Holme supplied information from a book about the Rigibahn.

On 12 July 1899 Aitchison had submitted his report to Banner. 'I have now in my possession what purports to be a copy of the contract between Messrs Holme & King and the Winterthur Company. Dated December 1894. From it, it appears the engines were never ever designed or intended to do the work they were asked to do at the start. As neither the line was designed or constructed with a gradient (maximum) as specified nor were the carriages built to the requisite weight or the number of passengers limited to the number intended.

'I send you a comparative report based on the *supposition* that the copy I have is correct in its details. I have also written to the Swiss firm to ask if Messrs Sir Douglas Fox knew of these particulars and approved and I am writing the Lancaster Carriage & Wagon Company to ask if they had any instructions as to the limit of weight.'

SLM's locomotive specification, not included in the Fox volume, had contained a guaranteed performance clause: 'The engines must be capable of driving a load consisting of two cars and passengers up a maximum incline of 18% at a speed 6-7 kilometres per hour, the weight of each car empty being estimated at 4,500Kg and the load due to passengers at 7,800Kg.'

Aitchison converted the figures: 18% gradient = 1 in 6 and 4,500Kg = 4tons 8cwt 2qtr 8lb 13oz. The steepest Snowdon gradient is 1 in 5½, the carriages weighed 5ton 10cwt 3qtr. He discovered that the weight of passengers was calculated on an average of 75Kg, 52 persons per carriage, 104 per train. Snowdon carriages accommodated 56 passengers plus the guard and four more passengers in the coupé. With regards to the gradient he said that the Swiss mountain railway engineers and locomotive builders had a maxim, that an engine had to do twice the work taking two cars up 1 in 5 as in taking one car up 1 in 6. He summarised: 'The gradient is steeper, the carriages are heavier and the carriages hold more passengers than was ever contemplated ... or the locomotives were designed [for].'

He wrote to SLM and on 19 July was told that the builder had not had a performance agreement with the contractors, neither had they, SLM, corresponded with Fox about it. On 8 August 1894, the contractors had, however, given SLM a specification stating that the maximum gradient would be 1 in 5½ and the train would consist of a locomotive and two carriages carrying about 56 passengers. 'The locomotives we offered were in many respects altered by Messrs Rinecker, Abt & Company and so, after all, we had to furnish locos different from those we offered at the beginning.'

So it seems that Rinecker, Abt had more influence on the locomotives than they had claimed in 1896. There is no written record of the outcome, if any, to Aitchison's report and its associated correspondence, but the physical consequence is clear to see: two full-sized carriages were not used on Snowdon trains.

With the trains having such a low capacity, it is no surprise that the company imposed a restriction of the minimum number of passengers to be carried for a train to run. In the early years it was four; in later years it was 25. Most of the time passengers would not be affected by this rule but occasionally one was. The *North Wales Chronicle* (7 October 1899) contains a letter from an irate would-be passenger. Having travelled 37 miles, from Rhyl perhaps, he and his wife had arrived at Llanberis intending to travel on the 1.42pm departure, only to be faced by a booking clerk saying that it would not run without four passengers. The timetable indicated that some trains were so restricted, but the 1.42pm was not one of them. The booking clerk explained that it would not pay to

take only two passengers, adding that it did not pay to take four either. The writer, who signed his letter 'Visitor', thought it was scandalous that a company would refuse to run an advertised train because it 'didn't pay'. In September Aitchison had been instructed not to run trains earning less than £3 3s in fares, more than four passengers.

By the end of the 1899 season the company had a positive balance, £30 13s 5d, to carry forward for the first time. In November Aitchison told the directors that 'if it was intended that a second open car should be ordered for next season no time should be lost as all the works were so busy he had ... so far failed to get drawings or estimates.' The shareholders were told that the carriage was 'to enable the increasing traffic to be dealt with more easily.' No details were recorded concerning the carriage's manufacturer; J.I.C. Boyd (see Bibliography) thought that it was the Ashbury Carriage & Wagon Company in Manchester, which is where railway companies often went if they wanted something made cheaply. Delivered in 1900, it had four compartments and a brake platform.

The only known photograph showing both open cars together, the four-compartment vehicle leading as the train approaches the summit.

With the railway operating smoothly and covering its costs the directors met less often, seven meetings in 1899 being followed by four in 1900. In consequence there is less information available about the railway and its operation, but newspapers often give insights into operations.

Devices to attract revenue and traffic were constantly being sought. In January 1900 the directors agreed to a 'photographic studio' being erected on ground near the river bridge at Llanberis by R.C. Symonds, a local photographer who paid £5 5s annually for five years. Born in Bath in 1867, he had photographed the railway during its construction and on the first day. He died in Ilkeston in 1948.

Only generalisations about traffic were made in the annual reports. From these it quickly, and obviously, becomes clear that traffic was very weather dependent. Poor weather was noted as affecting traffic and revenue in 1900, 1901, 1903 and 1908. In 1900 an increase in working expenses was also blamed on increased fuel prices, a not unfamiliar excuse in the 21st century.

At Llandudno, a kiosk promoted the railway and offered tickets for sale. Discounted tickets were made available to tour operators, including the Polytechnic Touring Association and Messrs Cook & Company. Holme was always keen to arrange advertising in Liverpool and Manchester newspapers, but the other directors did not always agree with his proposals, especially in his absence.

Considering the practicalities of reopening at Easter, in January 1902 the directors took the pragmatic view that 'Owing to heavy snow and the poor traffic at Easter and during April in previous years the manager was authorised not to trouble to cut out the railway or open for Easter unless circumstances changed and he considered it advisable to do so.' On 12 March 1904, the directors decided to run one train a day during April, except on Easter Monday and Tuesday, 'as far as the snow will permit without digging out'.

Installation of HRH Prince George, the Prince of Wales, as chancellor of the University of Wales at Carnarvon on 8 May 1902 brought a royal party back to Llanberis and Dinorwic on 10 May. On 3 May the directors had authorised Aitchison to 'expend some money on decorations … and to have an engine and carriage in readiness', but the party did not stop. After it had inspected the quarry workshop at Gilfach Ddu, the Princess of Wales set off a massive charge, two tons of black powder. Again the party left for Port Dinorwic on the private railway (*Carnarvon & Denbigh Herald*, 16 May 1902).

Aitchison brought the issue of his salary before the directors on 15 November 1902, pointing out that the commission agreed five years previously had never produced the anticipated amount. He left the meeting with his salary increased to £500 free of income tax, backdated to 1 July, the tax apparently reimbursed by means of an expenses claim.

The coronation of King Edward VII on 9 August 1902 was thought to have been the cause of reduced passenger numbers compared with previous years, reported the *Western Mail* (26 November 1902). When the coronation had been scheduled for 26 June, the King's illness had caused it to be postponed, plans had been made for a summit bonfire to be lit in celebration and Aitchison had said that he would run a train, but no reports of it have been found. The bonfire material had been taken up the mountain to mark the relief of Mafeking in 1900 but on that occasion the team sent to light it got lost (*Carnarvon & Denbigh Herald*, 11 April 1902).

Unable to get a position on the front row, the photographer photographed the crowd waiting for the Prince of Wales to pass the LNWR station on 8 May 1902.

Although the railway had closed on 11 October for the winter, special trains could be run up to the snow line on giving notice the previous day and guaranteeing a minimum of twenty fares, the *Western Mail* added.

As part of the hotel business, the company inherited and operated a fleet of road carriages, including an omnibus; the latter was 'unfit for use' in 1898 and Aitchison was authorised to replace it. On 5 September 1903 he was instructed to 'continue his inquiries this winter re motor cars and if possible to inspect the cars used by the Great Western Railway at Helston in Cornwall after they had been in service some time.' The GWR motor bus service between Helston and the Lizard had been started on 17 August 1903 and was the first regular road service run by a UK railway company. The company did not buy a motor bus. Although it had refused an offer to buy a charabanc from the Rycknield Engine Company on 9 September 1905, it was in a position to sell one for £21 in 1911.

On 14 November 1903 Aitchison 'was authorised to obtain what was necessary for repairs to engines and rolling stock and to keep the duplicate stock up to requirements,' the first time rolling stock maintenance had been mentioned for four years. A year later Aitchison 'was authorised to purchase the necessary repairing [sic] for the railway and also to experiment with other tubes if found necessary.' It appears that there was no formal strategy for maintaining the stock. From 1903 a depreciation fund of £946 15s 7d had been maintained on the balance sheet without explanation but presumably for railway assets as the auditor always noted that no allowance was made for depreciating the hotels' equipment.

In one respect, 1904 was the year of the motor car, with two teams of drivers testing the capability of their vehicles by driving them along the railway track to the summit. They were, according to the *Globe* (3 February 1904), inspired by a Captain Deasy, an explorer, who drove a 14hp Martini tourist car from Caux to Rochers de Naye on the Chemin de fer Glion–Rochers de Naye, a Swiss 800mm Abt railway with a summit station 6,463 feet above sea level, in October 1903.

The first attempt on Snowdon, made by Harvey Du Cros (1872-1928) using a 15hp Ariel on 26/7 January 1904, was abandoned due to the presence of snowdrifts near the summit (*The Times* 28 January), but a second attempt using a 25hp Daimler was successful on 26 May (*Manchester Guardian*, 27 May). The car was unfit to be driven back to Llanberis however, and was returned by the train that had followed it. Born in Dublin, Du Cros's father had founded the company that became the Dunlop Rubber Company.

The second team comprised Charles Jarrott and W.M. Letts, whose request to the company for facilities had been dealt with on 14 May. Also followed by a train, their 5hp Oldsmobile driven by Letts reached the summit on their first attempt, on 6 June. About half a gallon of petrol and very little water were used, in contrast with the Du Cros attempt that used three gallons of petrol and three of water for a much heavier car (*Manchester Guardian*, 11 June).

Judging by the lack of comment, Aitchison's position with the North Wales Narrow Gauge Railways gave the directors no cause for concern and when, on 9 January 1904, they were informed that he had been offered an appointment with the North Wales Power & Traction Company they approved it without demur. They even agreed to recruit a hotels manager to give him time for his new position but required him to take a £70 reduction in salary. Joseph P. Pullan (1859-1934) was appointed to the hotels post by 12 March 1904: salary £150, plus 10% commission on net profits over £700; his father ran the Royal Oak at Betws y Coed.

The Power company, which was about to take over the parliamentary commitments of the Portmadoc, Beddgelert & South Snowdon Railway, had ambitious plans for developing both an electricity transmission network and electric railways connecting

Portmadoc with Bettws y Coed, Corwen and Carnarvon via Beddgelert, the first link including the Croesor Tramway and the last the NWNGR.

Less relevant to the railway story perhaps, Pullan introduced some innovations to the hotels and left to take over the Royal Goat Hotel, Beddgelert, in 1908; reading between the lines, he had an 'interesting' private life that Aitchison and the directors did not know how to deal with. He was replaced by Mary Pryce Jones (1868-1948) at the Royal Victoria and Bessie Timothy (1867-1939) at the Padarn Villa. The former, born in West Felton, Shropshire, had held the Padarn Villa license for seven years. The latter had been born in Liverpool.

Share transfers approved on 10 September 1904 confirmed the position of the contractors as major shareholders in their own right, 591 shares being transferred to King and 441 to Holme.

G.W. Duff Assheton-Smith, the landowner, was interred in the family mausoleum at Vaynol when he died on 22 November 1904, aged 56. With his effects valued at £1,449,198 6s 4d, the estate passed to his brother, Charles Garden Assheton-Smith who was created a baronet

in 1911. The second and third baronets, his son and grandson, reverted to the name of Duff.

On 14 January 1905 Aitchison 'reported a temporary arrangement he had made with respect to office accommodation for the company [the Power company] who are taking over the working of the NWNG Company and asked for confirmation.' The company reserved the right to terminate the arrangement if it needed the premises.

Arranging this would have entailed Aitchison negotiating with himself, as would dealing with the wayleave requests that he put to the directors on 8 April 1905. They agreed to allow the transmission route to cross ground near Dolbadarn Castle for £2 10s and across the railway between the waterfall and the river bridge for £5, each sum being paid annually. In February 1906 the Power company was allowed to route telephone wires on the tramroad pole route, paying a wayleave of 1s per pole and terminating it at the office that it rented.

There was joy at the summit in August 1907 when the wife of the summit hotel manager gave birth to a son. The proud parents, William Thomas and Eileen Merwyn Evan, asked the

Harvey du Cros and his 15hp Ariel car poses for a photograph with the following train on 26 May 1904, his second attempt to drive to the summit.

George William Duff Assheton-Smith, the landowner who influenced many activities in Carnarvonshire, including the construction of a railway on Snowdon, was interred in the family mausoleum on the Vaynol estate. Unfortunately, it is both neglected and vandalised. Built in 1880, it is grade II listed by Cadw, the Welsh heritage agency. Assheton-Smith's wife, Laura Alice, and their daughter Enid, were also interred here, and his father, Robert George Duff (born 1817) had been interred here in 1890.

Train going up Snowdon

A train on the upper viaduct, circa 1905. The Dinorwic quarry hospital is on the far side of the lake. (James Valentine)

Archdruid to name the child and he chose Aerwyddfa – heir of Snowdon. The parents called him Roger. The Rector of Llanberis baptised the child at the summit on 30 August.

Serious damage to No 4 was dealt with by the directors on 11 July 1908. Aitchison was instructed to order a new firebox and tubes from the Hunslet Engine Company, Leeds, and to have them fitted. It might be reasonable to interpret this requirement as arising from an incident where the boiler water was allowed to run low, a situation that could have had serious and possibly fatal consequences. Another locomotive problem was manifest on 8 May 1909 when Aitchison was authorised to adopt a policy of ordering 'copper coated tubes when requiring any as it was considered that this might overcome the corrosion difficulty.'

There was an unspecified problem, probably unpaid rent, with the use made of railway facilities by the Power company during 1909. By 10 July the room had been vacated without notice being given and by 11 September Aitchison reported that the company had received payment in lieu. He subsequently arranged for the company to take over the Power company's telephone.

Receiving salaries from the Power company, the North Wales Narrow Gauge and the Portmadoc, Beddgelert & South Snowdon railways, as well as the railway, Aitchison was apparently quite well remunerated. On 16 February 1907 he had informed the directors that as an agent for insurance companies he also received the commission on the company's policies. In February 1910 the directors awarded him an honorarium of £50 for 1909 on account of the £70 he had relinquished when he took on the Power company appointment and Pullan was appointed. On the death of his father-in-law in later in 1910 he resigned from the company to take over the family firm; he referred to his departure as retiring. His notice expired in October but the directors gave him paid leave until 30 November, thereby paying him until the end of the company's financial year. They

also agreed to pay him £210 annually, plus expenses, to continue as the company's consulting engineer.

On 10 September 1910, the directors had no hesitation in accepting Aitchison's recommendation and appointing J.R. Owen to be his successor as 'secretary, traffic manager, superintendent of the line and works in charge of the railway and businesses other than hotel management'. Owen's salary was £156, payable quarterly, much less than Aitchison was paid. Mary Pryce Jones was given responsibility for managing the hotels for a salary of £80. When Owen had married in 1907 the directors had subscribed £4 for a present. Both he and Jones were instructed to maintain contact with Aitchison 'on all important matters'.

In the weeks before Aitchison left, two fatalities occurred on the railway within a few days of each other. Fireman Benjamin Hansford Roberts, aged 26, died on 15 September, caught between a loco and a pole when he was sanding greasy rails as the loco reversed out of the shed. The inquest jury recorded a verdict of accidental death (*North Wales Weekly News*, 23 September). A claim for compensation and costs made on the company's insurance resulted in the directors wanting to know why the £5 5s doctor's bill had not been settled on 14 November.

Benjamin Hansford Roberts, the 26-year-old fireman who died on 15 September 1910, three days after he had been crushed between a loco and a pole at Llanberis, was buried in St Peris's churchyard, Nant Peris. Aged 16 he had been an 'engine driver at quarry'. The headstone must have been made by his father and/or his brothers, who were all quarrymen.

The other fatality, on 19 September, was indirectly a consequence of the habit of local people to spend a Saturday night at the summit in September to watch the sun rise. *North Wales Express* (23 September) said that hundreds participated. In this instance William Morris Griffith, a 19-year-old quarryman from Groeslon, was with a group of friends descending on the Sunday morning when he placed a large boulder on the rack somewhere near Clogwyn and sat on it to slide down the mountain. Someone else placed another boulder on the rack and pushed it down behind him. Gaining speed, it hit Griffith and knocked him off with such force that he turned a somersault. His thigh was broken, and he sustained internal injuries. Taken to the quarry hospital, he died later.

At the inquest Aitchison said that the crowd had done a lot of damage to the railway, breaking fences, pulling up gradient posts, pulling down [telegraph] wires and interfering with the track. The same thing happened every year. He had to send a train up the line to check for damage; this was on a Sunday, when there were no trains. The jury returned a verdict of manslaughter, the cause of death being recorded as 'That while the deceased was sliding down the Snowdon Railway he was struck on the back by a stone someone had unlawfully put to slide on the rails behind him. Feloniously killed by some person to the jurors unknown.'

Two men admitted placing a boulder on the rack but said it would not slide so they removed it. Nevertheless, William Robert Jones, a draper's assistance of Carnarvon, was charged with manslaughter and Carnarvon magistrates decided that there was a case to answer although no proof was submitted that Jones had placed the boulder on the track that had killed Griffith. This point was accepted by the jury at the assizes and he was found not guilty, the decision being greeted by cheers (*Evening Express*, 17 October 1910). Aitchison was instructed to ask the chief constable to take steps to protect the company's property. That officer's response was reported to the directors, but the details were not recorded.

A fire at Halfway on 26 September 1910 destroyed the timber station building and its contents, including the telephone and the wiring to the staff instruments. The directors instructed that the railway's buildings should be insured and the cabin replaced by a brick building. Saunders recommended changing the instruments for automatic miniature instruments, but on 14 February 1911 the directors resolved that the instruments should be repaired by the Railway Signal Company. Following Owen's July 1911 report on the fire, he was instructed to obtain two extinguishers for the loco shed.

To mark Aitchison's departure, his successor, J.R. Owen, and foreman driver William Pickles presented him with a suitcase on behalf of the staff (*Yr Herald Cymraeg*, 18 October 1910). Pickles had been No 1's driver on 6 April 1896.

The Snowdon Summit Hotel Company's lease included an option for the company to buy the property for £3,250. During 1911 the Hotel company offered to sell for £1,625. Following some six months of negotiation by Aitchison, the company secured it for £1,100, including the furniture and effects; the draft contract was signed on 20 January 1912 and the cheque was issued on 11 May. Voluntary liquidation of the hotel company was started in June and completed in January 1916.

In May 1911, the directors rejected the Cambrian Railways' proposal to offer through bookings as 'we are unable to accept through bookings from the LNWR.' The value attached to the business brought by the Llandudno charabanc drivers may be judged by the award to them of a present of 10s each on 9 September 1911.

On 13 May 1911, the directors accepted the £18 offer of a Mr Francis of Carnarvon for the summit bookstall rights. On Aitchison's suggestion, he was invited to be the company's summit agent on condition that if he sold fewer postcards than the average of the previous three

Passengers happily pose for a photographer and the driver oils No 3's motion as they wait for a train to pass at Halfway.

Glyn Padarn has two connections with the railway. It was for a time occupied by W.W. Cragg, one of the first directors, and was probably taken by Aitchison, the first manager, following Cragg's resignation in 1906. Located just outside the village, it was built circa 1840. Photographed during the period it was used as a youth hostel around the 1950s, it was listed Grade II by Cadw, the Welsh heritage agency, in 1968. Since the picture was taken the walls have been painted white and its attractive porch replaced by an open structure. When he moved to Llanberis, Aitchison lived in Glyn Peris, which is nearby, on the opposite side of the main road, a property how used as a guest house. (A.W. Hutton)

years he would receive no commission; otherwise he would be paid 20%. 'Mr Francis' was probably Thomas Pryce Francis (1879-1936), who ran a stationer's shop in Llanberis. From 11 May 1912 the price of postcards was reduced to 2d from 3d.

The only time a carriage came to the directors attention was on 14 February 1911, when one of them was reported as requiring renovating and repairing; it was sent to the contractors' yard at Ince, near Wigan, for the work to be done. The lack of explanation leads to speculation that to need renovating when the remainder did not, the carriage concerned had been in an accident, and might possibly have been one of those derailed in 1896. However, it had been returned in June, when Aitchison saw it being tested and taken through the points at Hebron. Fitted with new wheels, its pinion did not mesh properly with the

One fine day at the summit, two gents with cameras watch the driver with his oil can. In this view the station building is considerably weather-beaten.

No 4 entering Hebron. Only the buffer stop and a short section of rack teeth reveal the location of the siding installed for the non-existent goods traffic.

rack; he ordered the packing plates to be removed and the brake to be adjusted.

In January 1912 the auditor had pointed out that there had been nothing written off against the company's preliminary expenses and suggested reducing the amount by £1,292 2s 2d, leaving a balance of £1,000, appropriating the existing depreciation fund, £946 15s 7d, and £345 6s 7d from the profit and loss account for the purpose. He then suggested that there was sufficient credit in the profit and loss account to justify paying a 1% dividend, a recommendation the directors adopted. This dividend, and ½% paid for 1912, were to be the only returns the original shareholders received unless they attended the annual meeting and took advantage of the train ride offered.

Two complaints were dealt with by the directors on 9 September 1912. Claiming £2 15s, one passenger had written that he and his wife had travelled on one of the open cars when 'owing to the force and direction of the wind a hot cinder was blown from the loco's chimney and dropped between the claimant and his wife burning a hole in both their coats.' A Mr J. Gray claimed a refund of 10s, the cost of two tickets from Llandudno, because on 3 September, 'owing to force of wind' the train could not make the complete ascent; the other passengers had accepted a 1s refund in respect of the incomplete journey. Gray had refused it and demanded the full amount. Both claims were settled in full. The author is sceptical about the first, given that apparently it was not reported at the time and no evidence was submitted.

The company bought back and cancelled debentures, £700 in 1912 and £2,300 in 1913, the transactions making a capital loss of £1,179 for the investors, the company having paid 45% for £500 and 50% for the rest of the 1912 purchases and 65% for £1,000 bought from Banner and £1,000 from Cliff's executors. In 1913 the investors' loss was applied to the depreciation fund and the remainder of the preliminary expenses, £1,000, were written off. On 14 September 1912 the *Cheshire Observer* had carried an advertisement offering 30 £10 shares for sale by auction.

Owen's salary was increased by £25 from 17 February 1913 and a further £50 from 1 December 1915. On 12 July 1919 it was increased to £400.

N.P. Stewart, Assheton-Smith's agent who had played a key part in the railway's creation and one of the first directors, had retired on the death of his employer in 1904. Born in Blair Athol, he died in Bangor on 8 March 1913, aged 76. Bequeathed £20,000 by Assheton-Smith, his estate was valued at £12,430 3s 10d.

No 3 was the subject of attention on 11 September 1913, with Aitchison reporting that its outer firebox had a crack and was leaking. Although a repair in accordance with the insurance company's requirements was authorised, it was 3 February 1914 before an instruction was given to send it to the Hunslet Engine Company in Leeds.

£50 set aside for distribution amongst the 'regular' employees on 3 February 1914, 'in recognition of their services with extra traffic', was conditional on Owen having £20 of it, the remainder being divided as Aitchison and Owen thought best. Not knowing that two-fifths of it would go to one person, the *Llangollen Advertiser* (20 February) was highly complimentary of the bonus and thought that other companies should follow the example. On the same occasion the directors resolved to ask the shareholders, at the general meeting, to approve their own payment, £50 each and £70 for the chairman.

'The start of the European war had sadly affected the company's receipts,' Owen reported on 2 September 1914. Railway revenue had been reduced by £805 10s 2d compared with 1913, the total reduction being £1,313 2s. Faced with having to raise £16,000 to redeem the debentures on 1 July 1915, the directors resolved to ask the holders to extend their investment for a further five years at 5% interest. Only four holders, representing £1,700, refused. The company's offer to redeem at 70% was also rejected although one holder was prepared to settle for 90% and another for 95%. Because of the requirement for all debenture holders to agree to the rearrangement, a meeting was held on 16 July.

The outcome was a resolution to extend the debentures until one year after the end of war, and that if any debenture holders disagreed a receiver was to be appointed with a recommendation that Owen was to take that post if required. This time all the debenture holders agreed to the extension.

An unpaid bill of £6 15s by Wyman & Sons, the newsagents, for guides supplied in 1912/3 prompted the company to join the Liverpool Trade Protection Society in November 1914. Following the society's intervention, the bill had been settled by 10 February 1915.

After a valuation of the company's property was carried out to determine its liability for investment value duty in 1915, Aitchison's firm, Smith, Woolley & Wigram, was employed to check the government's figures.

Owen reported an increase in traffic revenue when the directors met on 8 November 1915. He attributed a reduction in business at the summit to the lack of trains taking walkers to the area, saying 'the bulk of the people who visited Llanberis were the better class, who made the journey by motors, and ascended the mountain by train, requiring little or no refreshment at the summit.' He also reported having increased the fares by 20%, to 6s adult return, during the two weeks that trains ran in October with the result that revenue had increased when compared with the same period in 1914. The increase, the first since 1896, was made permanent on 14 February 1916, when Owen was given discretion to reduce them if it was found to affect receipts.

William Pickles, the railway's first driver and No 1's driver on 6 April 1896, had stayed with the company, becoming foreman driver. On 14 February 1916 Owen reported that he was 'in extremely failing health and that a good deal of time was lost by him.' Following his death on 26 September, aged 63, he was replaced by John Sellars, another 1896 veteran, despite the instruction given to Owen when he reported Pickles' poor health 'to recruit another man to be trained up with a view to him taking charge of the locomotives when it became necessary.'

By this time, the railway had lost its younger staff to the war. When Aitchison's call-up had been noted on 18 November 1914 the directors had agreed to keep his position open until he returned, and to pay him until 30 November. The 'plate-layer ganger's' departure was recorded in May 1917; the work was being carried out by casual labour. On 26 November 1917 Owen reported that the staff was much reduced and the men remaining had not only been in the company's employ for 18-20 years but were working for pre-war rates of pay. (Aitchison, incidentally, ended the war with the rank of Lieutenant Colonel and did not resume his association with the company, although he did return to

Visitors on an excursion from Llandudno smile at the camera as they wait of their journey to the summit to start on 8 September 1915, a rare photograph taken during wartime. The picture also shows that the roof boards carrying the company name have been removed, the lettering being placed along the underframe girder, above the running boards, instead.

William Pickles, the railway's first driver who drove No 1 on 6 April 1896, was buried at Culcheth Newchurch, Lancashire, with members of his wife's family. Despite what the stone says Joseph Moors and Sarah Dickinson had not been married. Their son George was the father of William Dickinson, who had been Pickles's fireman in 1896.

work for the North Wales Narrow Gauge Railways.)

Increased travel restrictions affected traffic during the war, although Owen reported that train revenue in August 1916 had exceeded £1,200, £150 more than 1915. By November, however, limits on the use of petrol were responsible for a loss of £300 on the traffic. A fare increase had generated £375 in additional revenue, a 'considerable assistance' as expenses had been higher. Assuming the fare increase was applied pro rata, some crude arithmetic suggests that 7,500 passengers had been carried.

One expense that was not increased was that for maintaining the signalling system, Saunders' application for a 50% increase until the war ended being refused on 27 November 1916.

Presumably an attempt to attract revenue, on 12 February 1917 Owen was told to ascertain if the railway could be of service to the government; in September he reported that the War Office had rejected the offer. Seeking land for allotments, Llanberis Parish Council did not like the terms offered and complained to the Vaynol estate, which pressured the company to release land on the council's terms.

The impact, literally, of a different new technology was considered by the directors in 1916, Owen reporting that he had, acting on instructions, insured the company's property against aircraft risks on 6 May. The directors appeared to have second thoughts about the risk, for they cancelled the £36 policy when it became due for renewal.

An early Easter and lack of travel facilities in 1917 prompted a decision not to start operating until May. When the directors met on 26 May Owen explained that despite deferring the service until 21 May, there had been no passengers. The situation was hampered by the impossibility of displaying posters and printing guide books and handbills. In July Owen reported that he had been unable to get the LNWR to agree to run more trains to Llanberis or to get the chief constable to agree to the company running a charabanc service from Llandudno. By November revenue was reduced by £1,674 7s 8d compared with 1916.

The directors were despondent when they met on 18 February 1918. The company had a debit balance of £1,511 6s 11d on 1917's trading, little money in the bank, and they saw no hope of improvement while the war continued; 'the company was in a serious predicament'. Owen was instructed to consult the solicitors to establish the company's position with regard to its leases if it was put into voluntary liquidation, and to have the plant valued.

By 25 May he had offers of £13,000 from Marple & Gillott Ltd of Sheffield for the railway and £8 per ton for the rails from Muirhead & Co. His conversation with a local bank manager had produced an offer from a Llandudno estate agent to act as agent for a sale on 4% commission. Owen suggested the directors should seek £24,000 for the railway alone or £26,000 for the railway and hotels.

Saunders & Company gave notice that they would terminate their agreement to maintain the signals and telegraphs when it expired on 30 June 1918. As it was unlikely that the staff instruments would be required, said Owen, he would endeavour to make other arrangements for the telephones to be worked for the present season, thus setting in train the situation whereby block working was abandoned.

Banner had produced a possible purchaser when the directors met on 9 July 1918. Sir Thomas Salter Pyne (1860-1921) had been chief engineer to the Afghan government and responsible for introducing many industries to that country. He had been knighted in 1894. He was told that he could have the ordinary shares for £1 each and the debentures for a sum that would produce 5% interest. Negotiations dragged on though, and despite Pyne's office saying, on 12 February 1919, that the sale would be completed within ten days, on 12 July the directors gave up hope of it when they were told that the securities lodged to support the sale had been returned to their owners.

When the 1919 annual report was released on 23 February 1920 the shareholders were told that, the company having had a good year, the best of its existence, their shares were worth more than Pyne had offered. They were also told that as the rolling stock and buildings had not been maintained in the best order during the war, extensive repairs were now required that would absorb the credit balance. A fare increase, to 7s 6d, approved on 12 July, probably contributed to the year's trading success.

Another opportunity of a transfer of control, if not ownership, came from a different direction a few days later. On 16 October 1919 Banner informed Owen that he had been approached by Samuel Gawith Bibby (1860-1950), chairman of the Dolgarrog-based Aluminium Corporation, suggesting a share and debenture exchange between the companies, and told Owen to research the Corporation and its prospects. The suggestion seems a little bizarre, for the Corporation was more than four times the size of the company by capital value so it could not have been a merger of equals. By the end of the month Banner was chasing Owen for information so that he could reply but on 9 December he told him that Bibby was considering making a cash offer. If details of these negotiations were given to the other directors, it was not recorded in the minutes. Nothing came of them.

On 20 October 1919 Banner had responded to Owen's regular report, referring to the section dealing with the locomotives and asking him to 'consider the question of applying electricity to the railway and merely putting the present engines into proper repair.' On 30 October he asked if the existing stock would need to be scrapped: 'If we used electric engines, could we not use both? I see it done on the London railway lines.' The London & South Western Railway informed Owen that its own electrification schemes had cost £8,660 per mile including sub-stations. He also wrote to the Berner Oberlandbahnen. SLM quoted £33,000, including four 300hp overhead-wire locomotives at £6,000 each. The directors rejected this as too expensive on 15 December 1919; any surplus funds, they decided, should be used to redeem debentures.

Meeting on 13 October 1919, the directors had thought that as the 'existing locomotives are getting old and may at any time give way' they should consider acquiring a new locomotive but had deferred a decision until Banner's opinion could be obtained. The stock was more than twenty years old, there was insufficient room to store all the carriages under cover, and none of it appears to have received a strip-down overhaul. It would be interesting to know if pinions had not been renewed before 1919, for under current conditions they are replaced after 18 months in service. The lack of heavy maintenance would have been taking its toll on service reliability for some time, not just during the war.

An order for spares, eight rack pinion wheels, twelve piston rings and four pairs of spindle glands, was placed with SLM on 4 November 1919. The forged pinion rings were sub-contracted to an English company and SLM hoped that a target price of £60 per ton would not be exceeded.

Owen returned to the topic of another locomotive when the directors met on 12 July 1920, saying, 'four locomotives [are] on the road and ... in case of a breakdown we [have] nothing to fall back on ... owing to the increase in traffic and the fact of the charabancs arriving at Llanberis at about the same time the demand on all days, in all probability could not be met.' He should have offered some of the parties a discount to travel at a different time. Quotations were sought from the Hunslet Engine Company and SLM, the former writing on 4 September that it could not supply for at least eighteen months and declining to tender.

SLM submitted two quotations on 30 August: £5,700 for a loco as already supplied, and £6,050 for a loco 'which offers important advantages in comparison with your existing type, for instance: double-armed rocking levers ... instead of single-armed levers, and the engine working with superheated instead of saturated steam. A smooth run of the train results from the former and a considerable economy of fuel and water from the latter improvement.' After being told that the prices were high, on 1 October SLM blamed the exchange rate and offered a credit note for the difference if it moved in its favour. The Swiss company's response to the directors' decision that £5,700 was prohibitive was to reduce it to £5,100 by 15 December.

SLM must have been keen to get the work, eventually reducing its price to £3,500 and complaining that it would make no profit. On 24 October 1921 Owen was instructed to order a 'new steam rack locomotive of improved type' to be delivered in April 1922. The £2,000 deposit had been transferred into a joint account with SLM by 16 January 1922. When the loco's boiler had been tested this money and the interest accruing were paid to SLM. A further £800 was paid when the loco was ready for shipping at Antwerp and £700 six months after delivery 'as a guarantee of sound material, good workmanship and satisfactory working', together with 5% interest accruing from the date of shipping.

Knowing that their continued involvement with the company was going to be short, as negotiations to transfer control of the company to new investors were well advanced, the outgoing directors instructed SLM that they should attach brass nameplates that honoured the company's chairman from 1896, *Sir Harmood*.

With the need to renew rolling stock and redeem debentures the directors had been prepared to sell the Padarn Villa Hotel, reviewing a £1,500 offer when they met on 16 February 1920. Their £2,500 counteroffer was accepted by 15 May; the furniture fetched £570 11s. Bessie Timothy, the manager since 1908, lost her job with the sale so she was given six months' salary in lieu of notice and permission to live at the Royal Victoria Hotel during that period while she remained unemployed. After the Padarn Villa lease had been extended in 1906 the company had sold building plots on the site, the proceeds seemingly being applied to revenue rather than capital. The 1920 proceeds were applied to the depreciation fund.

Profits made in 1919 had produced bonuses totalling £42 for the heads of the commercial departments and weekly bonuses of 17s each for the other employees on 16 February 1920. Owen's salary was increased to £500; on 15 May he also received a bonus of £100 in respect of 1919.

A train on the lower viaduct.

When bonuses for 1920, another record year according to the annual report, were considered on 21 March 1921 the four departmental heads received £27 between them and Owen received £200 free of income tax. Traffic in 1921 got off to a rocky start though, the directors learned on 21 May. The railway had opened at Easter and was then closed for a month due to a miners' strike. When services resumed the locos burned timber until the coal supply was restored.

The prospect of a sale to Pyne had resurfaced on 15 May 1920 when shares were transferred to his nominees: Harry Shaw (135), Betty Shaw (3,299) and James Douglas Moffat (428). Shaw was considered for nomination as a director but as there was some doubt about his eligibility legal advice was sought; he and Moffat were business partners. Despite additional transfers of small numbers of shares to Pyne nominees, the likelihood

of him taking control came to an end with the transfer of the Shaws' holding, 3,583 shares, to Sir John Henderson Stewart Bt on 21 March 1921.

Pyne died in Devon on 3 September; there is no sign of any will or grant of probate, so he was probably not as well off as the directors thought (*Coventry Herald*, 9 September / 16 September 1921).

With Henry Joseph Jack and Evan Robert Davies, Stewart was one of the Welsh Highland Railway promoters. In 1921 he had taken control of the Aluminium Corporation's railway assets (January) and the Festiniog Railway (July). He owned a wine and spirits business in Dundee and had made substantial profits during the war. His baronetcy, for public services, had been awarded in 1920 and may not have been unrelated to a £50,000 donation that he made to an 'unidentified' political party, which had been repaid to him in 1922, in order that he, and the party, should avoid embarrassment. He had probably met Davies when he attended a musical soiree at Downing Street on 21 July 1920 and it is very unlikely that he ever visited Wales.

There was also a connection between Stewart and Pyne's nominee Harry Shaw, for in July 1920 they had both been directors of Commercial Amalgamations Trust Ltd, which was being floated to raise £500,000 to invest in post-war company reconstruction (*Lancashire Evening Post*, 28 July 1920); it was wound up in 1921. The Earl of Northumberland's 1922 accusation (*Northern Whig*, 31 August 1922) that Shaw was involved in the sale of honours might also be relevant to Stewart's baronetcy.

Davies was a solicitor from Pwllheli and lifelong friend of the politician David Lloyd George; he had worked in George's personal office during the war and might have met Pyne there, as in 1915 he (Pyne) had been appointed to assist George in running the newly-established Ministry of Munitions.

Jack had had a varied career in England before managing a furniture store in Edinburgh. From there, in 1909 he moved to take charge of the Aluminium Corporation when it was being restructured following a financial crisis. Expanding the company's power generation capacity, he created one of the largest companies in Wales. He is known to have been in contact with Davies regarding what became the Welsh Highland Railway in 1919. In 1923 (*North Wales Weekly News*, 28 June) he said that he had first met Davies on a train.

The Aluminium Corporation's railway assets were the Portmadoc, Beddgelert & South Snowdon Railway, acquired in 1918 with the purchase of the North Wales Power & Traction Company, and the North Wales Narrow Gauge Railways, control acquired in 1920. The PBSSR comprised the Croesor Tramway and partly built sections of railway around Beddgelert intended to connect the tramway to the NWNGR at Rhyd Ddu, to create a railway connecting Portmadoc to Carnarvon.

The corporation's railway assets had been acquired to enable them to be incorporated into the Welsh Highland Railway. At a time when the nation's main-line network was being amalgamated into four groups, the trio created their own group of narrow-gauge railways. Whereas control of the Festiniog Railway was necessary to ensure the WHR's development, acquiring control of the Snowdon company was most likely opportunistic, based on the fortuitous availability of Pyne's shares.

Stewart's shareholding soon became little more than nominal however, reduced to just 38 shares after 25 were transferred to Jack, 25 to Davies and 3,500 to Branch Nominees Ltd, a subsidiary of the National Provincial Bank, on 21 May 1921.

It is most likely that the shares registered to Branch Nominees were being held as security for loans obtained by Stewart for his own purposes. On 24 October 1921, 90 of them were transferred to nine persons, 10 each, including Gwilym Lloyd George, Walter Cradoc Davies, Davies's brother, and several employees of the corporation, and on 16 January 1922 the remainder, 3,410, were transferred back to Stewart.

The company's 1920 offer to redeem debentures at 70% had received a poor response, with only £2,000 of acceptances. Another £600 was redeemed at 75%, including Fox's £400 holding acquired via a broker who received 2½% commission. There was a better response in 1922 when 90% was offered, attracting acceptances of £3,600 from contractor King's daughter, £1,000 from Banner and £3,500 from Holme.

Stewart's takeover of the company was well underway when the directors met on 18 March 1922, Banner announcing that he was negotiating with Jack and Davies to sell 'certain shares' for £3 each. Davies agreed to buy 1,500 shares at that price by 27 March, leading to his and Jack's election as directors subject to confirmation at the general meeting.

On 18 March, the directors had also dealt with bonuses for 1921, awarding £33 to the heads of departments and £100 to Owen, the last act of direction of the old regime.

It seems appropriate here to mention the changes to the board. Directors who resigned or died were not always replaced immediately. W.W. Cragg resigned in December 1906, F.W. Turner had died on 13 May 1908, aged 61, and H. Clegg on 26 November 1909. Born in Oldham in 1842, Clegg had been a solicitor who retired to Plas Llanfair, Anglesey, where he took an active part in public life on the island and in Carnarvonshire, estate £204,428 16s 11d. C.W. King, Holme's partner as contractor, became a director from 11 May 1907 and died on 25 December 1916, aged 89, estate valued at £25, a big difference from his partner; presumably the debentures redeemed by his daughter in 1922 were overlooked. William Coltart Cross, an India rubber manufacturer from Liverpool, was a director from June 1910; another Anglesey resident, he died on 19 March 1925, aged 77, estate £11,036 19s 10d. Holme died on 8 July 1912, aged 71, estate £25,524 2s 10d, and was replaced by his nephew, Clinton James Wilson Holme (1863-1931), from 9 September.

Francis Wynne Turner, one of the first directors, was buried in the churchyard at Llanfairisgair, between Caernarfon and Bangor.

This ornate memorial marks the burial place of Harry Clegg, another of the first directors, and other members of his family, in St Nicholas's churchyard at Llanfairpwllgwyngyll, Anglesey.

Contractor Charles Wilden King was buried with his eldest daughter and other members of her family in the churchyard of St Nicholas, Harpenden, Herts.

King's contracting partner, Arthur Hill Holme, was buried in Liverpool's Anfield Cemetery. His father, buried in the same plot, had the same names.

The railway's first chairman, Sir John Sutherland Harmood Banner, was buried in Toxteth Park Cemetery, Liverpool.

J.S.H. Banner, chairman from 1894 until 1922, died on 24 February 1927, aged 80. A respected accountant with experience in company reconstruction, he had been a member of Liverpool City Council from 1895 until 1912, Unionist MP for Everton since 1905, Lord Mayor of Liverpool in 1912, knighted in 1913 and created a baronet in 1924 (*The Scotsman* 25 February). His estate was valued at £449,279 10s 11d. His accountancy firm continued after his death but lost its independence after its part in the London & County Securities Bank's collapse in 1973 was subject to criticism.

Sir Charles Douglas Fox, the engineer, had died at his daughter's house in Sevenoaks, Kent, on 13 November 1921, aged 81, estate £49,164 12s 3d. His brother and business partner, Sir Francis Fox, died on 7 January 1927, aged 83. A pioneer in the use of grout to stabilise old buildings, his work on Winchester Cathedral had brought him a knighthood in 1912. His estate was valued at £40,615 10s 2d.

Sir Douglas Fox was buried in the churchyard extension at St Nicholas, Sevenoaks. His brother, Sir Francis, was buried in a section of Putney Vale cemetery that has been subject to substantial vandalism.

Holme & King's agent, T.W. Rigby, had died on 1 January 1924, aged 67, estate £3,038 7s 6d, and was buried in St Bartholomew's churchyard at Westhoughton, Lancs. Fox's resident engineer, Frank Oswell, died on 22 June 1936, aged 73, run down by a lorry while cycling in Chalford, Gloucestershire, estate £8,948 9s 2d. He had worked with Fox on the Mersey Railway tunnel. His father, William Cotton Oswell, had been an explorer and friend of David Livingstone.

G.C. Aitchison, the first manager, died on 25 October 1928, aged 65, estate £34,113 12s 3d. With his management of the North Wales Narrow Gauge Railways and the North Wales Power & Traction Company as well as the railway, he played an important part in the history of Welsh narrow gauge railways.

Owen Morris, the builder whose works included the Llanberis station buildings, died on 7 February 1917, aged 75. He also built houses, chapels and schools in the Carnarvon area.

Since 1894 the founding directors, and their successors in some cases, worked hard

This simple slab marks the grave of Gowrie Colquhoun Aitchison, the railway's first manager, in the churchyard at South Collingham All Saints'. He shared a plot with his first wife; his brother was buried nearby.

Targeted marketing in the *Manchester Guardian* on 6 July 1915.

to construct the tramroad, to create a viable and sustainable business, but despite their efforts the business was only marginally viable and was probably not sustainable in the long term. The annual reports only contain the minimal information required by statute so include nothing about turnover or operating expenditure. All that can be gleaned from them is that the company earned enough to pay the debenture interest and to redeem more than three-quarters of the debentures, but it rarely paid a dividend.

Nevertheless, it did overcome the setback of a serious accident on the first day of public operation and the railway did become an essential feature of a visit to Snowdon for thousands of tourists, restoring economic viability to Llanberis, just as the landowner G.W.D. Assheton-Smith and his agent N.P. Stewart had hoped.

Now the company needed a new team to take the railway forward into the second quarter, and beyond, of the twentieth century.

No 4 crossing the bridge over the Llanberis path near Clogwyn.

TRAIN NEARING SNOWDON SUMMIT

THE SUMMIT AND ITS BUILDINGS

Right: Cropped and coloured for use as a lantern slide, this photograph probably dates from the 1880s. The 'old original' hut is on the left and the summit hotel on the right. There are two umbrellas and two bags on the ground in the centre of the picture.

Below left: This view taken on another occasion shows more detail of the 'old original' building and ornate geometric patterns on the hotel porch. In 1886 the Ordnance Survey mounted a 12-inch theodolite on the cairn when it was making a trigonometrical survey of the surrounding mountains (*North Wales Chronicle*, 9 October 1886).

Below right: By the 1890s both properties have been altered, with the porches of both buildings having pitched roofs. The sign over the hotel entrance offers a bazaar and refreshments.

Soon after the railway was opened, the station building is freshly whitewashed, with no sign of weathering. An interesting feature of this picture is that no one is looking at the photographer.

The summit station building looking more than a little weather-beaten. The photograph emphasises the difference in the levels of the terminal tracks.

The summit station showing its relationship with the refurbished summit hotel. (Francis Frith)

SNOWDON SUMMIT FROM THE AIR (5383)

An aerial view of the original station building and the summit huts. (Photochrom)

The first phase of Clough Williams-Ellis's building under construction. (Photochrom)

The incomplete terrace.

W.662.   ON THE SUMMIT OF SNOWDON

The flat roof in use as intended, in 1936, but there are no barriers and there is a nasty trip hazard. How times have changed. The use of the roof by visitors did not last long. (James Valentine)

The summit station in 1936 with No 2 and one of the Swiss carriages painted in one of E.R. Davies's bright colours.

The poster published in 1935 to promote excursions to the railway and its new hotel. (Davies collection)

A few of the girders prepared at the Festiniog Railway's Boston Lodge works awaiting transfer to a road vehicle for transport to Llanberis.

The completed building in 1938. In front of the centre doors is one of the height posts. (Davies collection)

The Williams-Ellis building in 1938, a view that shows the large amount of glazing that he intended it to have. But already the edging to the flat roof has sustained weather damage and the new first floor does not look as fresh as might be expected. The summit huts are still in situ. (Davies collection)

The café in 1938. The signs hanging from the ceiling beams advise that visitors consuming their own food will be charged 6d. As well as advertisements for the railway there are signs telling visitors not to litter the countryside. (Davies collection)

Another view of the interior showing the oil lamps used for illumination. Water damage to the ceiling can be seen. (Davies collection)

The bedrooms were targeted at different classes. This was the largest, with a double and a single bed, handbasin, armchairs and a mirror. (Davies collection)

A smaller room with a double bed. (Davies collection)

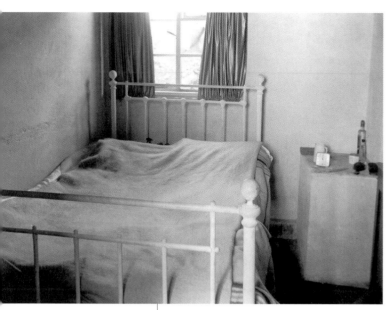

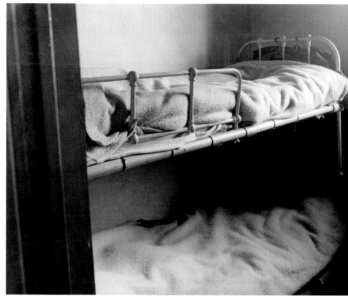

A room with more basic facilities, or perhaps this one was for staff. It will be noticed that the quality of the décor declines with the quality of the bed. (Davies collection)

Either for the lowest end of the market or for staff. (Davies collection)

The guests' lounge and dining room.
(Davies collection)

A pre-war view of a train arriving as seen from the café roof. (J. Salmon)

An aerial view of the summit circa 1948, the Air Ministry's Nissen hut remains in place, obstructing one of the platforms and terminal tracks. (Aero Pictorial)

Snowdon, the Summit

13134

From this angle changes to the building can be seen. The terrace door has been converted into a window, and the terrace removed, and one of the ground floor windows has been made smaller. (Aero Pictorial)

No 3 in the summit station in the late 1940s, a view that shows how the building's end wall has been bricked up leaving just a single door.

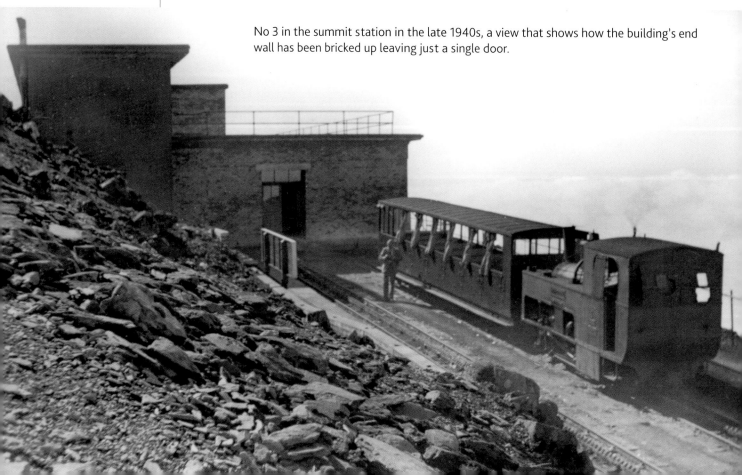

Two trains in the station on 7 September 1953. The nearest carriage has had its coupé glazed, whereas the far one has been rebodied while retaining its half-doors.

This view published in 1955 shows how all the original windows and doors have been replaced. The dish and aerial on the roof might be connected with a BBC broadcast made from the railway in 1954. (James Valentine)

SNOWDON SUMMIT HOTEL

W 5969

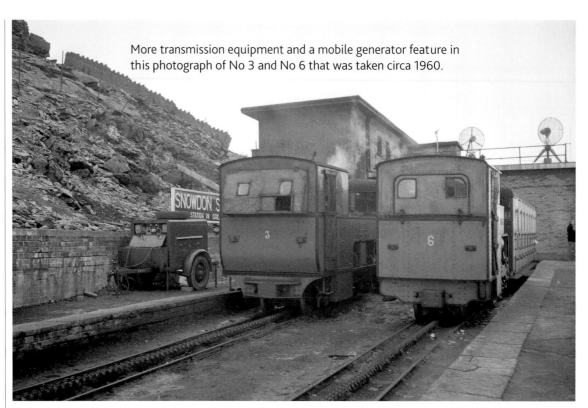

More transmission equipment and a mobile generator feature in this photograph of No 3 and No 6 that was taken circa 1960.

Another aerial view, this one dating from 1966 and showing a long queue waiting for the train. It also shows the generator house built alongside the platform and that some of the guest room windows have been bricked up. The low wall shown in the previous picture has been replaced by a substantial stone structure to stabilise the slope.(Aerofilms)

No 2 and *The Snowdon Lily* wait for passengers on 31 May 2013.

A reminder that for several months each year the summit is snowbound. This was the scene at the station on 19 January 2020. (Ian Andrew)

CHAPTER 7

UNDER NEW MANAGEMENT

Stewart, Davies and Jack formally took control of the company at the general meeting on 6 May 1922. J.S.H. Banner, A.H. Holme and W.C. Cross received £350, probably £150 to Banner and £100 each to the others, as compensation for their loss of office.

The new regime's first board meeting had taken place on 12 April, when H.J. Jack and E.R. Davies had formally accepted Banner's resignation and elected J.H. Stewart a director and chairman. Despite his investment, Stewart did not attend any meetings.

Owen was instructed to pay all accounts by cheque where possible and to cash a cheque to pay the wages. He reported on the condition of the infrastructure and rolling stock and said that the new locomotive was delayed. He was instructed to organise maintenance of the company's

Henry Joseph Jack

Sir John Henderson
Stewart Bt

lines, telephones and staff instruments and arrange for the GPO to install a telephone (Llanberis 223). Share transfers included 750 to Jack and 763 to Davies. Holme retained 86 and Banner 195. The source or sources of the shares concerned were not recorded. Davies reported that he had been in touch with the LNWR and Red Garage concerning combined bookings; his attempts to generate business were to be a key feature of his involvement with the railway.

Courtesy of the 1921 Finance Act, Owen was able to report a refund of £606 16s 2d in overpaid passenger duty. Fares had also been exempted from the duty if they were less than the, unspecified, minimum ordinary fare.

Over the course of meetings held on 12 April and 6 May, Davies and Jack

Evan Robert Davies

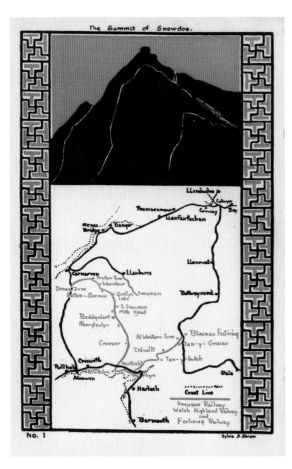

A map showing the three railways controlled by Davies, Jack and Stewart.

Surveying the railway on 27 May and 5 June, Davies and Jack recorded their objectives for the business at a meeting held on 24 June 1922. Concerning the railway: on the summit, the 'old original' building was to be used solely as a tea room, the former Snowdon Summit Hotel partly as a refreshment bar and partly as accommodation, and the small shed as a bookstall; a new hotel on the station site, made of concrete and with a flat roof, was to provide covered railway accommodation, seating for 250, lounge, kitchen, 'sanitary conveniences' and bedrooms for fifty guests; posts indicating the height above sea level were to be erected at half-mile intervals; the existing lavatories at Llanberis were to be converted into a bookstall and new lavatories to be provided adjoining the old offices; the Llanberis refreshment room was to have French doors giving access to the platform and its balcony was to be modified to give access to both the platform and main road; the riverside platform was also to be extended and widened.

Concerning rolling stock, prices for new locomotives and carriages were to be obtained. Owen was to develop afternoon excursions to increase late afternoon and evening traffic, 'even at reduced fares'. Davies was to organise the publication of a 'new book containing extracts from eminent authors dealing with the

made it clear that they would take a more commercial approach to the company's trading activities. Told that his bookstall agreement would not be renewed, Mr Francis countered with an amended offer of £40, more than double what he had been paying since 1911. He was told that he could have the right to sell Goss, crested, china for £40 but that the company would sell other gifts, including china, and that the company would review the arrangement at the end of the season, giving no pledge to renew the agreement. Davies arranged for stocks of suitable goods to be sold at Llanberis and the summit; two or three girls were to be employed, dressed in Welsh costume, to sell them. Two girls were soon employed but without the Welsh costumes. In 1934 Davies arranged for a schoolgirl in Welsh dress to act as station mistress at Beddgelert on the Welsh Highland Railway.

This poor image is the only one known to show that E.R. Davies did succeed in finding someone to work at the railway wearing Welsh dress.

Snowdon district and illustrated' and to arrange for the insurance policies to expire 'at midsummer'. Renewing policies would be easier when income was high than during the winter when it was almost non-existent.

It was to be more than ten years before the summit got its new building and then it was much smaller than described.

The business's fire insurances were itemised in detail. Of particular interest, with valuations, were the 'two small carriages', £300 each; five large carriages, £600 each; five locomotives, £1,500 each. The risk of damage arising from the use of steam boilers was covered up to £3,500 each. Third party cover put a limit of £20,000 of claims in any one year. Insurance for five locomotives informs us that No 6 had been delivered by this date; its arrival was not otherwise recorded.

The stations were listed as: station house, waiting room, dwelling room, storeroom, domestic offices, 'all under one roof or communicating known as Waterfall station', £300; Hebron and the summit station were similar, £300 each. Llanberis station comprised: booking office, booking hall, waiting room, porter's room and lavatories, £500; furniture and fittings, £50; refreshment room, bar and store, £1,200; engine shed and fitters' workshop, £1,500; dwelling house, offices and store, £600; office furniture, fittings, books, stationery and instruments, £200; store adjoining, £50. The house and store were stone-built with slate roofs, the other buildings being timber with slate roofs. Clogwyn signal cabin was brick-built with a corrugated iron roof, £50. Davies's legal practice arranged the insurance and took half of the commission.

Jack's ideas for timetables and increasing locomotive water capacity, to avoid having to take water en route, do not appear to have impressed Davies. The former was left for Owen to deal with and Jack volunteered to consult Fox regarding the latter.

Other issues dealt with on 24 June included the transfer of the registered office to Davies's office at 7 Victoria Street,

London, and the appointment of William Richard Huson (1854-1936) as secretary, a role he performed for the other railways in the Davies / Jack / Stewart empire; he was a solicitor. Owen continued as general manager without any change in salary.

A consequence of the change in office was that Owen ceased to attend the board meetings, and to write the minutes; since 1894 there had been only three meetings not recorded in his hand. Previously the minutes had been mostly recording matters arising from Aitchison's and Owen's reports, now they were to reflect the directors' concerns and there was, in consequence, less minutiae about operational matters recorded. Judging by the small amount of correspondence that survives, Owen and Banner had been in regular contact, writing several times a week.

Finally, on 24 June 1922, Davies reported a meeting that he had had with Sir Douglas Fox & Partners and SLM's London agent about new rolling stock in London two days before. SLM had quoted £3,750 for a new locomotive to be delivered in 1923. Discussing the need for additional safeguards, Fox had said that the railway would be quite safe running carriages with a capacity greater than sixty. Fox was appointed, or re-appointed, the company's engineer two days later.

An accident had occurred on 9 June 1922, when a casting broke and the loco 'shot forward' at Clogwyn Coch. The automatic brakes came into effect and the train stopped (*Carnarvon & Denbigh Herald*, 16 June) but a Mr Wade broke his leg when he jumped off the train. His letter of claim was passed to the insurance company to deal with. The *North Wales Weekly News* (15 June) said that he was unhurt until another jumping passenger landed on top of him.

On 11 August 1922 Davies was asked to negotiate with SLM for two locos and a carriage. Davies and Jack, together with

One of the height posts soon after installation at Hebron. The photographer noted that the locomotive was No 2 and it can be seen that the carriage also bears that number. Not only is the screen separating the passengers from the guard's coupé glazed but the side panels have been glazed too. (S. Wood)

one of Fox's engineers, were to inspect Swiss mountain railways to decide on the best type of carriage, to determine the best method of increasing capacity, 'by providing more passing places or otherwise', and observing the latest developments in mountain railway practices and amenities. This visit might not have taken place, for on 27 August 1923 Davies alone was instructed to visit Switzerland with a similar brief. He must have departed straight after the meeting, for on 19 February 1924 he said that he had visited Switzerland 'last August and September'. In addition to being shown the SLM works, he 'inspected and travelled upon' several railways and funiculars, noting that several lines ran trains of two or three carriages without problems. He had been assured by SLM representatives that the new locomotives were quite capable of 'taking a train of two coaches'. To test this claim, trains with two carriages were to be run in 1924, but there

is no evidence of them; the subject was not mentioned again.

The opening of the Welsh Highland Railway to Portmadoc on 1 June 1923 prompted the revival of the company's scheme for a new summit hotel. The 'somewhat unsightly' huts would be removed and replaced by a Swiss chalet-style building with a veranda (*Westminster Gazette*, 26 June) but it was to be another ten years before any work was done.

Railway wages were the topic of a meeting held by Davies and Jack at Dolgarrog on 29 September 1923, Davies and Owen having discussed the issue at Llanberis the previous day. They considered a list of the personnel concerned, seven of whom were still being paid the bonus introduced in 1919. New rates, as listed, were introduced from 1 October, removing the bonus and paying a small increase over the basic rate. A train crew returning to Llanberis after 4.30pm would be paid an extra 2s 6d each.

Name	Duty	Wages	Bonus	Total	Proposed
John Sellars	Driver	£3 8s	17s	£4 5s	£3 10s
T. Williams	Driver	£3 3s	17s	£4	£3 5s
C. Parry	Driver	£3 3s	17s	£4	£3 5s
E. Roberts	Driver	£3 3s	17s	£4	£3 5s
R. Williams	New driver	£3	Nil	£3	£2 5s *
W. Thomas	New driver	£2 5s	Nil	£2 5s	£2 *
B. Griffiths	Fireman	£1 10s	Nil	£1 10s	£1 10s
John Hayes	Bailiff	£2 18s	17s	£3 15s	£3
H. Williams	Conductor	£2 13s	17s	£3 15s	£2 15s
E. Hughes	Conductor	£2 8s	17s	£3 5s	£2 10s
H. Jones	Conductor	£2 15s	Nil	£2 15s	£2 5s
O. Griffiths	Ganger	£2 18s	17s	£3 15s	£3
Mr W. Edwards	Station master			£4	£3 10s

* for winter

There are some queries about this list. The bailiff, not mentioned elsewhere, was presumably the estate manager. Most likely the ganger was employed full time and had the assistance of additional labour on

a casual basis. William Edwards had been appointed stationmaster on 13 May 1911, wage £1 2s per week.

The order for two more locomotives, 'similar to the one last supplied and

known as *Sir Harmood'*, was sealed on
1 December 1922. The price was £3,500
each, payable in four instalments by
1 October 1925, 5% interest being payable
on the deferred payments. Reflecting Jack's
concern, tank capacity was increased after
the order had been placed, the additional
cost of £24 per locomotive being approved
on 12 January 1923. The existing rolling
stock was reviewed on the same date,
Davies and Jack agreeing to pay £25 for
an SLM employee to overhaul and test it
before it was put into service later in the
year. There can be no doubt that the stock
required qualified attention, but it must
be doubtful that the time available was
adequate.

Loco names were also considered on
12 January, *Aylwin* and *Eryri* being chosen
for the new machines. No 6's tenure
bearing the former chairman's name
turned out to be brief, for the decision
to rename it *Padarn* was recorded at the
same time. An order for two replacement
plates was placed with SLM on 23 January.
Costing £3, they were designed to use
the bolt holes originally occupied by the
Sir Harmood plates and were shipped with
No 7. No photographs are known to exist
showing No 6 at Llanberis with its original
name.

Removal of rock at Llanberis to improve
access to the yard and create more space
for charabancs had been carried out in
December 1922. The blasting risk was
insured for £7 10s and the employer's
liability at 7½% on wages estimated at
£300.

Davies and Jack considered
improvements to more of the railway's
infrastructure on 12 January 1923, reporting
discussions with Ralph Freeman, of
Sir Douglas Fox & Partners, on installing
a second track from Llanberis station
to a new loco shed and the provision of
additional passing places. None of this
work was done.

They were obviously confident about
the ability of the business to fund these
investments, and the new locomotives,
merely arranging a £7,000 overdraft from

the London City & Midland Bank; it was
increased to £9,000 by 27 August 1923.

Owen's proposal to reduce the fares 'in
view of the general reduction of fares on
railways and in view of the reduction in
wages on this railway' was considered on
2 February 1923. The new adult fare was
to be 8s, railway and charabanc companies
paying 5s 6d before 8 July and after
15 September. In the summer, the party fare
of 6s would be available before 11am and
after 3.30pm.

Sir Richard Bulkeley's attempt to
sell his Carnarvonshire property in
1921 gave the company an opportunity
to expand its business by buying 100

An advertisement
placed by SLM's
British agent
featuring locomotive
No 6 with its original
name, *Sir Harmood*.

No 6 at the summit on 30 August 1926. The *Padarn* nameplates were made to use the same bolt holes used by the *Sir Harmood* plates previously carried. (H.C. Casserley/Dave Waldren collection)

acres of land that included part of the Aberglaslyn pass. First mentioned in August 1922, on 2 February 1923 Davies said that it offered 'particular and exceptional advantages for laying out a pleasure park and tea gardens, possessing great natural beauty.' He was authorised to negotiate up to £2,000 for it. The likelihood of the Goat Hotel at Beddgelert also being offered for sale was also considered; operated in conjunction with the Royal Victoria Hotel, its value 'would be greatly enhanced by the opening of the Welsh Highland Railway.' An offer to buy it, including fishing rights, for £6,000 was rejected as the vendor wanted £6,500.

Further expansion of the business in association with the group's railways progressed when Jack obtained exclusive rights to operate refreshment rooms and bookstalls on the Festiniog and Welsh Highland Railways at a rental of £50 for each from 1 August 1923. Bookstalls were provided at Blaenau Festiniog, Tan y bwlch, Minffordd, Beddgelert and Snowdon, and combined bookstalls and refreshment rooms at Portmadoc, Dinas and South Snowdon. The inclusion of Snowdon and South Snowdon, both names given to Rhyd Ddu on the WHR, in both lists may appear to be an error but it was intended to provide two rooms for refreshments and one for the bookstall there. On 21 July 1925, annual ground rent of 10s for the refreshment rooms at Blaenau Festiniog, Portmadoc, Beddgelert and Dinas was agreed.

The Blaenau Festiniog bookstall cost £85; Portmadoc New, £400; Beddgelert, £75 and Dinas, £375. The latter was partly on land leased from the LMS by the WHR for £1 per year. The Tan y bwlch bookstall building was transferred from Llanberis and a temporary refreshment room was provided at Minffordd.

Two carriages had been ordered from SLM by 14 April 1923, the maker having tendered £1,350 per vehicle. A price had been requested from the Metropolitan Carriage & Wagon Company too, but that company had either declined to bid or its price was too high. SLM gave the company deferred terms again, a total of £2,621 to be paid by 1 October 1925. Sub-contracted to Société Industrielle Suisse of Neuhausen, delivery was expected by 20 June 1923.

The new locomotives were despatched promptly, No 7 on 24 March and No 8 on 10 April; the delivery notes survive at Llanberis. Following inspection and testing by Swiss Federal Railways' engineers, they had been shipped via the LMS at Antwerp, the journey taking eighteen days in the case of No 8. 'Erector' Ekhardt commissioned them for SLM. Unlike the original locos, the new ones, including No 7, had superheated boilers and Walschaert's valve gear, which made them more efficient. The larger tanks, as proposed by Jack, meant that Nos 8 and 9 could reach the summit without taking water en route, while No 7 could reach Clogwyn. Operationally, this extra capacity was of little value when the original locos still had to take water at Halfway.

An order for new carriage brakes, 'to provide additional safety', had also been placed by 14 April 1923, £110 per vehicle, total £770. An SLM engineer was to commission the new locos and carriages and to fit the new brakes. It is not clear if this was in addition to the engineer who was going to overhaul the stock or instead. On 19 February 1924, Jack and Davies considered a bill submitted by SLM, agreeing to pay £500 in addition to £500 paid in December and to pay the balance of £1,057 5s 3d on 1 July 1924.

No 7 *Aylwin* with one of the 1923 carriages at Llanberis in 1938. (H.W. Robinson/Dave Waldren collection)

No 8 *Eryri* at Llanberis sandwiched between Lancaster carriages. The larger water tanks are a distinguishing feature of Nos 7 and 8. (H.W. Robinson/Dave Waldren collection)

Due by 20 June, the brakes, which took the form of an overspeed device, took over a year to be delivered, due to 'certain difficulties ... by reason of negotiations between the Swiss company and Sir Douglas Fox & Partners.' SLM agreed to fit them for £1 15s per day plus expenses, sending Herr Habegger to Llanberis for five months from April 1924.

Some fine tuning might have been required though, for on 22 August 1924 when 'not far from the summit [the] engine and passenger coach parted company, and a few minutes later the coach crashed heavily into the locomotive. Passengers were hurled against one another, though without more serious injury than a few bruises and a bleeding nose or two.' The report, from the *Manchester Guardian* (25 August), noted that a new automatic brake had recently been installed. Under the heading 'a slight mishap', the *Carnarvon & Denbigh Herald* (29 August) quoted this report in full and obtained a statement from the railway.

The incident had actually demonstrated the efficiency of the braking systems, it said, in that the carriage had stopped, the collision occurring after the brake had been released. Two or three passengers in the compartment nearest the loco had been alarmed, sustaining 'nothing more serious than a bump'. The statement concluded: 'Since it was opened 26 years ago the Snowdon Railway has enjoyed almost complete immunity from accidents. A slight mishap occurred last year but that also went to show that, owing to the efficacy of the brakes, under no conceivable circumstances can the train get out of control.' No explanation was given for the locomotive and carriage separating sufficiently to activate the carriage brake. And in the present day the statement's compiler, Owen surely, would be sent on a media awareness course to learn how not to make a situation seem worse than it is.

In the directors' report for 1923, issued on 27 November 1924, the shareholders were told that 'as the [carriages] were not available until the close of the season, they made no contribution to the earning capacity of the company.' The following year they were informed that 'Owing to the wet weather experienced during the summer, full benefit of the two additional locomotives and coaches was not derived.' Numbered 8 and 9, SLM had photographed the latter on a wagon ready for despatch on 30 August 1923.

Reviewing 1923, Davies continued to seek publicity. By 2 February, the book that he had proposed in 1922 had evolved into the *Snowdon & Welsh Highland Holiday Book*. A substantial number of advertisements had been received, worth £243 12s 6d, and both the Festiniog and Welsh Highland Railways had agreed to pay £50 'in consideration of space and illustrations being devoted to the attractions of their railways and the district through which they pass', which would not have been too difficult in view of the positions that he and Jack held with those railways. 20,000 copies were printed and W.H. Smith & Son, Wyman & Sons Ltd, and other booksellers agreed to stock it. There were two printings.

During the year Davies also approached main-line railway companies and charabanc operators in search of traffic and encouraged Thomas Cook & Sons, the Polytechnic Touring Association (later a constituent of Lunn Poly), American Express Company and others to promote seven-day inclusive tours based on the Royal Victoria Hotel. The holidaymakers would pay £8 8s per week and the tour companies would receive 10% agency commission.

He also arranged a visit by thirty journalists and railway officers that

SIS carriage No 8 soon after it had been repainted in 1938.

The circumstances surrounding the rebodying of No 3 in a similar style to Nos 8 and 9 are not known. It is seen being propelled by No 4 *Snowdon* soon after it had been repainted in 1938. (H.W. Robinson/Dave Waldren collection)

No 6 with one of the SIS carriages waits for a descending train at Clogwyn on 30 August 1926. The down home signal (left) has lost its finial to the weather. (H.C. Casserley/Dave Waldren collection)

started from Paddington courtesy of the GWR on Friday 22 June 1923. The party was routed via Blaenau Festiniog where it travelled on the Festiniog Railway to Portmadoc, then by the Welsh Highland Railway to Beddgelert and by road to Llanberis, where the company provided accommodation at the Royal Victoria and other local hotels. The next day it was taken to Carnarvon by road and then to Beddgelert on the WHR, viewing the Marconi radio station at Waunfawr en route back to Llanberis. After lunch, the group travelled on the railway. The lack of organised activity on the Sunday, before the LMS returned the party to London on Monday, serves as a reminder that there were no trains on that day, although evening entertainment was provided by the Llanberis Male Voice Choir on both Saturday *and* Sunday. Afterwards Davies reported that the visit had resulted in articles in twelve newspapers and a film shown in 1,200 cinemas.

This was not the first time that Davies had engaged with the media to promote tourism in Wales, for in July 1914 he had been involved, under the aegis of the Cambrian Resorts Association, with hosting a visit by French and Belgian journalists who had travelled on the Festiniog Railway.

Not mentioned elsewhere but shown, without comment, as capital expenditure in the 1924 annual report was £85 0s 11d spent to buy 'road direction posts', the increase in motor traffic making such items essential.

In December 1923 there had been several transfers involving Stewart's shares. At the beginning of the month he held 3,443 shares in his own name and 1,634 deposited with Branch Nominees. On 6 December 3,410 of his shares were transferred to A.B. & M. Bank Nominees Ltd. By 13 December 2,000 of these shares had been transferred back to Stewart and then to Jack. Similar transfers were being made with his Festiniog Railway shares at the same time.

Seriously in debt, Stewart had made vast profits during the war but had not

The hay harvest is in full sway on Ddol Isaf as passengers leave the train after their journey to the summit. The land was leased by the company from the Vaynol estate but was never used for railway purposes. In the foreground, motor car owners try to get their vehicles as close to the train as possible. (Lilywhite)

planned for the downturn that followed. He committed suicide on 6 February 1924. When Davies and Jack met on 19 February 1924, they not only recorded his death but also his resignation, dated 12 December, as a director. The December share transfers were registered at the same time. Jack became the chairman.

On the company front, George Westall, a brewer who had become a surveyor and valuer and who had connections to the Power company, was appointed a director on 1 April 1924, just fourteen days after he had become a director of the Festiniog Railway Company, also a consequence of Stewart's death. Restructuring the company by increasing its share capital to £100,000, changing its name to Snowdon Mountain Railway Ltd, and revising the articles in relation to the directors and auditors was considered on 18 June 1924 but no action was taken.

Discussions with the Inland Revenue bore fruit in December 1924, when that organisation agreed not to assess the company as a railway for income tax purposes, saving £207 18s for the 1922/3 tax year. Agreement

Sir John Henderson Stewart Bt was buried in the parish churchyard at Kinnaird, just over a mile from Fingask, where he ended his life.

was also reached for the value of the company's plant and machinery being set at £23,091 and depreciated at 4% of that amount. A claim for income tax and profits tax of £1,951 19s 6d was settled for £1,200, paid in three monthly instalments from May 1927.

Capital Expenditure 1922-8

	1922	1923	1924	1925	1926	1927	1928
New locomotive cost and carriage	£3,649 15s 2d						
Additions		£12,839 16s 1d	£365 10s 1d	£385 11s 11d	£396 8s 9d	£1,577 19s 2d	£777 4s 11d
Additions, alterations and repairs	£2,813 6s 3d	£17,109 3s 6d	£6,001 17s 6d	£388 12s 6d			

With the objective of clearing the overdraft and funding capital investment, Jack had been charged with arranging a new debenture issue. On 19 February 1924 he reported negotiations with the Investment Registry, whereby £50,000 would be made available. IR would take £30,000 and the directors would place not more that £5,000, the balance to be issued when the company's requirements and revenue justified it. In the meantime, Jack had made a temporary loan of £4,000 at 8% against an agreement that no new debentures would be issued until the loan had been repaid. A Mr A.M. Williams had advanced £2,200 on the same terms; it was later revealed that this money was also Jack's.

There was no debenture issue. By June 1924 the overdraft stood at £10,500 and before the end of the year the bank was calling for its elimination. This placed the company in a quandary. If it settled the overdraft it could not pay SLM money due in August 1925. Reaching a settlement with SLM to pay half the debt in August and the remainder in 1926 with interest, the overdraft was reduced to £6,427 4s 7d by October 1925. The bank then agreed to accept £427 4s 7d on 1 November 1925 followed by four monthly payments of £200 from 1 January 1926, subject to an undertaking not to create any charge on the business or the property. Davies offered to 'find' the money to honour the undertaking if any loans he made were treated on the same terms as Jack's and Williams's – might he have borrowed money at, say, 5% to lend to the company at 8%? No such transaction was recorded.

A year later the overdraft was down to £4,600 and from 1 October 1926 was being reduced by £100 per month. SLM had been paid £728 14s 5d, leaving a balance of £4,200, plus 7% interest, to be paid in August 1927. Analysis of the company's ledgers on 3 November 1927 had established that Jack had lent £21,137 11s (including the £2,200 lent via Williams) and Davies £3,055 0s 3d. The overdraft was then £3,200.

SLM had to wait even longer for its money. Still owed £4,200 in October 1926, by the time of a special directors' meeting held on 3 November 1927 it had agreed to reduce the outstanding debt to £2,200 and for it to remain outstanding until the end of the 1928 season, subject to payment of 7% interest. A payment had probably been made in August 1927.

These manoeuvres leave the impression of the directors running a financial juggling act and struggling to keep all the balls in the air. Sooner or later something would have to be done to introduce a measure of stability into the company's fiscal affairs.

Following the success of the holiday book of 1923, several other publications were issued. Stocks of *The Book of Snowdon*, first issued in 1922, were exhausted by December 1926 when another 2,000 copies

E.R. Davies encouraged the LMS to promote excursions to Llanberis to win passengers for the railway. This advertisement was published in the *Manchester Guardian* on 9 June 1925.

were ordered from McCorquodale & Company. In 1925 the British Publishing Company had published an *Official Souvenir of the Snowdon & Welsh Highland Railways* at its own expense, giving the company 2,500 copies for sale at 6d. Reprinted for the 1927 season, the company then paid £59 for 5,000 copies.

The extreme weather experienced at the summit was demonstrated on 1 January 1926, three students from Bangor finding that gale force winds had not only damaged the hotel bulding, but scattered furniture and moved the heavy anthracite stove (*Manchester Guardian*, 4 January, *North Wales Weekly News*, 7 January). The Vaynol estate, concerned about the capital value of the license, refused to allow the hotel's demolition and replacement by a modified station building, which the directors proposed as the station site was sheltered and more accessible to those nervous about braving stronger winds to reach the huts. The Vaynol hut remained in use and the station building was adapted to serve refreshments in 1927. For 1928, the directors decided to provide five or six more beds for one of the huts and Owen was instructed to run 'sunrise' trips in June and July, but not to increase costs in doing so.

SLM was consulted over the repair to a crack in one of No 7's cylinders in the autumn of 1926. The railway had asked how the piston valve sleeves could be removed, adding that it must have been faulty when manufactured. SLM explained that the liner had been pressed into the cylinder and that 'for removing same a pretty considerable effort is necessary'. A drawing was supplied, explaining how the liner could be removed. SLM also pointed out that No 7 had worked perfectly well when it was handed over after commissioning in 1924 and that any fault could not be one of manufacture. The builder went on to suggest that the damage was caused either by too little cooling water being applied during a descent or by cooling water being applied to a cylinder that was already overheated.

A stylish, and stylistic, LMS poster promoting the railway.

Being unable to repair the cylinder at Llanberis, it was sent to Switzerland, SLM adopting a puzzled tone when writing on 10 January 1927, carefully suggesting that the company was not being entirely truthful about the damage, pointing out that fresh machining marks were visible on the bush. The valve rods were not straight, and the piston rings were not steam tight. The repair strategy proposed was presumably adopted. No other correspondence survives.

Davies's courting of the LMS paid off in 1927, when the directors attributed traffic levels remaining unaffected by the general strike, and the miners' strike that followed it, to the services provided by the main line railway. The *Cheshire Observer* (9 July) also described the 'trial run' of a circular tour from Chester run in conjunction with the GWR and the company that was to run daily from 11 July.

There was an unexplained hiatus with the 1927 general meeting. Called for 27 December, it was postponed until 19 January 1928 and then until 16 February. It is notable that Jack was not present and was only represented by proxy on the last occasion; it may be that those attending on the first two dates held insufficient shares to form a quorum. In May 1927 Jack had stood down as the Aluminium Corporation's managing director, saying that he was on the verge of a nervous breakdown, and earlier in December he had intimated that he would not stand for re-election as a director of that company. Although he had dealt with company matters during the year, most recently on 3 November, it may be that in December and January pressures were too much for him even to consider appointing a proxy to the meetings. With 4,143 shares, he was the largest shareholder. Surprisingly, Branch Nominees still held 1,648 shares, presumably the rump of Stewart's holding; acquired by Jack, they were registered to him on 6 December 1932.

The 16 February 1928 meeting was followed by an extraordinary meeting that was the first stage in several changes made to stabilise the railway's position. The shareholders resolved to divide the existing £10 shares into 10 £1 shares, to increase the capital to £100,000 by the creation of 30,000 7% cumulative £1 preference shares and to rename the company the Snowdon Mountain Railway Ltd. The resolutions were confirmed on 1 March. No explanation was given for the change of name, but it did put the emphasis on the railway and suggests that no expansion of the hotel business would be entertained. The decisions were found to be invalid however, because the interval between the meetings was too short.

At the directors' meeting on 28 March 1928 Jack proposed that Davies should become chairman when the change of name had been approved and be acting chairman in the meantime. He also suggested that Hubert Lander Westall, director Westall's youngest son, an accountant, should take over from Huson as secretary.

The company had still not eliminated its overdraft or its indebtedness to SLM. In the case of the former, Davies reported that he obtained approval to overdraw an additional £250 until Whitsun, 27 May 1928, and to reduce the outstanding amount to £3,000 by 30 June and to £2,000 by September. Regarding SLM, the directors agreed to ask if payment of £1,000 on account during the summer would be acceptable.

The Inland Revenue was also owed money and Davies had negotiated a settlement whereby £100 would be paid 'now', followed by three equal instalments in May, June and July, the current liability being met by two equal instalments in August and September. A demand for payment of £740 being considered on 6 November 1928, the directors resolved to offer £100 then, £100 in March 1929, and the balance in three equal instalments from July 1929.

The reconvened extraordinary meeting was held on 18 April and the resolutions were confirmed on 7 May 1928. The increase in capital was registered on 9 May and the change of name on 16 May 1928.

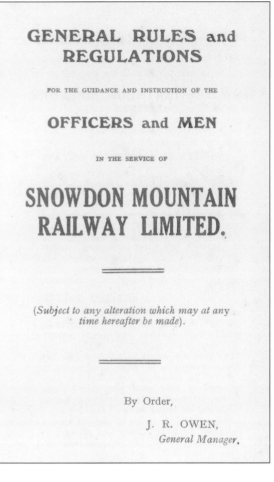

GENERAL RULES and REGULATIONS

FOR THE GUIDANCE AND INSTRUCTION OF THE

OFFICERS and MEN

IN THE SERVICE OF

SNOWDON MOUNTAIN RAILWAY LIMITED.

(Subject to any alteration which may at any time hereafter be made).

By Order,

J. R. OWEN,
General Manager.

The title page of the rule book produced after the company changed its name.

Following Jack's departure as chairman, he remained a director, several employees of the Aluminium Corporation and the North Wales Power Company disposed of their shares; there is no way of telling if the events were related. On 24 October the directors resolved to buy 'three pieces of antique furniture ... a motor lawn mower, garden roller and two or three other articles' for the hotel from Jack, paying him £450.

As chairman, Davies took to contributing a report to the board, reviewing the traffic in some depth on 6 November 1928. It had been better, 'not only in the sense that more money was taken but the undue crowding that had been experienced in previous years was largely avoided, because instead of relying upon the railways and charabancs as heretofore, there is increasing business every day from private cars which is distributed over the whole day.' As private motor-borne traffic would often travel in the afternoon when the weather had been off-putting in the morning, trains would be run at 5. 00pm and 5. 30pm in 1929.

Through bookings from the LMS had ceased during August because the train reached Llanberis thirty minutes later, about noon. After 23 September the through booking fare had been reduced to 4s, from 5s, and charabanc operators had paid 6s to include lunch; the extra traffic had not justified the reduction and the 5s end-of-season fare would be applied in 1929. The use of canvassers shared with the LMS at Llandudno, Colwyn Bay and Rhyl 'worked very satisfactorily as regards Llandudno, a little better than last year at Colwyn Bay but [was] quite unsatisfactory at Rhyl.' Passengers from the latter were negligible, 'though large numbers of Rhyl passengers passed through Llanberis daily in Messrs Brooks' charabancs.' The railway had shared a canvasser with the Festiniog and Welsh Highland lines to work the resorts between Pwllheli and Aberystwyth in August and September; the GWR would not participate.

A car park attendant had been employed to control traffic in the station yard. Paid by tips until mid-August, he was then paid £1 per week plus one third of the takings above that amount. In 1929 he was paid £1 15s plus one third, generating £87 6s 6d for the company on a turnover of £151 16s 6d.

The requirement for visitors travelling to Llanberis by train or charabanc to return to their North Wales coast accommodation for their early evening meals was undoubtedly responsible for traffic from these sources peaking around midday.

At the summit, a new refreshment room had made good profits. One of the huts had been repaired and would be provided with eight or ten sleeping berths before the 1929 season; supper, bed and breakfast and the rail ascent would be offered for £1 5s.

The problem of passengers taking space in the Llanberis refreshment room, only buying drinks to accompany their own food was considered. The woodland at the rear of the offices, the present car park, could be converted to be a tea garden with facilities to serve hot drinks and light refreshments, where a charge could be levied on the seats occupied, he suggested.

Discovering that the Lake District was visited by Americans, Davies had approached Atlantic liner companies, American tourist agents and the US minister of labor, a Welshman, to arrange for distribution of the company's literature in the US. He had also made representations to the LMS to arrange excursions from Chester, a haunt of Americans, to Llanberis. This effort seems to have been rewarded, for in 1930 he told the *Walsall Gazette* (14 June) that the railway carried as many Americans as British. While this claim is almost certainly overstated, the number of Americans being carried clearly stood out.

For the first time since Davies and Jack took over, gratuities were awarded to staff. Owen was the only railway employee so rewarded, with £20. At the Royal Victoria hotel, Mrs C.E. Watson, manageress, received £20 and Miss Marion Thomson Jones, housekeeper, and Miss Elizabeth Jane Jones, assistant general, each received £5.

Despite having made a profit of £6,523 2s 6d and carrying forward £4,166 2s 11d after allowing for interest and tax in 1928, the company was still unable to meet its financial obligations. At the meeting held on 22 May 1929 the directors decided to try to defer the bank payment due that month until June. The Broughton & Plas Power Coal Company had written about its unpaid bills; the secretary was to pay the February statement. £220 due to William Hope & Sons at Carnarvon for boiler repairs was to be paid immediately.

The crunch came, though, when Jack had complained to Davies that not only had he been compelled to sell securities on a falling market to compensate for interest he had not been paid, he had been compelled to refuse several investment opportunities because his capital was committed to the company. He was not, therefore, willing to continue the loan on the present terms. The directors' immediate response was to pay the interest due from 1 January 1929 free of income tax, but that was only a sticking plaster solution. By 1 December, the overdraft had been reduced to £1,700 and the SLM debt to £854.

Director George Westall died in Manchester early in 1930, aged 81, and his place on the board was taken by his son, the secretary, the appointment being confirmed at the general meeting on 2 September 1930. Westall appears to have had insufficient resources to trouble the probate office.

A further change in the share structure was approved on 30 September 1931, when the general meeting gave the directors permission to divide the £1 shares into four 5s shares.

There were no board meetings between 30 September 1931 and 29 September 1932, both dates those of the general meetings.

Highlights from Davies's 9 June 1933 report include: a seven-day visit by the

Alpine Garden Society in October 1932 being followed by a 14-day event in June 1933, and society members donated plants for the hotel garden; a psychic science conference in April being so successful that bookings were being taken for a repeat event in 1934; and the LMS producing 5,000 copies of a poster of Llanberis lake and Snowdon by Orlando Greenwood at a cost of £150, the company to contribute £50 over two years. The LMS placed the original on loan to the hotel later in the year.

Under the heading 'general scheme of decoration', on 28 July 1933 Davies described recent works carried out to improve the company's property. 'The railings and the wood and iron work of the station and neighbouring buildings have been painted green and cream. Four of the coaches have been painted red, grey, green and orange and attract considerable attention. A red line has been introduced into the painting of the locos. The summit

Seen in 1933 the carriage in this picture has obviously been repainted in accordance with E.R. Davies's desire to make things brighter, but it is not known which colour it is. (J.B. Rotheram/Davies collection)

buildings have also been painted and the refreshment room at the terminus made more attractive.' At the same time, complaints had been received about 'the lack of adequate sanitation at the summit'. A water tank was erected there to collect rainwater to flush the urinals and water closets. In 1934 Davies had the Festiniog and Welsh Highland Railway carriages painted different colours too, 'to develop the holiday spirit'. None of them were orange.

A way out of the financial juggling act was reported by Davies on 18 August 1933. With the aid of a stockbroker he had negotiated a £30,000 5½% loan from the Prudential Assurance Company. To be secured by a first mortgage debenture giving the lender a first charge on the railway and hotel and a floating charge on the other assets, it would be repayable over 30 years by 60 equal half-year payments of £1,026 12s. A £100 guinea arrangement fee was payable and the broker paid 1% commission on the loan for his trouble. The Prudential had the option of taking the company's insurance business.

The sum borrowed was £32,000, repayable in half-yearly instalments of £1,095 0s 10d over 30 years. Completed on 22 November 1933, legal costs totalled £800, of which £480 was paid to Evan Davies & Co. The money was used to redeem the outstanding 1895 4½% debentures (£2,900) and Davies's and Jack's loans (£26,011 11s 10d).

The Aberglaslyn land purchase had been completed for a total of £2,300 in October 1933, the vendor having agreed to forego his claim for interest, a move of some generosity considering it had taken some ten years for him to be paid. Despite not having completed the purchase, the Nantmor Copper Company Ltd had given the company a three-year tenancy on some of the land in December 1925, the company paying interest on the balance to the vendor. In an unusual example of environmental concern for the times, the company required the copper company to provide safeguards against polluting the river.

The eventual settlement with SLM was not recorded but the relationship was sound enough for an enquiry to be made about a new locomotive. The locomotive builder wrote on 2 October 1933 that an engine the same as the last three supplied would cost SFr66,000 instead of SFr88,100 because material and labour costs had gone down, but the exchange rate was against the company so that in Sterling it would cost £4,151 instead of £3,520. Construction would take up to six months from the date of the 'esteemed' order.

The directors treated the loan as a depreciation reserve and on 21 March 1934 told shareholders that the balance of any profits could therefore be distributed to them; on 3 May they agreed to pay a 5% dividend for 1933. Employees also benefitted, wages being 'restored to the level as at October 1931', subject to them working to a roster prepared by the manager and subject to review on 30 September.

At an extraordinary meeting held on 29 December 1933, the £1 shares were formally divided into four 5s shares and authority to create 7% cumulative preference £1 shares was modified in favour of 6% non-cumulative shares. The shareholders also agreed to various items with a book value of £3,032 being written off.

A new building at the summit was first mentioned on 8 February 1934, when Davies reported that it, the installation of electric lighting at the hotel, and draining and levelling the Aberglaslyn land, would cost approximately £5,000. He had therefore arranged to borrow another £3,000 from the Prudential on the same terms as previously obtained; the loan was to be repaid by 21 August 1934.

Although a new building had been promised in 1923, nothing had been said about it since. In 1929 the newly formed Council for the Preservation of Rural Wales had made the conditions at the summit one of its first priorities, contacting the company and mentioning it in its first annual report (*The Times*, 29 March 1929).

No doubt this, and clearing the structural debt, combined to provide the incentive and the capability to do something about it.

An application to Portmadoc licensing sessions on 9 February 1934 was better received than those made by Aitchison in the 1890s and revealed that Clough Williams-Ellis, 'the well known architectural artist' (*Liverpool Echo*, 10 February), had been commissioned to design the new building.

Albert Kirkham, Williams-Ellis's assistant, told the *Manchester Guardian* (16 February) that the building would be a modern, flat-roofed structure made of reinforced concrete and glass, designed to withstand severe frosts and built on a ledge below the summit so that it would not be seen on the skyline. Actually, it would be built on the station site and incorporate the station building into the structure. Schemes to get electricity and water to the site were being devised, he added; and to enable visitors to see the sunrise, sleeping accommodation might be provided in 1935.

Williams-Ellis circulated a 'note' referred to in the *Carnarvon & Denbigh Herald* (2 March), saying that the railway 'is becoming increasingly popular' and the 'existing agglomeration of timber and corrugated iron hutments ... are inadequate ... as well as dilapidated.' The new building would concentrate the facilities on one site and the station and restaurant should be in service during the summer.'

The walls of the building would be largely of glass, because of the view, he said. The supports of the flat roof, which would form a terrace, would be steel and concrete, the roof being reinforced hollow tiles covered with asphalt.

He also explained that the building 'is a frankly modern, functionalist erection, designed to do its necessary job in the most convenient and economical fashion,' as if rehearsing arguments that were made seventy years later, continuing, 'It might be argued by some that if a building has to be put up in such a place it should assimilate itself to the mountain by being built with Cyclopean blocks of the native stone. My own feeling, however, is that quite apart from the prohibitive cost ... and the fact that the mountain top would have to be quarried and despoiled to yield the stone, any attempted competition with its background in the way of mass or ruggedness would be rather futile.' Quite what he would have thought of stone being imported from Blaenau Ffestiniog and Portugal to clad a summit building, as was the case with the 2009 building, can only be imagined.

Davies told the *North Wales Chronicle* (2 March) that the 90 x 70-foot structure would contain a station hall, cloakrooms, conveniences, a large restaurant and a kitchen. Sleeping accommodation would be provided on the upper portion. He hoped that it would be finished by June or July. On 1 June, however, the paper reported that heavy snow had delayed the start of work until the previous week.

Also on 2 March 1934, the directors agreed to let the contract to Messrs Gregory of Carnarvon on the basis of cost plus 10%. Good progress was being made, Davies reported on 21 August 1934, and he had 'hopes' that the building would be completed by the end of September. If no unforeseen difficulty arose, the directors resolved, an additional refreshment

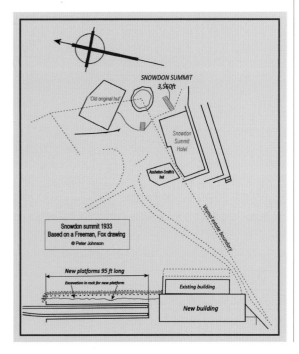

A plan of the summit showing the position of the new building. (Freeman, Fox)

A reminder that Snowdon is sometimes about snow. In the spring newspapers often reported on the railway's operating status as affected by the weather. This picture dates from 1930. (Topical Press)

kiosk would be built 'at the end of the lavatory buildings'. The roof was 'nearing completion' on 2 October, when it was proposed to leave the final coating until the spring. Shutters were to be fitted to the windows. Eighty-three girders were drilled and had base plates attached at the Festiniog Railway's works.

Another matter dealt with on 2 March was the health of J.R. Owen, the manager, who had been on sick leave for some time. Davies had commissioned a doctor's report, which recommended that it would be in Owen's interest to be relieved of responsibility, and had found a temporary replacement, a David Henry Roberts,

who was to be paid £6 per week. Born in Llanyblodwell, Shropshire, Roberts had worked in administrative capacities for the GWR at Chester and the LNER at Manchester and Liverpool.

Owen's 'lamentable' death on 20 April, aged 60, was recorded on 26 April; low blood pressure and chronic interstitial nephritis, a kidney disease, had caused it. Davies attended the funeral and sent a letter of condolence to Owen's widow. Roberts' temporary position was made permanent from 1 May, with a salary of £250 plus £50 expenses. While his position was temporary, he had been allowed to have his meals at the Royal Victoria Hotel.

It might be reasonable to suggest that the bricks in the wagon were destined for use in the construction of the new summit building. The carriage has had its rear quarter panels replaced with glass. Notice No 4's ad hoc cab wind shields, and the glazed cut outs in the rear panel.

A train at the summit while the first phase of the new building was under construction.

Another long-serving employee, John Sellars, No 2's driver in 1896, left the company during 1934, apparently of his own volition. He had become responsible for locomotive maintenance, and on 25 July 1934, after he had left, Davies said that he had been satisfied with Sellars' performance. However, a locomotive requiring 'a special repair under rush conditions' had been sent to the Port Dinorwic Dry Dock Company, a subsidiary of the Dinorwic quarry. The directors resolved not only to employ a new fitter but also to make greater use of the Port Dinorwic facilities 'in connection with the repair and overhaul of the company's engines'. Davies's careful choice of words and his tribute to Sellars indicates that there might have been a connection between the latter's departure and the

locomotive in need of 'a special repair'. He died on 29 July 1939, aged 81, effects £87; his son George was also a loco driver.

When the loco had reached Port Dinorwic it 'had proved to be in a very unsatisfactory condition' and required a new boiler. Approving the expenditure on 21 August 1934, the directors resolved that the rolling stock should be kept in perfect condition and to accept the Prudential's offer to inspect the stock annually at a cost of £2 2s for each locomotive and £1 1s per carriage.

Another of Davies's ventures was approved on 21 August 1934. He had started a Welsh woollen department at Llanberis and had arranged to rent premises at 60c Guildford Street, off Russell Square, London WC1, for nine months from 29 September to promote it.

As slate quarrying at Dinorwic became more profitable so the private harbour and the facilities at Port Dinorwic were expanded, including a dry-dock, a power station and a workshop capable of repairing and manufacturing locomotive boilers. In 1892 three iron-hulled steam ships designed to carry slate without damaging it were commissioned from S. McKnight & Co, Ayr, and the second of them, *Velinheli*, is seen here on the right, circa 1907. (James Valentine)

The Docks, Port Dinorwic

An advertisement for 'superfine Welsh woollens', with the address 'Department T, Snowdon Railway, Llanberis', appeared in *The Times* on 15 September. Nothing more was said of it.

The year 1934 had been one of change for the directors. Jack had changed his name to Henry Jack Macinnes on 2 June 1933, his co-directors being formally notified on 6 April 1934. On 2 March 1934 he had transferred 137,720 shares to Davies. On 25 July, the latter was awarded a salary of £400 for his services as managing director, although he saw little of it, for he died on 2 December, aged 63, intestate. Earlier in the year he had arranged for the Festiniog Railway to lease the Welsh Highland Railway, and it may be that with the effort involved in running the three railways, a legal practice in London, and as a politician, he had overreached himself. His eldest son, Cynan Evan Davies, also a solicitor, took his place as managing director and Macinnes resumed as chairman.

The minutes covering the period from the end of 1934 until 1940 are missing. Some insights into the company's activities have been extracted from the annual reports and newspapers. Capital expenditure amounting to £131 3s 11d in 1936 was unexplained, as was £30 compensation received from the county council the same year and placed to the capital account. Also, in 1936, a locomotive renewal fund of £500 per annum was established. Dividends were paid at 5% each year.

With no provision made for rolling stock maintenance when the railway was built, heavy lifting had to be done outside. A boiler in transit to Port Dinorwic on 12 June 1935.

Evan Robert Davies was not only influential in Welsh narrow gauge railways but also in developing tourism and in Caernarvonshire education. He was buried in Pwllheli's public cemetery.

Cynan Evan Davies

One effect of Davies's death was that on 21 July 1935 Sunday trains were run for the first time (*Liverpool Echo*, 17 July). In 1930 he had told the *Walsall Observer* (4 June) that he respected the 'old Puritan spirit' with regard to 'the blessings of the Sunday rest', despite knowing that the company could make a lot of money by running on Sundays, saying that if trains ran on Sundays Llanberis would be crowded with cars and charabancs and its Sunday peace would be destroyed.

Despite protests by the Free Church Council, the services were well supported. D.H. Roberts, the new manager, told the *Carnarvon & Denbigh Herald* (26 July) that the decision to operate was not just the financial result but the company had been pressured by visitors from England and South Wales. The council had previously failed to prevent the Corris and Vale of Rheidol Railways from running trains on Sundays.

Having taken ten years to complete the Aberglaslyn land purchase in 1933,

the enterprise came to an end with the property's sale to the National Trust in 1935. The land had cost £2,300 and £212 11s 1d had been spent on the car park at Nantmor but the whole was written down to £1,450 in the 1934 balance sheet, not a very productive exercise. How much the company got from it is not known; the National Trust was given a donation to make the purchase and the company applied the payment to revenue. The *Manchester Guardian* (5 August) demonstrated the media's traditional lack of understanding for railway matters by claiming that 'the land ... will be purchased from the Snowdon Mountain Railway Ltd (whose line goes through the gorge here in a tunnel).'

The new summit building, on which £3,791 had been spent, was opened on 19 July 1935, a year late. The *Carnarvon & Denbigh Herald* (26 July) did not comment on its tardiness, merely saying that it was fitted with all modern conveniences and 'presents a beautiful sight'. It had nowhere near the capacity of the earlier proposals.

Expenditure on the building finished in 1937, when £6,158 9s 11d had been spent; beyond recording the expenditure, the directors did not deem it necessary to give the shareholders any information about it. However, a newspaper report, source unknown, of 2 July 1938, states that the accommodation had been brought into use 'this season'.

Describing the hotel as 'most attractive and well-appointed' it said there were seven bedrooms for visitors and staff and a lounge, the accommodation was gas lit and centrally heated. It was managed by Charles Gibson, and his wife, both from Liverpool, who had worked at the summit for four years, previously living in one of the huts. Manager Roberts explained how he had designed a tank to ride on a wagon such that it remained horizontal on the steepest gradient; it was used to carry 800 gallons of water to the summit on alternate days; it held 400 gallons. Drinking water was carried in cans, and gas for lighting in cylinders.

The contractors had not tidied the site when No 4 was photographed at the summit on 4 July 1935. The new building was opened on 19 July. (H.R. Norman)

Clough Williams-Ellis's summit building as designed, with its first floor accommodation section.

No 2 shunting the first caboose at Llanberis. The tank used to carry water to the summit is to the right of the loco.

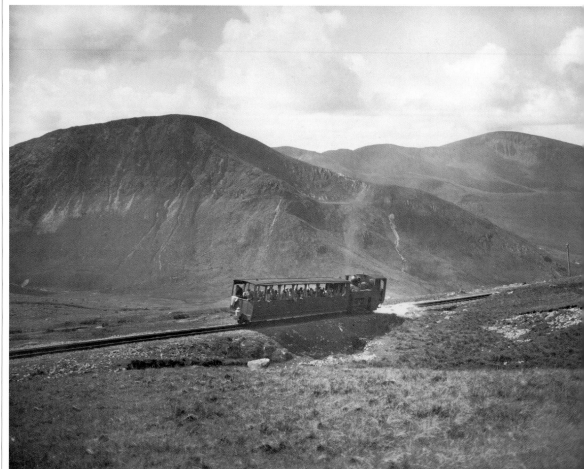

In this view of a train nearing the summit a can of drinking water for the summit hotel is being carried on the front of the carriage.

The *Manchester Guardian* (2 July) added that there was accommodation for eight guests, an open fire in the dining room, a wireless in the lounge, and a drying room. The writer was also shown the kitchen and the boiler house. Photographs show that at least one of the bedrooms had bunks and another appeared to be quite spacious, with a double bed and a handbasin.

The huts were removed at the end of the 1937 season, just forty years after A.H. Holme had said this was the company's intention. Clough Williams-Ellis, writing as the chairman of the Council for the Preservation of Rural Wales, told *The Times* (5 November) that he had been to the summit a few days earlier, in a snowstorm, and could confirm their removal. However, he continued, the company had not removed the platforms on which the huts had stood, which he thought was a good thing, they were convenient level places for visitors to stand on and he thought that the landowners should build low parapets around them in the interest of safety. Earlier, the CPRW's secretary had told *The Times* (20 September 1935) that at a meeting held in 1934 E.R. Davies had promised that not only would the huts be demolished but that all traces of their foundations would be removed too. Williams-Ellis acknowledged the part played by the railway company in acting as summit caretaker and for carrying away far more rubbish than could be attributed to its passengers.

Williams-Ellis's letter prompted Edmund Nelson, a retired clergyman from Harrogate, to say (10 November) that he had taken the train to the summit in 1936 and was 'amazed' to see evidence, beds and blankets, that one of the huts was still being used as accommodation. He recalled staying in one for a night in the 1890s and the experience had not been very pleasant.

The outbreak of the second world war in September 1939 found the railway having to deal with very different circumstances and, in comparison with the first, was much more affected by it. Closure of the railway, summit hotel, bookstalls and refreshments were advertised in the *Manchester Guardian* (5 September). The Royal Victoria Hotel was expected to remain open but it, and the Llanberis bookstall and refreshment room, were immediately requisitioned for military use; they were handed back on 16 December.

Thomas Gibb Jack (1899-1990), who had been appointed locomotive superintendent after 1935, was called-up in 1939. The son of John Jack, who had been Penrhyn slate quarry's engineer, he had served his apprenticeship at Penrhyn as a 'quarry engine fitter'.

The remaining railway staff was kept on at the normal reduced winter levels and hours until 5 January 1940, when a five-day week was introduced as an economy measure.

A link with the railway's beginnings was lost with the death of Assheton-Smith's widow, Laura Alice, for whom the first loco had been named, on 22 February 1940, aged 70. She had married George Lewis Holdsworth, a cavalry officer, in 1907 and died at their Sussex home. Her £322,814 13s 2d estate attracted £106,212 duty.

In 1940 the train service was started at Easter and was moderately successful until a government veto was placed on holidays. In June a cash flow forecast produced a deficiency of £45 by the end of July so arrangements were made to reduce staffing levels by 50%, partially by not replacing those who had left for other work. The Prudential loan payment due on 22 May was deferred, by agreement, until 30 September, 5% interest being payable until it was paid. Closure of the railway from 21 September for the remainder of the season was announced in the *Liverpool Daily Post* (19 September). In their report for the year the directors said that a restricted service had been run and that the rolling stock, track and buildings were being maintained, which contributed to an operating loss of £1,881 13s 5d, nearly doubled when £1,667 16s debenture interest was taken into account.

In May 1941 prospects were so poor that the directors decided a train service would not be viable. The summit hotel was to be opened from 31 May as a trial however.

Roberts had resigned on 30 April, his wife had been ill, and Westall stood down as secretary due to his own ill-health; despite remaining a director, he probably attended no more meetings. Ninian Rhys Davies, E.R. Davies's second son, was appointed assistant secretary from 1 June.

Necaco Ltd, a company 'engaged on work of national importance in Llanberis', operating an observation post on Derwlwyn, was given permission to run a telephone wire from Llanberis to Hebron on payment of 1s per annum per stay, pole or bracket used.

Revenue from the summit during June, £162 4s 2d, exceeded that of the same month in 1940, £107 3s 2d, and demand for a train service was such that the directors decided to reopen the railway for two months from 14 July, re-employing Roberts to manage it. With the employment of another driver or fireman, staffing was sufficient for two trains to be run daily. With revenue exceeding £900 by 6 September, the service continued until 29 September.

Another contribution to the war effort was agreed on 10 September 1941. The railway's lathe and drilling machine were hired to the Britannia Foundry in Portmadoc at an annual rental of £40, backdated to 1 September; the arrangement seems to have lasted for about a year. By the end of September, the company had £1,280 in the bank, was entitled to an income tax refund in the order of £600 and awaited £700 compensation and rent from the War Department. Employees retained during the winter were: Robert John Williams (clerk); Evan Roberts (driver); Thomas Hughes (platelayer) and W.C. Jones (gardener). Consideration of payment to Prudential was deferred until May 1942.

The refreshment room and bookstall were requisitioned again from 29 September 1941, occupation being given to the Air Ministry. Advance notice was given when the summit hotel was required for three weeks of experimental wireless work by the wireless regional office in April and May 1942. Exclusive use was granted for £10 per week with one train per week charged at £5 or two for £7 10s.

Considering the circumstances, a surprising amount of loco work was approved on 31 March 1942. No 7 received a complete mechanical overhaul and Nos 5 and 8 were re-tubed; the Board of Trade approved the steel for the latter. One of No 7's driving wheels had also been sent away to be re-tyred. Nos 3, 4, 5 and 6 were laid up and the insurances relating to them cancelled. The railway was reopened at Whitsun, 24 May, and Roberts returned to manage it. The employees were: R.J. Williams (clerk); Evan Roberts (engine shed foreman and driver); Thomas Hughes (platelayer); Hugh Jones (fireman and platelayer's assistant) and John Owen (fireman and platelayer). They were given a 'small' pay rise.

Learning that services, daily except on Sundays, were being operated, the *Manchester Guardian* (30 May) asked if it could really be essential travel and if anyone could answer 'yes' if asked if their journey was really necessary. At the end of the season (23 September) it quoted Roberts as saying that it had been 'splendid'. There had been two trips daily excepting Sundays, a third of the normal number, consuming 8cwt of coal on each trip. Trains ran until 27 September.

H.L. Westall's death on 28 February 1942, aged 63, had been recorded on 28 July. Macinnes acquired 1,400 shares from his estate and transferred them to his (Macinnes's) wife, Charlotte Pauline. She and Walter Cradoc Davies, E.R. Davies's brother, were appointed directors. 6,000 shares held jointly by the Davies brothers, inherited from their father, were divided between them in December 1942 and N.R. Davies became secretary from 1 January 1943.

From 29 September 1942 trains were run for the benefit of the Air Ministry, which had requisitioned the summit building and started making alterations to it. This traffic caused James Williamson (1871-1967), the Festiniog Railway's engineer, to be commissioned on 2 October to inspect the railway and report on it. Following a three-day inspection, he submitted his report on 23 October. Generally, the track was in poor condition, he said. Before the war 'a ganger and four men, and a boy for rack-lubricating, were fully engaged during the summer months.' Now the track was neglected and rough. Drainage gullies were silted up and did not serve their function, affecting the sleepers, 200 of which needed replacing. The rack had not been lubricated for two years and showed signs of friction and wear. Much of the track was out of alignment. All the fishplates were rusted in place. The points were badly worn and required replacing. The embankments were suffering from erosion such that sleeper-ends were unsupported.

He also commented on the method of train working. 'All the safety appliances have been dismantled and removed ... the traffic ... is now passed along the line by telephone control and what seems locally known as the 'interval' system; I have no knowledge of such working and if the telephones fail it must be a serious position. I have never heard of any authority who would give permission for such working, where two or more passenger trains would occupy the same section at the same time and I personally would refuse to permit the same without written consent of some controlling authority.'

In a handwritten footnote he said that the railway would deteriorate more rapidly if it was closed down and that it would be better to run a skeleton service, but that a skeleton service could not be run indefinitely.

On 21 December 1942, the directors were concerned because the ministry's works had been abandoned before completion and without notice being given. They did not comment on Williamson's report and obtained an itemised one, not seen, from a Thomas Barratt that included the rolling stock. Abt had submitted a report on the track in 1936, incidentally, of which only the title page survives; assuming that there were recommendations, they appear to have been disregarded.

The requisition was formally terminated on 8 January 1943, leaving the company to claim compensation to restore the building. In addition to £1,467 5s 4d expenses incurred, including £400 for improving the track, the company sought £500 as a fee for the use of its facilities. No details were recorded about the changes made to the building, but they were enough to affect the railway's alcohol license and needed to be undone. The treasury solicitor was not impressed to learn that Davies had claimed expenses for dealing with the requisition, saying that he should be paid both for work done as secretary and as solicitor.

Several changes to the company's office arrangements were agreed on 18 February 1943. The payment made to C.E. Davies as managing director was ceased, to be replaced by an annual fee of £250 paid to Evan Davies & Company. In return, the company would have access to the facilities required by the Davies brothers to exercise their functions of managing director and secretary. £50 of the payment would cover the services of an accountant. The Davies brothers could also claim expenses incurred when travelling on the company's business. As chairman Macinnes was paid £250, backdated to 6 April 1942, presumably to compensate him for the £250 previously paid for allowing his London office to be used as the company's registered office.

A comprehensive set of minutes was typed up for a meeting in 1943 but the date was left blank; approval to reopen the summit hotel on 31 May points to it being held, or intended to be held, earlier in that month. The arrears of interest due to the Prudential had reached £3,185 12s by 31 December 1942.

Transcribed into this minute, N.R. Davies had written to Macinnes on 12 April 1943. There were 40 tons of coal in stock, Billingtons would supply 30 tons before the end of April and Broughton & Plas Colliery in Wrexham would contract to supply 100 tons at 20 tons per month, enough to operate a similar service to 1942. He had met Williamson and inspected the track, on foot, with Hughes, the platelayer, and R.J. Williams, the clerk. There were 100 sleepers in stock, he was trying to obtain more, and a gang comprising Hughes, Hugh Jones, John Owen and John Morgan would install them. A greaser would be employed. Jones might have to work as a fireman when trains were run. The remainder of the train crew were Evan Roberts (driver) and R.J. Williams (conductor, and clerk). The last time sleepers had been purchased, in 1933, they had cost £1 1s each; now new ones cost £2 5s.

There were four locomotives available for service subject to boiler work being carried out on two of them by Port Dinorwic personnel. Williamson would supervise the operation for two days a week at the same rate paid to Roberts for full time; this was expensive 'but Williamson is not in need, is 72, retired with a good pension and … points out he will have to pay away in tax half whatever we pay him.' Williams would be in charge in Williamson's absence. 'I have every confidence in him and after all right through the winter he had sole charge of the running for the Air Ministry and managed it all without a hitch and we ran five to six trains a day.'

Subject to track maintenance continuing, Williamson thought that a limited passenger service could be operated. Davies proposed a service using a single train leaving Llanberis at 1.15pm and 4.00pm to avoid using the loops, and the worn turn-outs. The *Western Mail* (12 May) announced the start of services from 31 May 1943.

Directors' reports for the years from 1942 until 1945 were not issued until 7 December 1946, with the explanation that because property had been requisitioned from 1940 and the railway run for various services and government departments, claims made for compensation, rental and dilapidations had only recently been settled. Profit in 1942 (£1,503 10s 8d), 1943 (£1,500 8s), and 1944 (£1,411 14s 9d), had been more than offset by the annual debenture interest payment of £1,667 16s. No doubt the

£3,487 10s profit in 1945 included delayed payments and compensation for previous years.

From 1942 until 1945 the army used live ammunition during training exercises in the mountains. Although the exercises were not held near the railway an indemnity was obtained from the War Department and warning notices were posted in the booking hall and on the trains. An announcement in the *Liverpool Daily Post* (9 May 1945) saying that there would be a daily service until 29 September was followed by some newspapers, including the *Birmingham Mail* (19 May), declaring that 'Snowdon had been "liberated" to the public', which caused some concern for the authorities.

On 21 May, the *Liverpool Daily Post* carried a report saying that the police and military authorities were worried that the mistaken belief that Snowdon had been 'liberated' could be responsible for loss of life. While the railway had resumed services and the summit released by 'service ministries', it remained unsafe for visitors to stray from the footpaths, it said. Most of Snowdonia and the Welsh mountain ranges were still sealed firing areas and a risk to anyone entering them. Visitors were advised to ask the police if particular areas were safe to visit.

The paper added that during the war four services and ministries had used the summit building for secret work at different times, saying that it had been linked to anti-invasion planning and plotting enemy submarine movements. 'Last winter' Admiralty staff had been snowbound for three weeks and trains had not run, which made the replenishment of supplies both difficult and hazardous.

T.G. Jack, the locomotive superintendent, returned from war service on 15 November 1945 but got another job and left on 30 April 1946.

There were no celebrations for the railway's 50th anniversary in 1946, but it was noted by the *Staffordshire Sentinel* (23 April), along with claims that George Bernard Shaw and the Late Lord Stamp, then chairman of the LMS, had been passengers. Today, the name of the former will resonate with readers, whereas that of the latter almost certainly will not.

There were no more board meetings until 5 June 1946, when W.C. Davies and C.E. Davies met to deal with the aftermath of Macinnes's death on 2 January, aged 77. His executors, his widow and Herbert Aubrey Crowe, transferred 15,000 shares to the latter. On 7 August Macinnes's widow, Charlotte Pauline Macinnes, acquired 4,800 shares from five individuals and 111,580 from the estate, giving her control of £29,095 of the issued capital. Her appointment as a director was not recorded; she attended her first meeting as such on 10 October 1947. Crowe, Macinnes's solicitor, had been articled to Evan Davies & Company.

Henry Jack Macinnes (born Henry Joseph Jack) was buried at Ann's Hill cemetery, Gosport, with his only son, who had died in Gosport when learning to fly in 1916. Buried in the same plot are both his wives, a brother-in-law and Hilda André, a woman with whom he had probably had a relationship.

Pauline Charlotte Macinnes

CHAPTER 8

THE DAVIES ERA

The company emerged from the war in quite a good position, albeit at the expense of getting into arrears with the Prudential and of not paying some bills. The same could not be said of the locomotives and rolling stock however. With a good proportion of it fifty years old and receiving only routine maintenance and running repairs it would have been quite run down. And it soon became clear that something would have to be done about improving the passenger accommodation.

At the first directors' meeting since 1943, on 16 December 1946, C.E. Davies was elected chairman and became managing director, he and his family taking responsibility for the railway's wellbeing for the next 38 years. In 1946 the directors appeared to be much more confident about the company's prospects than their predecessors were in 1918.

They first had to deal with the railway's management. James Williamson, the consultant engineer, had followed T.G. Jack and resigned on 30 September 1946.

Philip Harris Jackson, formerly of the Southern Railway, was then appointed engineer and general manager from 17 December 1946. A civil engineer, he had started his railway career with the London, Brighton & South Coast Railway; his salary was £600. R.J. Williams, the clerk, was designated assistant manager. Williamson died on 21 May 1967 and was buried in Oswestry's public cemetery.

Financially, £150 compensation had been received for twelve acres of land at Ddol Isaf that the Gwyrfai Rural District Council wanted for housing. Located on the other side of the river to the station at Llanberis and leased from the Vaynol estate, consideration had apparently been given to extending the station onto part of it, but it had been sub-let for agricultural purposes instead.

The money was no help towards settling the arrears due to the Prudential however, which amounted to £4,865 17s 3d at 22 November 1946; the outstanding balance was £30,323 15s 7d. Taking into account the tax due on the interest, arrangements had been made to capitalise the arrears by increasing the amount covered by the debentures to £33,000. With six-monthly payments of £1,370 10s 10d the debt would be cleared on 22 November 1966.

On the railway, new points had been purchased and were being installed. An import licence had been obtained for new pinions ordered from SLM for delivery in June 1947 and orders had been placed for new bogie and carrier wheels. A licence had been obtained for timber with which to build a new carriage body. 'This latter work would be carried out as hitherto with direct labour,' the first reference to work being undertaken on the carriages. Eventually they were all fully enclosed, with droplights fitted in the doors.

At the summit the claim against the Admiralty for dilapidations had been settled but two quotes exceeded the amount. The license was current but inactive and would remain so until the repairs had been carried out to the satisfaction of the justices.

Staff conditions received the directors' attention when they met on 10 October 1947. At a cost of £12 per week to the company, wages had been increased to bring them into line with rates paid elsewhere in the locality. The permanent staff would henceforth receive fourteen days paid holiday, seven days to be taken at the end of the summer season and seven days at Christmas. An outing was arranged for the permanent staff; this became a regular event, but the venues were not recorded. Two long-serving – over thirty years – employees, Evan Roberts (driver) and Humphrey Williams (conductor) had been awarded pensions of 10s per week on the understanding that if they were re-employed by the company the pension would be suspended.

Despite not being a statutory railway, the company had issued privilege rate (quarter-fare) tickets to employees of main-line railway companies, 511 in 1947, such tickets being conditional on the holders not seeking compensation in the event of death or injury following an accident. The National Union of Railwaymen had negotiated for them to be brought into line with other tickets, and the Railway Clearing House had notified the company of the change. The directors decided that the company should not change its conditions.

Jackson, the new engineer, had estimated that it would cost £6,000 a mile to relay the line. Both he and C.E. Davies wanted a second opinion from SLM and expenditure of £100 for this purpose was agreed. Davies investigated the provision of a siding at Waterfall, to see if it would improve traffic flexibility, and the scope for improving the water supply at Halfway.

The gross takings to 8 October 1947 being £8,000 higher than in 1946, the directors decided to pay an interim dividend of 2½% at the same time as the 2½% dividend already agreed for 1946.

During 1948 'abnormal' repairs were carried out on the locomotives, using £300 taken from the £500 rolling stock repair fund created in 1947. The repairs followed another visit from SLM's Herr Habegger; he had installed the new carriage brakes in 1924 and returned to 're-assemble two locomotives and adjust others' in May 1949. £2,203 18s 9d had also been set aside for repairs to the summit building, of which £75 6s 9d was spent in 1948; the arrival platform was cleared

and reinstated before the 1949 season. The last item appears to refer to a Nissen hut erected over the platform and its adjacent track seen in an aerial photograph. In 1950 a quote for £4,500 was received for putting the summit building into a sound condition; its flat roofs were a particular problem.

For the first time in fifty years the railway came to the attention of officialdom. In June 1949, a Mr Jenkyns wrote to the Board of Trade from Llandudno: 'I wonder if you are aware of the general condition of the rails and joint-plates on the Snowdon Mountain Railway.' He went on to say that the original signals, interlocking and electric staff system had been scrapped 'without your authority, I believe' and 'the trains are sent up and down sometimes closely behind each other without any block working and the regulation speed of 4mph is often up to 9mph.' Claiming that there had been several derailments in 1949 he suggested someone be sent to conduct an incognito inspection.

Neither the Board nor the Ministry of Transport knew which of them, if any, was responsible and it took a while to track down the nineteenth century file because it had been deposited with the Public Record Office. His comment about trains being sent closely behind each other is surely a reference to the operation of 'doublers.'

The ministry took the initiative and wrote to the company with a transcript of the letter on 28 September 1949, C.E. Davies replying on 24 October. He explained that the track had been examined by someone from SLM in 1947, 1948 and 1949. Following the first inspection the directors had decided to relay part of the line, but it took until April 1948 to obtain the necessary licences. 2,200 sleepers were ordered from Robert Hudson & Company of Leeds and 4,320 yards of rail from Guest, Keen & Baldwins Ltd, enough for 2,160 yards of track. The rail was delivered in August 1948, but Hudson had only just started delivering the sleepers.

So far as the signals were concerned, they had been dispensed with circa 1921, he said. Until then the company owned and operated four locomotives. Then three more locomotives were acquired and the then manager 'saw fit to dispense with this system, presumably on the grounds that it was not suited to the traffic on the line having regard for the low operating speed.' The traffic was afterwards controlled by telephone. His comment 'I am given to understand that block signalling system has been discontinued on the majority of single lines in this country' attracted the marginal comment 'NO!!' Photographs show that the signals still appeared to be capable of being operated in the 1920s.

The automatic brake being effective at speeds over 5mph and the journey time of an hour for just under five miles combined to refute the claim that trains ran as fast as 9mph. He denied that there had been

any derailments in 1948 and described the company's inspection and testing procedures. He concluded by mentioning the timetable, normally 30-minute intervals but 'if a more frequent service is called for, an interval of five minutes between trains is maintained.' The ministry merely acknowledged Davies's explanation and took no further action.

C.P. Macinnes died on 16 July 1949, aged 58; she had not attended a board meeting since 10 October 1947, estate £63,855 6s 10d. N.R. Davies told the author that he had bought her husband's shares from her but such a transfer was not recorded in the minutes. By 25 September 1952, her holding was registered to Norman Ronald Aubrey Crowe and Monica Constance Mylne, her executors. On that date 15,000 shares were transferred to Crowe and Herbert William Bartlett, jointly, as trustees for David Edward Aubrey Crowe, Crowe's son, as a bequest. The remainder,

No 6 leaving Hebron with a rebuilt carriage in a brown and off-white livery in the 1950s. The post on the right is all that remains of the height post erected in 1922. Considering they were erected at half-mile intervals it is strange that only this one and the one at the summit have been seen in photographs.

102,780 shares, was retained by Crowe and Mylne. It is probable that Davies acquired these shares after 1960. Reverting to 1949, Crowe and N.R. Davies were appointed directors on 29 November and W.C. Davies's resignation was accepted at the general meeting held on 31 December.

P.H. Jackson's time as the company's engineer and manager ended on 31 December 1950. The directors had decided that as he preferred to spend time in his office rather than supervising the permanent way gang or producing the schedules of work expected of him, he should be dismissed, giving him a month's notice and two months' salary. R.J. Williams took over as manager with a salary of £500 on 1 January 1951, the board seeking a consultant engineer. Jackson died in Llanberis on 16 October 1951, aged 67, estate £1,316 4s 6d.

Ninian Rhys Davies

Passengers await their train on 6 July 1950. On the platform is one of the Swiss carriages in course of being rebuilt, while alongside it is one of the Lancaster vehicles with its panelling incomplete. Litter was clearly a problem throughout the railway. In 1949 the *North Wales Weekly News* had published two letters complaining about litter at the summit. (J.H. Meredith)

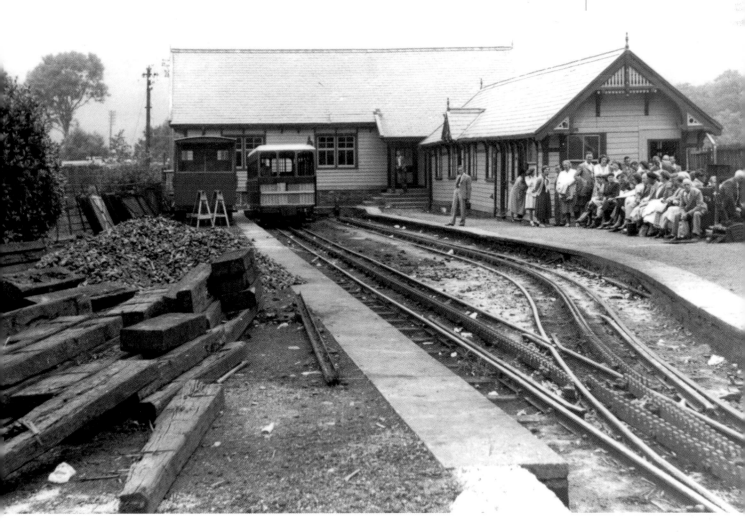

Carriage No 6 awaits departure after it had been rebodied, its doors remaining unglazed. Behind is one of the Lancaster carriages, up on blocks with its rebodying in progress.

On 10 October 1950 another letter was sent to the Ministry of Transport. A Charles Allen of Brixham had written to complain about his wife's experience when she had travelled on the railway on 27 September. The circumstances had been almost the same as those in 1898 when the Reverend Adler had complained, and it was almost exactly 52 years later. On this occasion Mrs Allen had travelled with a coach party. Despite poor weather the train had reached the summit and returned to Clogwyn without difficulty. There, on a ledge with a 2,000ft drop, said Allen, the gale force wind blew through the windows on one side of the carriage and, meeting the resistance of closed curtains on the other side, lifted it 'momentarily' off the rails. The few passengers on an up train transferred to the down and the ensemble returned to Llanberis without further delay or alarm. Allen claimed that the ticket seller had been heard to say that the conditions were so bad that he would not 'go up that day for all the money in the world'; if that

was the case, asked Allen, why weren't the passengers warned? Someone had put these lives at risk, he said, and passenger safety should be the company's priority, not its revenue. He concluded that he had consulted the clerk to the Brixham Urban District Council before writing.

Once again, the ministry copied the letter to the company, C.E. Davies replying on 24 October 1950. Three trains had been run on 27 September, at 10.10am, 11.00am and 3.00pm. Mrs Allen had travelled on the first. The only untoward occurrence was an obstruction blown onto the track at Clogwyn which was removed. There is no drop there and the 'lifting' sensation was caused by the carriage moving on its springs. After the passengers from the 11.00am had been transferred to the 10.10am both trains had returned to Llanberis. As to the remark alleged to have been made by the ticket seller, at that time the conditions were favourable, as confirmed by the Mr Allen's description of the ascent, so there was no reason for anyone to make such a comment. Davies concluded by taking exception to the claim that revenue took precedence over safety. No trains were taken higher than conditions permitted, and refunds were given if conditions prevented a journey being completed. A copy of the reply was passed to Allen and nothing more was said.

Acquisition of a new boiler was approved on 14 November 1950. The last one had cost £650 in 1936. Although the new one would cost £1,800, the 'expenditure would be justified in that it would give a seventh locomotive available for service during the height of the season and the revenue which the locomotive would earn would recoup ... to no small extent the cost of the boiler.'

Since the war, railway employees had started to join the Transport & General Workers Union, transferring their allegiance from the NUR that some of them had joined in 1934. The organiser successfully negotiated a pay rise, recorded on 20 December 1950: shed foreman, £6 5s; drivers, £6; driver/firemen, £5 10s; platelayers, £5; firemen, £5; foremen platelayers, £5 5s; carpenters, £5 15s.

Although nothing more had been said about the complaints made about the railway to the Ministry of Transport, the ministry had not forgotten it. On 30 March 1951 an officer wrote to C.E. Davies reminding him of the previous exchanges and continuing, 'it did not appear necessary to pursue the matter further at the moment, but it is felt that it might be desirable for an inspecting officer of railways to take an opportunity in the near future of inspecting the line under actual working conditions ... While it is appreciated that the minister does not have the same statutory responsibility for safety with regard to this line ... it is considered that such an inspection would not only be of interest to this department but that the interchange of views thus afforded would be useful to all concerned.'

Replying on 2 April, Davies answered that he would he pleased to arrange for

an inspection, suggesting that it should wait until the weather had improved. On 29 May James Briggs (1889-1978), recently recruited in replacement for P.H. Jackson and retired from British Railways' London Midland Region, suggested that an inspector should accompany him during one of his visits to the railway. Briggs shared his name and his profession with his father, who had been a Midland Railway civil engineer. He had started his career with that company and had also spent time with the Royal Engineers' Railway Operating Division.

Colonel Robert James Walker (1903-1979) eventually made his inspection on 13 September 1951, writing to Davies on 21 September that 'In general, I found it well run and well maintained.' The track, allowing for its age, was reasonably sound but reaching the stage where major renewal was required, particularly the points; most of the new rails and sleepers obtained in 1948/9 had not been installed. He was concerned about the railway's system of block working by telephone; telephones were unreliable, and messages could be misunderstood, especially if transmitted to drivers by seasonal staff. He thought that a better system should be employed and would advise if required.

Influenced by Briggs's ROD experience, a combined telephone and ticket system was devised, where a paper ticket authorised the train movement through a section. Special arrangements covered the first train of the day, where the stations were unmanned until it reached them, and for running relief trains, where a second followed the first at a five-minute interval. Davies was closely involved in drafting the rules and producing the tickets and was anxious to introduce the new system at Easter 1952, a target that was achieved. The rules were printed after the first season's experience had not revealed any shortcomings.

Coincidentally, the telephone cable from Halfway to the summit had been found to be deficient in 1950. The purchase of

4,400 yards of cable from Pirelli at a cost of £646 16s had been approved on 18 July 1951.

Faced with mounting losses by the Royal Victoria Hotel since the war – £13,000 was quoted in 1951 – during 1950 the directors had decided to sell it. The 16 years remaining on the lease being considered a hindrance to finding a buyer, an option to extend it by 21 years had been obtained from the Vaynol estate. Even then, hotel agents Christie & Company had failed to find a buyer. That company's representative had visited and thought that it was too big for the locality and could not be run profitably unless the rates were increased considerably. The directors decided not to reopen it in 1952.

The situation changed very quickly, though, and it was sold to a Jack Kushner on 31 December 1951. No value was attached to the lease and the furniture and contents were sold for £750, which sum was passed to the Prudential. The capital loss of £4,550 15s 8d was charged to the general reserve fund.

So, more than 50 years after starting in the hotel business and 23 years after company's name had been changed, the business had no hotels. Because there was no breakdown in the published accounts there is no way of telling the impact of the hotel on the business. It had benefitted from considerable revenue investment over the years – improved plumbing, furnishings and electric lighting are three examples – whereas the railway had suffered from the lack of it. The agent's comment about the rates suggest that it had accommodated the cheaper end of the market and therefore that investment had been made without any effort to increase returns from it. In the 1951 report the directors said of the disposal, 'the wisdom ... should become apparent in the accounts for 1952 and succeeding years.'

At the summit during 1952, a programme of works reducing the window openings and replacing the roof stanchions resting on the concrete floor with longer members that rested on solid ground were carried out, funded by the deferred repairs reserve, £795 0s 7d compensation for the damage done by the Air Ministry during the war. It seems that the accommodation had only been used by staff since the war.

The directors met rarely in the early 1950s, mostly to register share transfers, consequently the minutes contain even less information about the railway's operation than had previously been the case. On 28 July 1953 they agreed a rearrangement of the company's administration. Since 1943 Evan Davies & Company had provided management facilities for £250 a year, increased to £350 from January 1951. C.E. Davies had been paid a salary of £600 for his services as managing director and N.R. Davies had been paid £400 for his services as secretary. Under the new arrangement, backdated to 1 April 1953, the Davies brothers ceased to be paid their salaries and Evan Davies & Company was paid £1,700 for the provision of accommodation and services, including those of the Davies brothers as managing director and secretary. The author suspects that there was a tax benefit in the revised arrangement. All the directors were paid £100 annually for their services as directors, an arrangement that had started after Macinnes's death.

The crash of an RAF Anson trainer aircraft on the track near Clogwyn in low cloud and heavy rain at midday on 11 August 1952, killing its three occupants, stranded two trainloads of passengers at the summit (*Liverpool Echo*, 12 August). About 120 passengers bedded down where they could in the summit building for the night and returned to Llanberis the next morning. The *Western Mail* (13 August) told how guard Gwyn Roberts took supplies to the summit and sang to the passengers to cheer them up. From the 1950s there are regular newspaper reports of the railway being used to aid the recovery of individuals injured in falls on the mountain.

On the engineer's recommendation, approval was given to obtain sufficient materials to relay 100 yards of track annually and an order was placed with Robert Hudson & Company. In 1955 the principal fare was increased to 12s 6d and in 1956 to 15s.

Staff requests for a £1 a week pay rise in February 1954 were countered by an offer of 15s that was accepted. A year later a deputation met Williams and asked for another £1 a week and for an extra week's paid holiday, the latter to compensate for working on three bank holidays. C.E. Davies, as chairman, thought that the pay rise was unjustified, and that three days' extra holiday should be granted. Another £1 per week request in 1957 was negotiated to 4d per hour for a 44-hour week. Williams received a pay rise of £100 from 1 January 1956; he had been paid £550 since 1 January 1952. An increase of £300 to the payment made to Evan Davies & Company, to £2,000, was backdated to 1 January 1956.

A locomotive crisis arose in 1956, with five boilers requiring substantial repairs following adverse inspection reports. To give breathing space while the problems were resolved, the railway did not open until Whitsun, 21 May; the period from Easter was usually fallow the directors thought, and the closure would not only save money on fuel and some staffing costs but would also make time for shed and permanent way staff to carry out further works that could not be done when the railway was operating. By 5 April, the boilers of Nos 3 and 8 had been sent to the Hunslet Engine Company to be repaired and No 5's boiler was due to be sent there.

By July the three boilers had been repaired at a cost of £1,300 each for Nos 3 and 5 and £2,500 for No 8. The boilers of Nos 6 and 7, sent to Port Dinorwic to have their fireboxes removed for examination, required the same repairs as No 8, costing £2,500 each plus £450 each for new copper fireboxes. They were repaired in time for the 1957 season. When the order for the last boiler was approved on 15 October 1956 it was noted in the minutes that six locos would be available for service in 1957. The missing loco, No 4, having apparently been out of use since about 1938, had been considered for 'rehabilitation' in September 1955. By deduction, the loco that received the new boiler in 1950 had been No 2.

No 2 at Llanberis in the 1950s. It had been reboilered in 1950.

No 4 after it had been rebuilt by the Hunslet Engine Company in 1963.

No 7 with a silver chimney in the 1950s.

No explanation of the problem or expenditure, which cleared out the £2,000 locomotive replacement reserve, was given to the shareholders. Their 1956 dividend was reduced to 3% because of it though.

Another expense in 1956 had been the £600 purchase of Mrs Williams's, the manager's wife's, Vauxhall Wyvern saloon car, approved on 13 March. Remaining in Williams's custody and control and used by him on the company's business, the registration was transferred to the company and the company became responsible for its licence and insurance. It was depreciated at £120 a year; in 1961 the entry in the balance sheet became 'motor cars' and the amount increased to £2,115, suggesting an increase in the fleet.

A rating assessment of £3,500 following revaluation, increased from £128, had caused concern when levied in 1956. Many owners were seeing big increases (*Western Mail*, 26 June). Seeking advice, a settlement was reached reducing the claim to £1,000. As a result, the report for 1956 was not issued until June 1958 and those for 1957 and 1958 until July 1959.

Another link with the past was broken on 6 March 1959 when the landowner G.W.D. Assheton-Smith's only child, Enid Mary, who had dug the first sod in 1895 and had a loco named after her, died in London, aged 70. She had not remarried after her husband, John Grey Archdale-Porter DSO, whom she had married in 1915, was killed in France on 22 November 1917. There were no children. The £1,016,683 duty payable on her £1,299,634 9s 5d estate caused headlines as it was the highest amount due to the treasury from this source for nearly two years. The *Liverpool Echo* (29 April 1959) said she had been frail and shy, dividing her time between homes in Belgrave Place, London, and Gresford, near Wrexham. She was interred with her parents in the family mausoleum on the Vaynol estate.

The 1950s and 1960s were good years for the railway and its shareholders. After the 1956 crisis had been resolved the four original locomotives were sent to the Hunslet Engine Company to be overhauled, No 2 in 1958, No 5 in 1959, No 3 in 1960 and No 4 in 1963; seven locomotives were recorded as being in service in 1964, the first time this had happened for some time. No 4 was sent to Hunslet again in 1978. It is not known why it needed major works so soon.

With the passenger boom in the 1960s, before cheap holidays to places overseas with guaranteed sunshine became available, the railway increased capacity by running 'doublers', two trains running through each section at a time. This view at Halfway shows two trains going down crossing two going up. (Photo Precision)

In the 1960s a gantry was obtained to assisting in the lifting of the heavier components, a safer option than the shearlegs used previously. No 5 was photographed on 29 May 1967.

No 7 shunts No 6 after the gantry has been used to remove the latter's cab. 7 April 1980.

Financially, the company earned interest on money kept in a deposit account from 1957 and the Prudential loan was settled on schedule in 1966. Before that latter event was achieved, however, on 9 November 1965 the company had obtained a seven-year mortgage from Gwyrfai Rural District Council for £3,090, apparently to buy a house called Aylwin, in Capel Coch Road, Llanberis. Given that the company already owned R.J. Williams's, the manager's, wife's car, it might have bought the house for him too, but there are no minutes or reports available to confirm or refute this suggestion. Since 1946 dividends had been paid every year, reaching 8% in 1959 and 1960 and then 12% from 1961.

Andrew Owen Evan Davies, N.R. Davies's son, was co-opted to the board on 10 April 1962, and his uncle, C.E. Davies died on 9 November 1963. In the annual report, N.R. Davies acknowledged his brother's service as managing director for nearly thirty years, saying that he had 'rendered devoted service' to the company and 'laid the foundation for its present prosperity'. He was replaced by his son, Morys Lloyd Davies, on 4 November 1963 and N.R. Davies became both chairman and managing director. On 31 December 1963 R.J. Williams, the manager, was co-opted to the board.

Morys Lloyd Davies

Cynan Evan Davies, who succeeded his father as company chairman, was buried in Pwllheli's public cemetery.

Andrew Owen Evan Davies

Lord Snowdon, who as Antony Armstrong-Jones had married HRH Princess Margaret on 6 May 1960, was almost a local man. Plas Dinas, his family's home, is close to the Welsh Highland Railway station at Dinas. The creation of his title on 6 October 1961 prompted the company to mark the occasion with a gold medal that entitled him and his heirs free travel on the railway in perpetuity. It was delivered to him at Kensington Palace by N.R. Davies in May 1962. On 21 August 2005, following the publicity that accompanied the project to build a new summit building, railway personnel were surprised when he arrived at Llanberis unannounced, presented his medal, and exercised his right to travel. By then, of course, none of the railway's staff knew that it existed, telephoning the duty manager to make sure that it was alright.

The final break with the Vaynol estate occurred in 1967, with the sale of 21,000 acres to two property companies, jointly, for a reputed £1½ million. Vaynol itself, its home farm and some associated properties were retained by the heir, Sir Michael Duff Bt. The Dinorwic slate

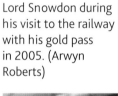

Lord Snowdon during his visit to the railway with his gold pass in 2005. (Arwyn Roberts)

quarries were owned by a family company and were also not sold. 'Family reasons' was the explanation given for the sale, but Sir Michael's obituary (*The Times*, 20 March 1980) said that it had been forced on him by high taxation.

The purchasers had bought the property with the intention of breaking it up and put several plots, including 13,000 acres of Snowdon land, on the market for sale by auction in October, which resulted in the Welsh Office buying the Snowdon property for £140,000 before the sale (*Birmingham Daily Post* 15 September / 8 November 1967). In 1971 a Welsh Office minister told a House of Commons adjournment debate that the summit would be kept in public ownership, that Caernarvonshire County Council would be allowed to buy the land it needed for tourist facilities, and that the tenants would be offered the opportunity to buy the land they occupied. (*Hansard* 10 June).

Publicity surrounding the sale had probably accounted for Lord Snowdon adding his name to a letter criticising the summit building and calling for its replacement by a modern building of

'architectural merit'. The signatories actually did not know who owned the building and sent it to British Railways' director of industrial design, who passed it on to Caernarvonshire County Council which passed it to the company (*Manchester Guardian*, 13 June 1967). Asked for comment, the architect, Clough Williams-Ellis, told the paper that it was "a poor utility building. My building was not properly finished off." His building had, of course, been much altered both during and after the war. It would take more than thirty years before it was replaced by a modern building of architectural merit.

Gillian Davies, N.R. Davies's daughter, became a director in 1972; unlike her board colleagues, all solicitors, she was a barrister, specialising in intellectual property law. M.L. Davies resigned on 26 November 1976 and was replaced by Claude Francis Jackson from 1 January 1978. N.R. Davies and A.O.E. Davies had become joint managing directors in 1977. Gweneth Elizabeth Davies, N.R. Davies's wife, was appointed a director on 1 January 1979. In 1976 ten members of the Davies family had held 166,051 shares, 59% of the issued capital.

C.F. Jackson had been appointed manager in 1970 when R.J. Williams retired. He, Williams, had joined the company as a carpenter in 1933, becoming clerk by 1941. He died on 24 September 1980, just after his 80th birthday, estate £39,971. Jackson had retired from the navy with the rank of Commander.

The appointment of Ralph Ernest Sadler as consultant civil engineer in 1963, apparently in succession to James Briggs, proved to be very successful. His recommendations enabled the railway to overcome longstanding civil engineering problems, including the regular flooding of some sections and poor water supplies at Halfway and Clogwyn. He had joined the Great Northern Railway in 1922 and worked for the LNER and British Railways before starting a consultancy. He died on 4 December 1977, aged 72, estate £194,802. On 4 October 1978, his wife named

Gillian Davies

Claude Francis Jackson

No 7 *Ralph Sadler* in his honour (*Railway Magazine* June/December 1978).

While the railway was making civil engineering progress under Sadler's guidance, it made mechanical engineering progress under Jackson's direction. His appointment as general manager brought with it experience and discipline, N.R. Davies told the author, being

Renamed after
the railway's late
consulting engineer
in 1978, No 7 was
photographed at
Hebron in 1984.

particularly complimentary about his contribution to the railway's wellbeing.

One project that Jackson did not take forward would have entailed regauging and rebuilding a 48hp diesel locomotive for use as a yard shunter. The Colwyn Model Railway Club acquired a 2 foot 10½ inch gauge Ruston from A.R.C. (Powell Duffryn) Ltd, limestone quarry operators at Llandulas, and moved it to Llanberis on 27 August 1971. Unaltered, it was transferred to the Llanberis Lake Railway on 24 October 1977.

Some idea of the problem faced by the company in managing the summit building can be gained from a report in *The Times* of 8 August 1972. The first train of the day, carrying staff and supplies for the summit, had to proceed slowly, with its crew looking out for stones and boulders placed on the track, and steel plates a quarter of an inch thick were placed over the windows when the building was closed, to deter vandals, after one eighth steel sheets and timber had proved to be inadequate. On a

clear day an estimated 5,000 visitors, 1,500 of them train passengers, could produce up to a ton of rubbish that the company would remove.

Each year, when railway personnel went to prepare the summit building for reopening after the winter, they did so wondering how much damage they would find, as there was always something to be repaired.

In 1977 the Countryside Commission issued a report with options for the mountain's management, saying that a professional management service committee should be established to improve visitor facilities. Regarding the summit, it recommended making a grant to the railway company to install piped water, mains electricity and a telephone, and to operate an improved sewerage and litter collection service. Saying that a new building was desirable, it called upon the company to improve the existing building and 'help tidy up the summit in general' (*The Guardian*, 2 November).

In 1972 manager Jackson had told *The Times* (8 August) that the company's consultants had estimated that installing the infrastructure to deliver water and electricity to the summit could cost £32,000.

Hitherto unknown parts of the business came to light as company accounts became more detailed during the 1970s. A chalet and Welsh craft shop in Llanberis, perhaps a successor of the Welsh woollens enterprise of 1934, made profits until 1981, when the entry disappeared following another change in accounts presentation. Expenses for two flats at Evan Davies & Company's office at 5, Catherine Place, London SW1, appeared in the revenue accounts for the same period, mostly incurring small losses tempered with an occasional small profit.

During times of strong winds, services were, and still are, terminated at Clogwyn. Even then, there are still occasions when the wind is too strong for the trains. To maximise revenue on such occasions a concrete platform was built in the sheltered location known as Rocky Valley; J.I.C. Boyd (see Bibliography) dated its introduction to 1974. At some as yet unidentified date a single platform was installed at Clogwyn to assist passengers of trains terminating there.

The 1970s were also good years for the shareholders, with a 12% dividend paid in 1972 and 14% in 1973. Underlying this apparent success, however, were deeper problems, with a bank overdraft of £8,107 in 1972 reaching £145,641 in 1982. Losses of nearly £40,000 were made in 1979 and 1980 and no dividend was paid in 1980-2. The business was increasingly in hock to the Midland Bank: a floating charge on the undertaking from 27 August 1975; a mortgage secured on the summit property on 2 May 1980; a mortgage on the land at Llanberis on 14 May 1980; a chattels mortgage was secured on the rolling stock on 31 December 1980 and a legal charge on

A train approaching Rocky Valley platform on 13 April 1998.

A typical 1970s scene at Clogwyn. No 6 with Swiss carriage (left) and No 8 with the oil tank on its cab roof with a Lancaster vehicle. 8 May 1977.

the summit business on 21 February 1983. It is a wonder the bank did not restyle the business as Snowdon Mountain Railway (Midland Bank) plc. Of 1983, the directors said every effort had been made to contain overheads and improve cash flow.

	1972	1973	1974	1975	1976	1977	1978	1979	1980	1981	1982
Turnover		246,349	291,134	384,530	442,849	478,522	554,827	541,128	584,864	612,488	
Overdraft	8,107	8,222	22,406	29,259	23,877	34,392	45,430	106,606	135,086	130,774	145,641
Bank loan	6,000	14,000	12,000	10,000	13,000	11,000	10,000	7,000	-		

Motivated by the earlier reports on the mountain's condition, by 1981 the Snowdonia National Park Committee had secured £600,000 funding to repair the six main paths to the summit and £7,500 to improve the summit toilets. According to the committee's consultants another £1 million was needed to deal with the summit building, £310,250 to rebuild the café and reclad the walls, £607,000 to install mains water, electricity and telephone, and £74,000 to replace the septic tanks. Faced with the knowledge that the company was not in a position to fund such an investment, the national park officer told the *Guardian* (17 January 1981) that the only other solution was to consider raising money by appeal to improve or acquire the building.

Increasing pressure to improve the situation resulted in the non-railway land and building being transferred to Gwynedd County Council, and the company taking it back on a 999-year

lease on 31 January 1983. The transfer of ownership allowed the council to invest in the property while it was managed by the railway; the length of the lease allowed the company to borrow against it if required. As rent, the railway would pay 7½% of gross revenue, excluding VAT, from retail sales. As owners, the council was able to undertake a £200,000 facelift straight away (*Liverpool Echo* 14 January). As the sale price was merely enough to cover the cost of conveyancing, it meant that the company sold the last of its three hotels and had made nothing from any of them.

There were other changes on the railway in the 1980s. William Ronald Whelan (1938-2015), a bullion and numismatic dealer, and Nicholas Peter Evelyn, a director of a marketing company, were appointed directors on 30 December 1981. Whelan resigned on 10 July 1984. N.R.A. Crowe died on 8 September 1983, aged 68, estate £152,629.

Anthony Constantine Joseph had been appointed secretary from 1 January 1978, replacing N.R. Davies. In turn, he was replaced by James Ralph Woollard Hyde MBE (1918-2011) from 1 April 1980. Hyde resigned on 9 July 1984 and was replaced by A.O.E. Davies.

C.F. Jackson retired as manager in June 1981 and as a director on 23 March 1984; he died in Hampshire on 8 August 1999, aged 84. Derek Rogerson had replaced him as manager and was appointed managing director in November 1984. With training at the Vulcan Foundry, locomotive builders, and SNCF, the French national railway operator, and experience in mining,

No 2 near Waterfall station on 25 May 1980.

Rogerson brought an engineering focus to the railway's management. He told the author that he found the railway in a poor state and struggling to keep going, introducing a five-year plan to deal with arrears of maintenance. Behind the scenes, a solution was at hand.

An event of national significance had affected the railway in 1981. A few days before the marriage of Prince Charles, the Prince of Wales, to Lady Diana Spencer on 29 July, it was subject to a vandalism attack at Hebron. The points were tampered with, bolts removed from the track, a store was broken into and sleepers strewn across the track. The damage was seen by the permanent way gang and put right before the train service started. In a phone call to the BBC at Bangor, responsibility was claimed by Mudiad Amddiffyn Cymru (Movement for the Defence of Wales), which objected to the railway's involvement in a celebratory bonfire at the summit (*Guardian* 21 July 1981).

Pursuant of the 1980 Companies Act, the company was re-registered as a public limited company on 30 March 1982.

The railway had benefitted much from the post-war passenger boom, with the locomotives overhauled and the carriages rebuilt with enclosed bodies. The shareholders had done well too, but there appears to have been no long-term planning to secure the railway's future. The investment in overhauls required renewal, but the borrowing restricted the options available to the directors.

No 8 descends with 'the truck' near Halfway on 6 July 1975.

CHAPTER 9

THE CADOGAN ERA

Sometime in the late 1970s, Nigel Keith Ross, a commercial estate agent carrying out a rent review against one of N.R. Davies's clients, expressed an interest in the display of books and memorabilia that he saw in the latter's office. Learning that the Davies family effectively owned the railway, he asked if he could buy it (the railway); this, he told the author, despite having 'no passion for steam' or interest in railways. The offer was rebuffed. The review took some time however, and the pair continued to meet. In 1983 Ross tried to introduce a purchaser but nothing came of it.

But in 1984 the situation was different, for on 9 April Ross told Davies that he and colleagues were about to take over Cadogan Properties Ltd, then a 'substantial' private property company, and they 'would like to be involved with the Snowdon Mountain Railway.' He explained that Cadogan owned a shopping centre in Yardley, Birmingham, which produced an annual income of £200,000, enabling it to engage in other ventures.

The railway company's position was serious. It had high levels of debt. The rolling stock required extensive maintenance. Derek Rogerson, the manager, had realised that capacity could be increased, and costs reduced if diesel locomotives were used, but the existing debt blocked access to fresh funding.

Discussions were started, and on 10 September Ross was in a position to outline the terms of a takeover, saying that an offer would be made on the basis that the company required £500,000 of fresh capital with which to purchase two diesel locomotives and a carriage and to fund the construction of new sidings.

Cadogan Properties Ltd therefore made its offer for the share capital, at £1.15 per share, on 31 October 1984; it was completed at a cost of £322,000 on 23 November 1984. The largest holdings were those of the Davies family, 163,478 shares, 58% of the issued capital, and the Crowe family, 32,000 shares, 11.43%. Company law specialist David Crowe, N.R.A. Crowe's son, advised the Davies family. On 23 November G.E. Davies and N.P. Evelyn stood down from the board and Ross and his colleagues Andrew Ian Jaye and Brian Ivan Leaver replaced them. Jaye took over as secretary from A.O.E. Davies. 90 years of independence and 38 years of the Davies family running the company had ended and the company was now a wholly owned subsidiary of Cadogan Properties Ltd. The years ahead saw the railway's fortunes revitalised.

Just before the takeover, on 29 October 1984, in one of the old directors' last acts, N.R. Davies was appointed executive chairman for life, with a salary of £7,000; the company also paid a £25,000 single premium contribution towards his pension, actions agreed with Cadogan. Also agreed had been the £1,600 salary paid to G.E. Davies and the sale of the 1954 Bentley owned by the company to N.R. Davies for £200. Just to wrap things up concerning the outgoing regime, a 4% dividend had been paid for 1983 and 6% for 1984.

One of the first actions of the new regime was to transfer the company's registered office back to Llanberis, which was effective on 1 January 1985. An executive board was formed, which comprised the Cadogan directors together with N.R. Davies, A.O.E. Davies and Rogerson. Gillian Davies and Alexander Donald Mackay were non-executive directors. Mackay was an insurance broker who had been appointed on 11 January 1985; he resigned on 8 November 1987.

A long lens distorts some of the curves near Clogwyn on 4 May 1999. In the background are some of the higher levels of the Dinorwic slate quarry.

The new owners quickly introduced plans for putting the railway on a sound financial footing. On 11 January 1985 the share capital was restructured: the 30,000 unissued 6% £1 preference shares became 120,000 25p shares; the capital was increased and reorganised to be £200,000 divided into 2,000,000 10p shares by consolidating every two existing 25p shares into one 50p share and sub-dividing those into five 10p shares – railway history does not get more complicated than this. Before the shares were divided, seven Davies family members, Rogerson and Elizabeth Hughes, who ran the office at Llanberis, reinvested in the business by subscribing to a total of 25,000 of the new 25p shares at £1.15 each. New articles of association were also adopted on the same date.

On 23 January 1985 these moves were followed by the launch of a prospectus offering 840,000 10p shares for sale at 80p each. Offered under the 1983 Finance Act's business expansion scheme, there were tax incentives for investors who left their investment in place for five years. The issue was oversubscribed and closed in eight days. Cadogan held 43.3% of the issued capital; the three Davies directors together spoke for 45,000 10p shares. (The 25p shares bought for £1.15 would have been worth £2.00 each: 2 x 25p shares = 1 x 50p share = 5 x 10p shares = 5 x 80p = £4.00 ÷ 2 = £2.00.)

The cover of the 1985 prospectus.

The declared purpose of the new capital was to buy two new diesel locomotives, install new sidings and improve passenger facilities, as previously agreed by Nigel Ross and N.R. Davies. Prospective subscribers were told that on fine days in July and August demand often could not be met. Capacity was limited by the seven steam locomotives and reduced if one was out of service. Further, they were inflexible and could not be put into service at short notice to cope with unexpected demand. The new locomotives would cost £428,830, £42,830 from current resources, £60,000 from a Wales Tourist Board Grant, £226,000 from a commercial loan and the balance from the issue. The balance of the proceeds of the issue would be used to extend, by acquisition, the company's activities in the tourist field, making it less susceptible to the vagaries of the weather.

The capital also allowed the overdraft and mortgages obtained from the Midland Bank between 1975 and 1983 to be satisfied, a process that was completed by 15 January 1986. A new floating charge on the business was created on 9 February 1987.

To expand the business, in 1985 an attempt had been made to take over the Llanberis Lake Railway, the 2ft gauge tourist railway constructed on the trackbed of Assheton-Smith's former 4ft gauge private railway, offering £25, then £60, for each £10 share. At an extraordinary meeting held on 25 May, the target company responded by altering its articles, requiring share transfers to be made at the directors' discretion for a period of five years, blocking the bid. To overcome any problems with shareholders who wished to realise the value of their shares, the company also took power to buy them back, paying a substantial premium.

Another expansion proposal was considered in 1985/6, putting the railway at the centre of a Llanberis visitor centre to be developed in partnership with the Royal Victoria Hotel and using land owned by the company, the hotel and the county council. It would have contained an information centre, shops and cafés and acted as a reception centre for the attractions in Llanberis, including the pumped-storage power station, Dolbadarn Castle, the slate museum, the Llanberis Lake Railway as well as the railway. Finding that neither the Central Electricity Generating Board, owners of the power station, nor the Arfon Borough Council would support the scheme it was abandoned. The architect's claim for £56,000 plus VAT as fees for the feasibility study went to court, with judgment given in the company's favour in 1991.

One diversification/expansion plan that did proceed was the acquisition of the former military airstrip, Caernarfon Airport, at Dinas Dinlle. A 125-year lease was purchased from the Glynllifon Estate Trust for £140,000 on 1 February 1986, the price including equipment owned by the previous operator. The control tower was refurbished and a new operations building built. A subsidiary, Snowdon Mountain Aviation Ltd, operated the business, a flying school was started and leisure flights using a De Havilland Rapide aircraft were offered. The company's articles were amended to include the carriage of passengers by air on 1 May 1987.

For a few years from 1985, the company's links with Llanberis were highlighted by sponsoring Llanberis Athletic Football Club, a member of the Gwynedd League. Then one of the most consistently successful clubs in the league, it was renamed Locomotive Llanberis for the duration of the sponsorship.

The 320hp diesel locomotives were delivered by the Hunslet Engine Company in April 1986. Their unusual appearance, with their exposed engines and revolving jackshafts, can be explained by Rogerson's desire, he told the author, to have locomotives with character, that were as much a visual attraction as their steam counterparts. He explained that Rolls Royce engines were specified because

Locomotive No 9, funded by the share issue, being unloaded in April 1996.

the arrivals platform, along with a new entrance into the station building, was carried out during 1986 at a cost of £65,000. Refurbishment of the summit complex carried out by the county council at the same time included installing a new heating system and increasing the café's seating capacity.

At the time of the takeover the company employed 53 personnel, 8 on management and administration, 37 on railway operations and 8 on ancillary services. In 1987 a funded defined-benefits pension scheme was created with Equitable Life Assurance.

The derailment of No 7 one hundred yards from the summit on 13 August 1987 was caused by the left-hand coupling rod breaking, which allowed the connecting rod to fall and jam against a sleeper and derailing the loco, which ran away for about 250 yards. The carriage was stopped by its brake working as designed. The loco crew, John McAvennie and Nigel Day, jumped off, the latter banging his nose, the only injury sustained (*Caernarfon & Denbigh Herald*, 21 August). A lot of damage was done to the track and the underside of the loco.

Tests found faults in the steel used in the coupling rod's manufacture and the railway's regime of non-destructive testing of motion components was increased, some components being redesigned to increase their strength. The next day, trains terminated at Clogwyn until No 7 was recovered and the track had been repaired.

The air museum built at the airport in 1988/9 was funded by a rights issue that raised £158,795 from shareholders. They were offered £68 of 3% convertible unsecured loan stock for every 500 shares held. The stock was convertible into ordinary 10p shares at 80p each until 31 July 1996. Any stock not converted by 31 July 1996 would be redeemed at par on 31 July 1997. Intended as an all-weather attraction at the airport, the company had obtained a £44,000 grant towards the museum's £200,000 cost from the Wales Tourist Board. The airport had accumulated losses of £676,902 by

most passengers would recognise the significance of the RR motif on the front. They proved to be ideally suited to the work required of them. The five-year loan of £225,947 obtained from Lombard North Central plc was registered on 2 May 1986.

The refurbishment of the buildings at Llanberis, including refurbishment of

Llanberis station on 28 September 1996. The arrivals platform, on the left, had been built ten years earlier.

Diesel and steam at the summit in July 1989, the image showing the cladding applied to the building by the Snowdonia National Park Authority.

Passengers mill around as they wait to be rescued after No 7 ran way on 13 August 1997. (Ralph Berry)

Ninian Rhys Davies and Gweneth Elizabeth Davies were buried near their home at Abersoch.

Ninian Rhys Davies, Gweneth Elizabeth Davies and Andrew Owen Evan Davies at Llanberis on the occasion that No 9 was named.

31 December 1991; when the business was sold on 28 February 1992 there was a cash inflow of £43,150.

N.R. Davies, a director since 1941 and chairman since 1963, died on 3 November 1989. The author remembers a man of great intellect. Others remembered his charm. David Crowe remembered attending company meetings held in Davies's office and being treated to lunch afterwards.

The letter to shareholders informing them, inter alia, of Davies's death, also told them that the season had been the busiest ever, 120,826 passengers carried, passing the 100,000 mark for the first time. The 100,000th passenger, a Daniel McDermid from Glasgow, had been presented with a free pass entitling him to free travel on the railway for life. The record number of passengers had required a record number of trains run, 2,243, the first time the 2,000 barrier had been broken.

Ross took over as acting chairman until he was formally elected on 23 January 1990. Elizabeth Hughes had replaced Jaye as secretary on 8 December 1989.

More additions to the rolling stock were made from 1988, when East Lancashire Coach Builders Ltd delivered a new carriage. Built to the limit of the loading gauge, it seated fifty-six passengers, had a centre gangway, which meant that it required fewer doors, and wheelchair access. A five-year loan from Forward Trust Ltd was registered on 11 April 1988. A third diesel locomotive was delivered

Shovelling ballast at Llanberis in 1989. With the construction of the lineside access that accompanied the 2009 summit building, such deliveries can now be made away from public gaze.

The permanent way gang pauses for tea when carrying out track repairs near Clogwyn on 29 March 1997.

Two trains approaching Clogwyn. The practice of staff hanging from trains was subsequently banned.

Carriage No 10 awaiting commissioning at Llanberis soon after delivery in 1988.

in April 1991. Built to the same design as the first two, it had been ordered from the Hunslet Engine Company and was built at Andrew Barclay's Kilmarnock works. With a contract price of £238,512, it was financed with a £200,000 loan from Lombard North Central plc that was satisfied on 29 February 2000. A fourth locomotive obtained in 1992 appeared not to require any external financing.

The diesel locomotives increased the railway's capacity considerably, being able to make four return trips in a day as opposed to the steam locomotives' three, enabling the railway to run more trains on fine days, up to ten steam and fourteen diesel trains. In 1993, good weather and four steam and four diesel locomotives in traffic enabled the carriage of 131,500 passengers, the best year recorded.

The advent of diesel traction was not the end for the steam fleet though. A new boiler was obtained for No 2 in 1992 and in 1994 two more boilers were ordered. Experiments with oil firing were started in 1992 and equipment was fitted to No 4 until 2001; there had been a trial with oil firing involving Nos 2 and 8 in 1971/2. Experiments with draughting saw a Lempor exhaust ejector installed on No 4 in 1994; it was removed some years later.

A modern scene
on the viaduct.
Locomotive No 10
and carriage No 10 in
1989.

A nameless No 11
crossing the Ceunant
at Llanberis, the loco
shed on the right.

Three out of the four diesel locomotives at Clogwyn on 6 April 1996.

No 2 with its cab roof oil tank near Clogwyn in the 1970s.

No 8 climbing the upper viaduct with its cab roof oil tank in 1976.

The first of the extra sidings forecast in the prospectus had been built on the opposite side of the line to the loco shed in 1985, the first new rack laid for ninety years. The need to remove rock to create level ground made it particularly expensive. A second, longer, siding was built in 1995 to accommodate the railcars. Simultaneously an area of hard-standing spanning both tracks was created to aid maintenance. Other works carried out during the 1990s included installing a Philips radio system for train control in 1990 (*Railway* Magazine, December), repointing the arches of the viaducts and installing mile posts, the latter task completed in 1997. The radio replaced an earlier system of unknown origins.

Two of the railcars pass the loco shed on 29 March 1997. The third railcar is stabled in the siding built to house them. The building behind the water tank houses a machine shop that appears to have been built circa 1980.

Railcar No 22 with its power bogie removed for maintenance, 21 June 1996.

No 8 at Waterfall station in 1975. The mast for the traffic control radio at the Llanberis end of the building. In the centre distance there are two trains at Hebron.

The locomotives are not often seen out on their own. On 23 August 1984, No 8 was taken for a trial run up to Waterfall following repairs.

The crossing equipment at Hebron was automated in 1991, with a wind turbine providing the power to operate the points and signals. Someone passing by must have guessed that the 60-amp cable used on the installation contained a lot of copper, for it and the generator were stolen the following winter. The Halfway loop was automated in 1995. These installations used track treadles to detect the presence of the trains and make sure that the points were set correctly. System upgrades saw solar panels installed to supplement the wind turbines, signals illuminated by LEDs, and the points operated by remote controls worked by guards going uphill, and drivers going downhill.

A train operating record was set on two days in August 1991, with five steam and three diesel locomotives in service. All trains left Llanberis full but by 1pm over 1,000 intending passengers had been turned away (*Railway World*, November 1991).

Two derailments were reported in the Health & Safety Executive's *Annual Report on Rail Safety 1994/5*. The first was at Halfway on 26 May 1994, when No 12 derailed a wheelset on points which had not been locked; a lapse in operating procedure by the train crew, the report said, which would be eliminated by the automation planned for 1995. The second occurred at Hebron on 23 July, when the leading wheelset of the rear bogie of a downhill train's carriage derailed on the upper points. Unusually hot weather had prevented them from operating correctly so previous trains had been crossed by using the loop as a siding, causing delay. In response, water from a steam was used to cool the points. It was thought that the quick contraction dislodged rail fastenings, which became jammed between the moveable rack and the stock rail. No one was injured in either incident.

A more radical approach to improving the railway's capacity problems was taken during 1994, when an order was placed with HPE Tredegar Ltd for three diesel-electric railcars. With seats for 108 passengers, plus wheelchair space, the railcar set had twice the capacity of a steam or diesel train and only required a crew of two. The increase in capacity would be significant, it was thought. Working four trips per day, the number of

Hebron station with its first power generating wind turbine in 1991.

After the first
wind turbine at
Hebron was stolen
its replacement
was placed in a
secure compound,
4 May 1999.

Halfway loop on
4 May 1999, after it
had been automated.

daily trains operated could be increased to the equivalent of 32, or 1,800 passengers. The contract price was £483,613 and Lombard North Central plc provided £360,000 of finance.

Designed to be operated in multiple, the first railcar was delivered on 15 May 1995, the second a few days later and the third in September. Each vehicle was equipped with an 8.3 litre 234hp Cummins diesel engine that powered a 440v generator supplying a 90kW synchronous motor mounted on the rear bogie.

During testing, the first, No 21, reached the summit on 4 July. They carried their first fare-paying passengers in October (*Steam Railway*, February 1996). Unfortunately, the builder had been placed in liquidation by the time the third vehicle had been delivered and was unable to meet its obligations for commissioning.

After an initial problem with vibration in the passenger saloons was resolved by fitting additional friction dampers, the three cars ran together on 'quite a few occasions', remembered manager A.P. Hopkins, speaking to the author in 2009. On two days in 1996 a record was created when the railway operated 31 out of its theoretical maximum of 32 trains, a feat that was only possible by running four trips with the three railcars.

On 1 September 1995 Rogerson retired as general manager, remaining managing director. He left on a high, with the diesel locomotives doubling capacity and his final year promising to break records (*Steam Railway*, October 1995). His replacement was Anthony Peter Hopkins, who joined on 11 September; he had previously been a projects manager at GEC Alstom, Preston. Twelve months later Hopkins became managing director and Rogerson retired, maintaining his connection as a non-executive director.

Both men played a part in arranging events to mark the company's centenary in 1996. The anniversary day, 6 April, Easter Saturday, was marked by the issue of an anniversary label for the railway's summit mail. A formal event took place on 21 June. Unfortunately the principal guest, Lord Tonypandy, former speaker of the House of Commons George Thomas, was ill so his place was taken by Gwilym Jones MP, secretary of state for Wales with special responsibility for transport. Rogerson calculated that the railway had carried 5½ million passengers during the previous 100 years. Guests included Derek Rogerson's predecessor as manager, C.F. Jackson, and Frau Heidi Abt, wife of Peter Abt, a great-nephew of Roman Abt, the inventor of the railway's rack system;

Two railcars approach Halfway on 6 April 1996.

On 21 June 1996 Gwilym Jones MP substitutes for George Thomas, Viscount Tonypandy, former speaker of the House of Commons, to unveil the plaque commemorating the railway's centenary. Behind him are Derek Rogerson, manager from 1981 until 1995, and Nigel Ross, who reformed the company's finances and enabled the railway to modernise.

Following a commemorative lunch the centenary guests enjoyed a journey on the railway, and at the summit they were invited to enjoy the view from the Williams-Ellis building's roof.

a college lecturer, Abt had been unable to gain leave of absence to be present himself.

An enthusiast event was held on 28/29 September 1996, when an all-steam service was operated and five locomotives were steamed, believed to be for the first time since 1992. The occasion saw the return to steam of No 3 *Wyddfa* after a 'part-time' overhaul that had taken two years. With a new boiler, cylinders, side rods, injectors, cab, bunker, regulator, chimney and blastpipe all being replaced, this was the most intensive overhaul ever undertaken by the railway. No 5 *Moel Siabod* had been returned to service following an overhaul in June. A record 156,000 passengers were carried during the year.

The second of two changes in Cadogan's ownership had unexpected consequences for the company. The 1993 report recorded that Cadogan was owned by Brian Ivan Lever and Haigside Ltd, another property company in which Ross and Jaye had an interest. Then in 1995 Cadogan was owned by Compco Holdings plc, in which Lever, Ross and Jaye also had an interest. Cadogan had actually made a reverse takeover of Compco, a much larger company. As a stock exchange listed company, Compco was made aware that the market liked focussed companies and could not understand why a property company should own a railway, especially as it had more employees than the remainder of the business. Compco came under pressure to dispose of it.

A buyer was found early in 1998. Kevin Ronald Leech, then a businessman with interests in biotechnology, was diversifying into landmark destinations, including Land's End and John o'Groats, on a personal basis. He had made his first fortune by expanding his family undertaking business, which he had inherited at the age of 21, into a 38-strong chain. When that was sold, he moved to Jersey and invested £50,000 in a pharmaceuticals company that owned patents for drugs used in dialysis

treatment, accumulating a 40% stake in a multi-million business, which gave him the means to invest in other activities (*The Observer*, 26 December 2004).

At the time of the railway purchase he was ranked 157th in the *Sunday Times* Rich List. His private company, Crockley Green Ltd, registered in Jersey, bought Compco's shareholding for 74p per share and made an offer for the remainder. On 14 August 1998 Leech and three of his nominees were appointed directors, the three Cadogan directors retiring at the same time; Leech was appointed chairman. By the end of the year Crockley Green owned 90% of the capital and acquired the remainder shortly afterwards. The takeover valued the railway at £1.33 million, just over four times its value when Cadogan had taken over in 1984.

The railway had been transformed during the Cadogan era, marked by new rolling stock, increased capacity, innovation and, for the employees, a pension scheme. With passengers carried ranging from 76,539 in 1986 to 156,944 in 1996, the centenary year, this surely counts as a success. Despite the failure of attempts to expand into other leisure markets, the company and its railway emerged well placed to face the challenges of the future.

The last years of Cadogan's involvement had been good for the shareholders too. Dividends of 2½p per share paid from 1991 until 1994 and 3p per share until 1997 equate to a remarkable 22½% and 30%. Although at 74p the shares had made a loss on the 1985 80p issue price, the realisation for those who had bought 25p shares at £1.10 was £1.85. Of his involvement with the railway, Nigel Ross told the author in 2009 that it was a 'pride of ownership' business, he enjoyed his time with it but it was very time consuming; the Cadogan team had visited Llanberis every six weeks.

Kevin Leech, then company chairman, posed for photographs during a visit to the railway on 25 May 2000.

CHAPTER 10

21ST CENTURY HERITAGE ATTRACTION

Outwardly, there were no changes to the railway, but big changes were made behind the scenes. On 25 May 1999 the company was transferred to Heritage Great Britain plc, a Liverpool-based business wholly owned by Leech, via Cherberry Ltd, another Jersey-registered company, which managed his attractions. Snowdon Mountain Railway plc was re-registered as a private company on 29 June 1999.

Derek Rogerson resigned from the board on 9 August 1999, followed by Andrew and Gillian Davies on 30 November, ending nearly eighty years of Davies family involvement with the railway. A.P. Hopkins resigned as a director on 31 January 2000. Rogerson died on 16 August 2004, aged 73, and Andrew Davies died on 12 October 2005, aged 69.

When Heritage Great Britain was reorganised on 31 January 2000 the company's 'trade, assets and liabilities' were transferred to another group company, Heritage Attractions Ltd, which had been incorporated on 26 March 1999. There was now no need for the railway company to exist and it was registered as dormant on 1 February 2000. Ownership of Cherberry was transferred to the trustees of a Jersey-registered settlement during 2001. Providing head office, management and accounting services to its subsidiaries, Heritage GB has a strategy of investing in attractions that attract more than 100,000 visitors annually.

It set out to transform the railway into an attraction that exuded quality. Over the following twenty years every aspect was addressed. Items not needed were disposed of or stored off site. The stations were tided, the liveries standardised.

The final break with the old management occurred in February 2001, when A.P. Hopkins was made redundant. Alan Kendall, an existing Heritage Great Britain employee, took over as general manager on 1 March.

Andrew Davies was buried close to his family home at Abersoch.

The new management turned its attention to presentation and marketing. When the Llanberis shop was refurbished in 2000 removal of false ceilings revealed original features of the building's roof structure for the first time in many years. A small museum display was created near the arrivals platform at the same time. The booking office was relocated to the former snack bar building in the car park and a new ticketing system was introduced in 2001.

Concern about the railway's future when Kevin Leech was made bankrupt in October 2002 proved to be unfounded as it was one of the assets that had been placed in the ownership of a private Jersey trust. Leech reached a settlement with his creditors and was discharged from bankruptcy in 2004 (*The Observer*, 26 December 2004). One of the directors of the Heritage companies is his son, Allan James Stuart Leech.

Conditions at the summit were a big concern, as they had deteriorated beyond the capability of any remedial works to resolve them. The Prince of Wales notoriously called it 'the highest slum in Wales' or 'in Britain' or 'in England and Wales' depending on the source, it has not been possible to identify precisely what he said or when he said it; the earliest reference to this much quoted remark, 'the highest slum in Britain', found by the author was published in the *Liverpool Echo* in 1979; a 1982 report in the *Guardian* attributes it to 'generations of conservationists', so perhaps the Prince was quoting someone else.

However, after many years of debate a resolution of the summit building problem was started in December 2004, when planning permission was given for a new building estimated to cost £8.35 million. Designed by Ray Hole of Furneaux Stewart Design, it was funded by the Snowdonia National Park Authority, the Welsh Assembly Government, the Welsh European Funding Office, Visit Wales, the railway, and contributors to a public appeal. £500,000 was removed from the budget when the appeal failed to attract much support (*Steam Railway*, February 2006). The railway's contribution was £217,000. The building was designed to resist the extreme weather conditions at the summit and to comply with modern environmental requirements.

Carillion plc was appointed the contractor and work started with the demolition of the old building in the autumn of 2006. The expectation was that the building would be completed during the summer of 2007 and opened in May 2008 but the loss of many days because of high winds and unseasonal snow delayed completion until September 2008.

As might be expected, the project had a considerable effect on the railway. All passenger trains were terminated at Clogwyn during 2007 and 2008. Many passengers took single tickets to Clogwyn, then walked to the summit and back to Llanberis.

A tracing of the outline of the 2009 summit building made from the plan submitted with the planning application. The island platform was not built.

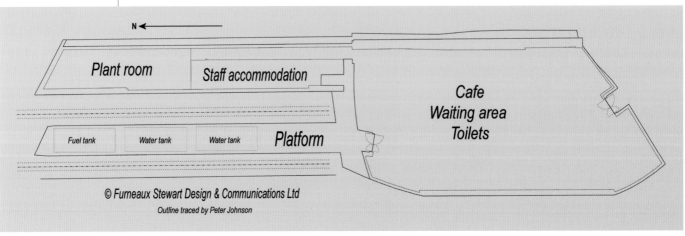

Plant room   Staff accommodation   Cafe   Waiting area   Toilets

Fuel tank   Water tank   Water tank   Platform

© Furneaux Stewart Design & Communications Ltd

Outline traced by Peter Johnson

On 12 October 2006, the day chosen for the park authority members and press to visit the summit construction site, there was a cloud inversion. Llanberis was in low cloud and the summit was in bright sun, although by the time the security barrier had been opened to allow the press to take photographs outside the compound conditions were changing and the cloud soon engulfed the summit.

A contrasting view of the finished building from the summit, 31 May 2013.

Carriage No 10 and its passengers set off for the summit on 12 June 2009. The carriage on the right is stabled on the loop line formed by extending the railcar siding to facilitate transporting supplies to the summit during the new building construction project. It is standing on the new river bridge required to make the loop. The road bridge that connects this location with the railway's car park is to the right, out of view.

At Llanberis, the car park became a site compound and a bridge was built over the Afon Hwch to give vehicular access to the railway for loading. Also bridging the river, the railcar siding was extended to the same area and connected to the main line by a remote-controlled solar-powered point, enabling loading to take place without interrupting the passenger service. With the departure of the contractors in 2009, these alterations were left in place with planning permission obtained to use the road bridge for fuel deliveries and the disposal of effluent from the summit.

Before work started, the Hunslet Engine Company built a 10-ton capacity 40ft flat wagon to transport materials and equipment. It was fitted with an electronic braking system that was monitored and controlled from the cabs of the diesel locomotives. During times of poor visibility, a CCTV camera mounted on it and a cab-mounted monitor were used to check that the track was clear. Up to four trains a day were run for construction purposes.

Taking the view that it would benefit from the new building in the long term the railway did not seek compensation for the interruption to its business. Not only did it lose fare income, with trains terminating at Clogwyn, but it lost revenue at the summit and the Llanberis car park too. The national park's planning did not appear to appreciate the gesture however, refusing planning permission for the railway's attempt to mitigate its losses by installing a temporary catering facility at Clogwyn, saying that it was contrary to the park's policies. Heritage Attractions attributed £80,000 reduced revenue during 2008 as mainly due to the non-availability of the summit outlet.

Facilities in the building include a café, kitchen, toilets, shop, staff quarters, and a plant room. The staff quarters include a single bedroom. Water tanks and a fuel tank are located under the platform. Not noticeable in the finished structure, the

lower part of the external wall against which the kitchen and the shop are located is the back wall of the 1896 station building.

The building, called Hafod Eryri, summer residence in Snowdonia, by the authority, was formally opened by the Welsh Government's first minister, Rhodri Morgan, on 12 June 2009. He walked there from Pen y Gwryd. The railway ran four trains for the benefit of the Snowdonia National Park Authority's guests.

Occupying the same ground area as its predecessor, the lack of a first floor means that the building is smaller. Features include a large viewing window and a smaller window on the east wall designed to give a view of the summit. The building is monitored remotely using a wireless link from Waterfall station. Operationally, the railway has the same two platforms as before.

There was great public enthusiasm to see what had been made, with over 1,000 passengers a day being carried in the first few weeks, and many turned away (*North Wales Live* 25 June 2009). Architect Ray Hole was awarded the Welsh National

Eisteddfod's gold medal for architecture on 1 August and the 'Welsh project of the year' award from the Royal Institution of Chartered Surveyors in 2010.

After more than five years out of use, the 1995-built railcars were scrapped in 2010. Changes made in 2002, to increase engine ventilation and to keep the electronics dry, had improved reliability but they could not be relied upon to work consistently. Taken out of service, they had been stored in the car park for several years, their bodies showing signs of rust. Their bogies and some other items were retained and put into store.

Severe damage was done to some of the railway's offices by fire during the evening of 6 November 2011. The cause was never established but it had started outside a 1970s-built extension and spread along a soil pipe. The thick walls of the adjacent building, Ty Clŵb, stopped it doing more than smoke damage in that section. As well as office furniture and equipment, the railway lost its archive photograph collection and some locomotive nameplates.

Railcars looking neglected in the car park on 22 May 2009. They were scrapped the following year.

The summit building
on 12 June 2009,
the day that it was
opened.

Two trains at the
summit on 12 June
2009.

A £1.5 million three-year programme to replace the carriages was started in 2012. Remarkably, the original carriages were still in use, although much altered, with only the 1988-built No 10 being anywhere near the standards required for 21st century passengers.

For the diesel powered 'traditional' service, four carriages were built by Garmendale Engineering Ltd of Ilkeston, Derbyshire, with bogies built by LH Group in Staffordshire, in 2012/3. Securing the order when traditional rolling stock builders had been unable to meet the railway's timescale for delivery, Garmendale has done work for other members of the Heritage Attractions group.

The vehicles are longer, higher and slightly wider than the original stock, seating 74 passengers instead of 56. They are also wheelchair accessible and provided with pull-out steps for use in situations where an emergency evacuation is required. Use of modern composite materials enabled the manufacture of vehicles with a contemporary and functional design. A £300,000 Welsh Government tourism development grant contributed to the £1,200,000 cost.

The carriages introduced a new red, white and black livery to the railway and the diesel locomotives were painted black to complement them. A gold version of the railway's logo was applied to the carriages' centre panels. Delivered on 5 November 2012, No 14 had to be returned to its maker for repairs and have its bogies replaced after it was damaged by flooding later in the month. Nos 15 and 16 were delivered on 5 March 2013 and No 17 on 13 March.

For the 'heritage' steam service, two of the original underframes were refurbished and received new bodies that acknowledged the original designs, also made by Garmendale. With a more spacious interior, they carry 34 passengers and attract a premium fare. The first, named *Snowdon Lily*, entered service on 1 June 2013. The second, *The Snowdon Mountain Goat*, was delivered on 15 April 2015, entering service soon after.

In connection with the heritage train service, with the carriages bearing the original company name, on 22 May 2013 Heritage Great Britain plc had registered Snowdon Mountain Tramroad & Hotels Company Ltd as a private company limited by shares. With one hundred £1 shares issued, it has been maintained as a dormant company since.

The first of the Garmendale carriages was delivered in November 2012. (SMR)

A few days later, on 16 November, it was possible to compare the ancient with the modern. The new carriage had not had its fleet numbers, or its gold logos, applied.

The new order, No 9 and one of the Garmendale carriages near the summit on 13 September 2019. (Chris Parry)

The first of the 'heritage' carriages, *The Snowdon Lily*, was launched on 31 May 2013. With No 2, it is seen just above Clogwyn. The railway's anemometer and the measures taken to restrain the embankment can also be seen.

When traffic warrants, the two heritage trains run together, as seen here at Clogwyn. (SMR)

The railway's management at Clogwyn for the launch of the first heritage carriage on 31 May 2013. From the left are Judith Pettit (retail and administration manager), Jonathan Tyler (Hafod Eryri manager), Vince Hughes (commercial manager), Alan Kendall (general manager) and Mike Robertshaw (engineering manager).

For the first time since the loco shed had been erected in 1895, in 2016 the amount of undercover storage space was increased at Llanberis, when a double-ended two-road shed capable of housing four carriages was constructed over the former railcar sidings.

Another enhancement at Llanberis was provided to accommodate visitors' basic needs in 2018, when an extension was opened that housed new toilet facilities, replacing those installed some 95 years earlier, and upgrading them to match 21st century expectations.

Alan Kendall, general manager since 2001, retired in May 2018. The position was not filled, commercial manager Vince Hughes, operations manager Marty Druce and engineering manager Mike Robertshaw overseeing the railway's management jointly.

A brief visit to the railway by global superstar Shirley Bassey on 17 May 2018 was the final instalment of a programme to name the four carriages acquired in 2012/3. In a ceremony at Waterfall station she named carriage No 16 after herself. The other carriages had been named after the opera singer Bryn Terfel (No 17, 10 April 2014), who lived near Caernarfon at the time, Team GB cycling manager David Brailsford (No 14, 6 December 2014), who grew up in the area, and singer Katherine Jenkins (No 15, 6 July 2015).

In September another visitor stayed for the entire month, a train, locomotive and carriage, from the Brienz Rothorn Bahn, a Swiss Abt railway, sponsored by the Switzerland Travel Centre. Built by SLM in 1891, the locomotive, No 2, had the distinction of being the oldest loco to run on the railway. To enable a service to operate, the safety rails were removed to a point just beyond Waterfall and the station was refurbished but the train only ran to the foot of the first viaduct. Over 2,000 visitors had free rides.

Having replaced and upgraded the passenger stock, the next issue to be addressed was the diesel fleet. With the oldest dating from 1986, aged in diesel terms, an innovative answer was sought. It was found at Clayton Equipment in

The shed erected on the stock sidings, photographed on 13 November 2016.

DAME SHIRLEY BASSEY DBE

Dame Shirley Bassey named carriage No 16 in a ceremony at Waterfall station on 17 May 2018.

Bryn Terfel at Llanberis on 10 April 2014. Each of the celebrities was presented with an SMR medal minted at the Royal Mint. (SMR)

Sir David Brailsford on 6 December 2014. (SMR)

Katherine Jenkins on 6 July 2016. (Eryl Crump)

the batteries ready for the next trip. A secondary brake provides a backup for the traction brake. The advantages are lower fuel use, reduced emissions and less noise. An unusual feature is a 12-seater passenger pod mounted on the front, adding an extra travel option and increasing the train's capacity.

The locos were delivered during the Covid 19 coronavirus crisis, which had forced the railway to cancel its plans for reopening in March. The situation changed rapidly, as shown in the table.

Announcement	Reopening
6 March	20 March
Normal services	
13 March	27 March
Deferred, otherwise normal services	
17 March	
Capacity reduced, screens installed in carriages	
19 March	1 May
Deferred, reduced capacity	
23 March	
Closure until further notice	

Reduced capacity traditional (diesel) services to Clogwyn did not recommence until 10 July, when the railway announced that as it would be impossible to implement safe social distancing measures at Hafod Eryri the building would remain closed for the rest of the year. Implementation of new Welsh Government restrictions saw the railway close completely on 16 October. In December it announced that it intended to resume service to Clogwyn on 21 March 2021.

This is a very uncertain time at which to end this story. The railway overcame the tragic accidents on its open day and the disruption of two world wars. Over the last forty years it has benefitted from some significant investment. It has owners and staff who care for it. It has the capacity to continue to play a significant role in the enjoyment of Snowdon and in the economy of Llanberis, just as its promoters intended 125 years ago. It deserves its success.

Burton-on-Trent, Staffordshire, in the form of a hybrid diesel electric design of loco developed especially for the railway. The £1.1 million order for two CBD30 locomotives was announced in October 2019 and they were delivered in June 2020, the first bogie locos to run on the railway.

Numbered 14 and 15, they are driven by electric motors powered by a 524KWh lead acid traction battery pack recharged by a 115kW Deutz Euro 5 low emissions diesel engine. On the descent the diesel engine is switched off while service braking recharges

A contrast in styles between Abt locomotives from two different railways, Brienz Rothorn Bahn No 2 and No 3 at Llanberis on 1 September 2018.

In anticipation that the Swiss visitor would be carrying passengers to Waterfall, the station building was made presentable and platforms constructed on both sides of the line.

The new normal. Clayton hybrid loco No 14 *Glaslyn* on test with one of the Garmendale carriages in August 2020. (SMR)

A diesel train climbs above Clogwyn on 13 September 2019. (Chris Parry)

SNOWDON RAILWAY ESTIMATE OF EXPENSES

In Parliament – Session 1872
Snowdon Railway
Estimate of Expense – of the Railway & works proposed to be authorised by the above Bill.
Length of Line 4m 1f 6ch
Whether single or double – Single

	Cubic yards	price p yd	£. s. d.	£. s. d.
Earthworks				
Cuttings - Rock	9,532	@ 2/-	953 4 0	
Soft soil	9,532	@ 1/-	476 12 0	
Roads	none			
Total	19,064		1,429 16 0	1,429 16 0
Embankments including Roads 9,587 Cub yds				
Bridges – Public Roads (none)				
Accommodation Bridges & Works				350 0 0
Culverts & Drains				300 0 0
Metalling of Roads & Level crossings				50 0 0
Gatekeepers' houses at level crossings				100 0 0
Permanent way including Fencing – cost price 4m 1f 6ch @ £3,644 0 0				15,305 0 0
Permanent way for sidings & cost of junctions				100 0 0
Stations				400 0 0
Contingencies 10 per cent				1,803 0 0
Land & Buildings				1,000 0 0
Total cost of line				£20,837 16 0

27 December 1871
Eugene Bucklin

PROJECTED CAPITAL EXPENDITURE 1895

Cost of land	£1,500	
Add 5%	£75	£1,575
Earthworks		£26,200
Permanent way		£17,973
Engineering	£2,808	
Add 5%	£140	£2,948
Law and other expenses		£1,500
Compensation to farmers		£100
Hotel at summit		£6,000
Architects' commission on hotel		£300
Furnishing hotel	£1,000	
Add 5%	£50	£1,050
Water supply to hotel		£200
Refurnishing Victoria Hotel including stock and valuation	£4,000	
Add 5%	£200	£4,200
Four locomotives	£6,400	
12 carriages	£4,800	
Four trucks	£800	£12,000
Syndicate		£6,000
Electric light		£1,500
Signalling	£1,500	
Add 5%	£75	£1,575
Underwriting		£4,500
Working capital		£2,000
		£89,621

ESTIMATE OF WORKING EXPENSES 1895

Worked with two locomotives – 130 working days		
130 days – two locomotives, including driver, cleaner, coal, oil and depreciation @	£2	£520
Two guards @ 6s	12s	
Two platelayers @ 5s	10s	
Four porters @ 5s	£1	
130 days @	£2 8s	£312
235 non-working days @	£2 8s	£258 10s
365 days – six carriages @	1s	£109 10s
Coal for station etc		£20
Secretary		£300
Contingencies		£50
		£1,570
Add for taxes, say 10%		£157
		£1,727
Two locomotives working five trips each per day would work 90 miles per day, 11,700 train miles over 130 days, at a cost of 2s 11½d train per mile		
Estimated revenue		£8,220
Less expenses		£1,727
Balance for dividend	8½%	£6,493

Worked with four locomotives – 130 working days		
130 days – four locomotives, including driver, cleaner, coal, oil and depreciation @	£2	£520
Four guards @ 6s	12s	
Two platelayers @ 5s	10s	
Four porters @ 5s	£1	
Booking clerk @ 6s	6s	
130 days @	£3	£390
235 non-working days		
One engine driver @ 6s	6s	
Two platelayers @ 5s	10s	
One booking clerk @ 6s	6s	

235 days @	£1 2s	
365 days – six carriages @	1s	£109 10s
Coal for station etc		£20
Secretary		£300
Contingencies		£50
		£2,270 10s
Add for taxes, say 10%		£227 10s
		£2,505
Four locomotives working five trips each per day would work 180 miles per day, 23,400 train miles over 130 days, at a cost of 2s 1½d train per mile		
Estimated revenue		£8,220
Less expenses		£2,505
Balance for dividend	7½%	£5,715

One day in the 1930s the guard and passengers pose for a photograph while their loco takes water.

THE MECHANICAL EQUIPMENT OF THE SNOWDON MOUNTAIN RAILWAY

Gowrie Colquhoun Aitchison, Assoc. M. INST. C.E.

The Snowdon Mountain Railway starts from Llanberis at a point some 350 feet above the sea level, and ascends with varying gradients, ranging between 1 in 20 and 1 in 5.5, until it reaches the upper terminus, which lies about 50 feet below the actual summit of the mountain, which is 3,560 feet high. The total rise of the railway from terminus to terminus is 3,140 feet, and the length is 4 miles 54 chains, the average gradient being 1 in 7.83. The system adopted is that known as the 'Abt,' and rack is used for the whole length of the line, and on all sidings and turnouts, as well as in the engine and carriage sheds. The line is single, but three passing places or turnouts are provided at practically equal distances, as well as a double track at each terminal station of sufficient length to hold a full train. The sharpest curve is of 4 chains radius.

Permanent Way — The permanent way is of steel throughout. The bearing rails are rolled to the Indian State Railway section; they are flanged, and weigh 41¼lb per yard. The sleepers are of rolled steel, 6ft long by 1in thick on the crown, gradually tapering off in thickness at the sides; their ends are doubled down, and they weigh 67lb each. The bearing rails are fastened to these sleepers by clips, which are fixed to the sleeper by hook bolts; each clip has a projection on its underside, which, together with the hook bolt, fits into an oblong hole through the crown of the sleeper.

The gauge is widened as required on the curves by this projection on the underside of the clip being varied in size. Sleepers are spaced regularly 2ft 11½in apart. The rack, which is double, is of mild rolled steel, and is carried down the centre of the line on rolled steel chairs weighing 12lb each, machined on the faces against which the rack bars fit. These chairs are connected to the sleeper by two finch steel bolts, the square heads of which are rigidly held on the underside of the sleeper by a channelled iron plate. Rack bars of varying strength are used, according to the steepness of the gradient: on gradients below 1 in 9, the thickness of rack bar is 20mm; on gradients of 1 in 9 and over, the thickness of rack bar is 25mm. The rack bars are 5 feet 10 inches long, and are so laid that the tooth of the bar on one side of the chair comes opposite the space of the bar on the other side. The weight per rack bar of 25mm in thickness is 67lb, and per rack bar of 20mm in thickness 53lb. All rack bars are 4⁵⁄₁₆in in depth. Two ¾in fish bolts fasten the rack bars to each chair.

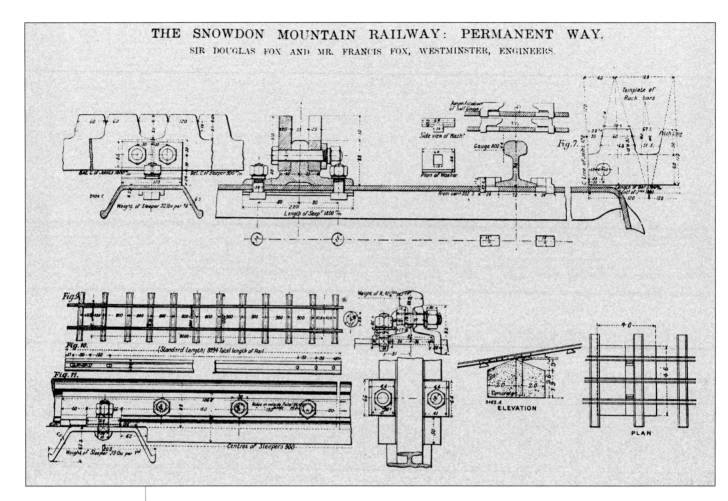

The following are the dimensions of the teeth:

Depth of tooth   50mm
Centre to centre of teeth   120mm
Length at pitch line   60mm

There is now on all gradients (but dropped off at the crossings) what may be termed a 'safety angle iron', an arrangement designed with a view to supplying an additional safeguard against the possibility of the cogs on the engine pinions mounting and thus losing or reducing their engagement with the teeth of the rack. This angle iron is of rolled steel, and attached to each side of the rack bars by the same bolts which hold the rack bars to the chairs. It is laid in various lengths to suit both vertical and horizontal curves, and dowel pins are inserted at the ends to secure correct alignment at the joints. In consequence of the variation in the thickness of the rack bars (as before described), a 5mm washer has to be introduced between the 20mm rack bar and the angle iron, in order that the latter should always be the same distance from the centre throughout. Two grippers are attached to each engine, and one, or in some cases two, to each carriage. These are so adjusted that they never come in contact with the angle iron unless there be a tendency to mount, when the gripper will at once come into action by catching under the flanges of the angle iron.

All rails, rack bars, and angle irons are fish plated. The bolt holes at the lower end of the bearing rails are round, but those at the upper end are oval, so that expansion takes place up hill. Each rack bar has four bolt holes, the two in the centre being round, while those at each end are oval, expansion being thus allowed for from the centre. To prevent creeping, iron stays or uprights are set at intervals in solid concrete blocks, and the lower side of a joint sleeper is allowed to rest against them. The spacing of these anchors depends on the steepness of the gradient. On the 1 in 6 gradients they are about 60yd apart.

The crossings adopted on the Snowdon Railway are of rather a complicated character, as the rack is carried right through, thus making a continuous track for the engine pinions. The switches are 12ft in length, the radius of curve being 151ft 3in, the rate of crossing about 1 in 4, and the angle 130. The rods and levers which work the points are connected with and work hinged portions of the rack, which are thus brought into correct position at the same time as the points are thrown over. This provides a continuous rack for the passing of the engine, and also clears a passage for the bearing wheels.

No crossing is placed on a steeper gradient than 1 in 10.

Locomotives — These were built by the Schweizerische Locomotiv und Maschinenfabrik of Winterthur, Switzerland. They weigh 13tons 5cwt when empty, and 17tons 5cwt when in running order with full load of coal and water. They were guaranteed to be capable of driving a load of 18 tons up a gradient of 1 in 5 at a speed of 6.7km per hour. Their IHP is 166. The cylinders are 300mm in diameter, and they are placed outside the frame. The stroke is 600mm. The motion is communicated to the cranks by means of a one sided rocking lever with upper and lower connecting rods. The throw of the cranks is thus reduced and tractive power increased. The fulcrum of the rocking lever is kept as low as possible.

The valve chests are above the cylinders. There are three axles, the leading and second each having pinion wheels attached, and being coupled together, while the third is on a trailing pony truck.

The wheels are carried inside the frames, and are all loose on the axles except one of those on the trailing axle, which is keyed. The first and second axles have solid forged disks in their centres; to each of these disks are attached two steel pinion rings, so set that their teeth alternate. There are fifteen teeth to each pinion ring. In order to hold these pinion rings in their relative position on the axle disks, and yet at the same time to allow some slight circumferential movement to prevent jarring, and also to allow for any slight irregularity in the pitch of the teeth of the rack bars, eight double horseshoe springs are inserted in the disk under each pinion ring. The upper ends of these springs project into countersunk spaces on the inner or under side of the rings. The maximum of play allowed is 3mm, and to avoid more play

being obtained in the event of one of these springs snapping or becoming weak, a solid iron tongue is introduced. The springs and pinion rings are held in position by the brake drums (which will afterwards be described), being placed on each side, and being firmly bolted through the solid forged axle disks with eight steel bolts 1in in diameter.

The teeth of the pinions on the leading axle are given a lead over those on the second axle of one quarter the distance between two teeth, in order that when the teeth of a pinion on the leading axle are about to leave engagement with the rack, the teeth of the corresponding pinion on the second axle are about to engage. Perfect and continuous engagement is thus secured. In order to keep the water level over the crown of the fire box as regular as possible, the whole boiler is set down by the head at a slope of 1 in 11 to the horizontal. The gauge glasses are placed halfway along the boiler, so as to register correctly on the varying gradients.

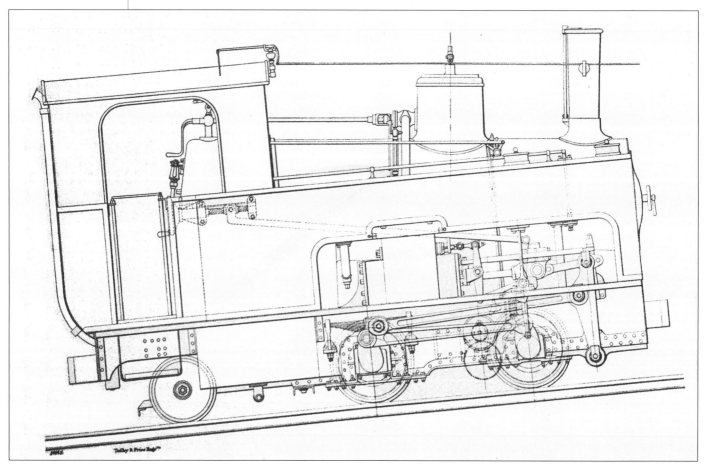

Gauge of rails	800mm	2 ft 7 in
Diameter of cylinders	300mm	11 13/16in
Stroke of piston	600mm	1 ft 11 5/8in
Diameter of pinion wheels at pitch circle	573mm	22. 56in
Pitch of teeth		4. 72in
Diameter of rail wheels on coupled axles	653mm	25. 71in
Diameter of truck wheels	520mm	20. 74in
Wheel base, rigid	1,350mm	4 ft 5ft 1/8in
Wheel base, total, total	3,000mm	9 ft 10 1/8in

BOILER

Number of tubes		156
Inside diameter of tubes	32mm	1. 26in
Outside diameter of tubes	35mm	1. 38in
Heating surface, fire box	3. 90sq m	41. 981sq ft
Heating surface, tubes	33. 00sq m	355. 220sq ft
Heating surface, total	36. 90sq m	397. 200sq ft
Grate area	0. 95	10. 030sq ft
Steam pressure when at work	14kg per sq cm	200lb per sq in
Hydraulic test pressure	20kg per sq cm	284. 4lb per sq in
Plates, cylindrical shell	11mm	0. 43in
Plates, copper fire box	14mm	055in
Plates, tube plates	25mm	0. 98 and
	20mm	0. 79in
Feed water in tanks	1,700l	374gal
Cooling water for brake	300l	66gal
Coal box capacity	500kg	10cwt
Water in boiler	1,150l	253gal
Coal in fire box, and tools	400kg	88lb
Maximum load per axle	6,000kg	5.90tons.
Tractive power	7,100kg	7tons

The boiler plates are of mild steel, the fire box is of copper with a circular top, and the tubes are of steel, with copper ends at the fire box end. The water tanks are on either side of the boiler, and run the whole length of the same. The leading dimensions of the engines are given in the Table.

A most careful test was applied to samples of all the materials used in the construction of these engines. The cost of the engines averaged about £1,475 each.

The two grippers are placed one in front of the leading axle and the other between the first and second axles in the centre of the engine.

Brakes — There are five brakes on each engine: Two separate hand brakes, one steam brake which can be applied by hand, one automatic brake, and one air brake.

Hand brake — On each of the driving axles (on each side of the pinions and securely bolted direct on to the axle disks

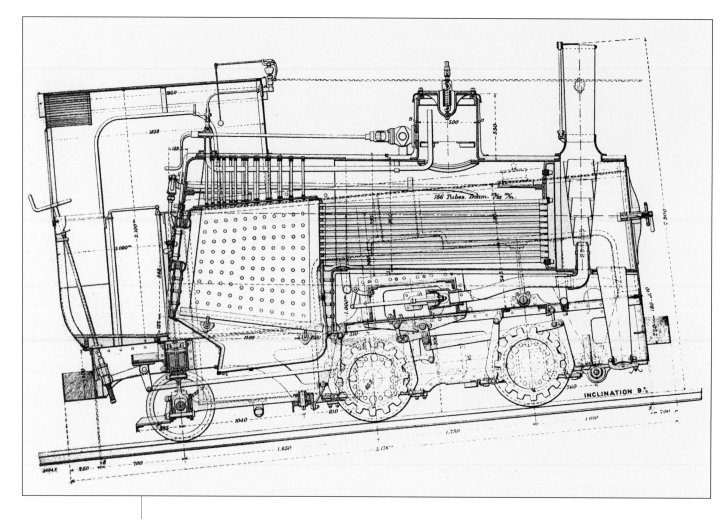

previously referred to) are two deeply grooved cast steel brake drums, upon which grooved cast iron brake blocks work, one on each side of each drum, thus there are four drums with eight brake blocks, the working face area of each block being 60sq in. These blocks are actuated by hand from the cab, there being two handles, one for the driver, which operates the four blocks on the right hand side of the engine, and one for the fireman, which operates the four blocks on the left hand side.

Steam brake — In addition to the hand arrangement above described, the four blocks on the right hand side of the engine are capable of being worked by steam, the driver being able to bring them into action by means of a hand lever rod, conveniently placed over the crown of the fire box.

Automatic brake — This is a brake which is designed to come into action automatically in the event of an engine travelling, from any cause, above a given speed. On the right hand side of the frame plate is placed a circular cast iron box, which is connected onto a small shaft which passes through to the inside of the frame plate and is there geared by means of toothed wheels direct onto the leading axle. Within the circular box is a governor block, to which a light coil spring is attached; this spring is controlled by a screw which may be tightened or loosened, and thus regulates the action of the governor block. On the maximum or limit of speed allowed being exceeded, the nose of this governor block projects sufficiently far to strike a trigger, which on being tripped releases a powerful coil spring, and this, in its turn, pulls down a rod which opens a cone valve, and steam is admitted gradually into the steam brake cylinder, which is fixed on the inside of the engine frame. This arrangement has to be most carefully adjusted and constantly tested, as it is absolutely essential that the action of this brake should not be sudden, as locking of the pinions too suddenly must be carefully avoided on such gradients as those on the Snowdon Railway. Before the engine can proceed, after this brake has come into action, it is necessary for the driver to leave the cab and put the lever back in position and reset the trigger and so cut off the ingress of steam.

Air brake — This brake is used to control the engine while descending the mountain. Air is admitted to the cylinders through the exhaust ports, and on becoming compressed controls the travel of the piston. The driver, in order to allow the engine to descend, allows the compressed air to escape through a hand valve, which is conveniently placed at the rear of the cab. All steam is cut off when the engine is descending, and when the air inlet to the exhaust ports is open the passage for the steam exhaust to the chimney is closed. To avoid excessive wear and tear, water is taken into the cylinder along with the air, from a spray pipe. This brake is most effective in its action, completely controlling the engine without the aid of other brake power, as long as everything in connection with it is kept in absolute repair, and all leakage is reduced to a minimum.

The author at first found it extremely difficult to accurately control the speed at which the drivers allowed their engines to travel; he therefore had 'speed indicators' attached to each engine. These instruments indicate the speed by a hand on a plain dial face, and in addition ring one beat on a gong to warn the driver that he is approaching his limit of speed, and three beats when he has reached or exceeded that limit. These indicators also register, by means of pin pricks on a paper roll, the variations of speed during the journey, and so an accurate record can be kept of each driver's performances. The instrument has the appearance of a clock and is fixed on the top of the right-hand side water tank, and directly facing the driver. A down shaft runs from the indicator, through the tank,

to a box or case which is supported by bolts to the engine frame; within this box are a pair of mitre wheels, one keyed to the down shaft, the other to a short shaft which projects through the side of the box, and at the end of which is a crank with a long slot. This crank is worked by a projecting pin connected to the crank of the second driving axle, the revolutions of the axle being thus transmitted to the indicator. The engines are fitted with right and left hand re-starting injectors and sight lubricators for the cylinders and valve chests; there is also an oil dripper arrangement in the cab which conveys a heavy lubricating oil direct to the teeth of the pinion wheels, but this is not sufficient in itself, and it is therefore essential that the rack bars should be kept thoroughly lubricated. If this is carefully attended to there is little wear and tear on either the pinion wheel or the rack, considering the work these engines have to accomplish during a season.

The coal consumption is heavy, the quantity used varying considerably with the load taken up and the quality of the coal. Unfortunately this last year, owing to trade complications, no really reliable tests could be carried out; but it is a fair average to say that from 6cwt to 7cwt of good quality quick steaming coal is burned on one journey.

The carriages are 38ft long over buffers, 6ft 6in wide and 9ft 4in high; they are open at the sides above the door level, and are divided into seven compartments, each holding eight persons, and a separate compartment in front for the guard.

Canvas curtains are provided for use in wet weather, hung on slender wooden rods, which would snap under very severe strain from wind. In order to obviate any discomfort to the passengers, owing to the gradients up which the carriages have to pass, the upper seats in each compartment are deeply hollowed on the sitting portion; by this simple arrangement the necessity of stepping the floor of the carriage, or having movable seats, has been avoided. The weight of each carriage is 5tons 13cwt now that grippers have been fitted similar

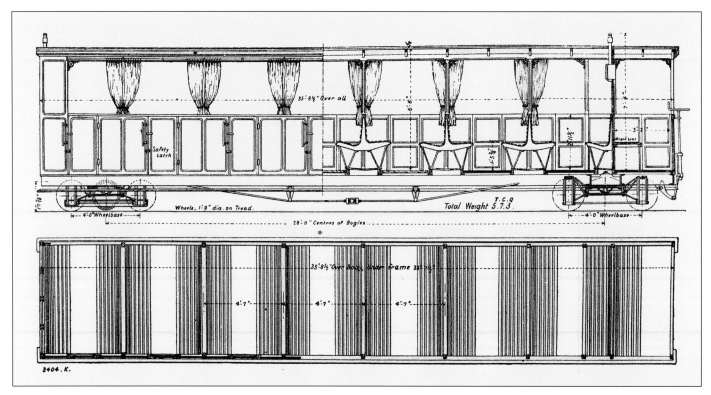

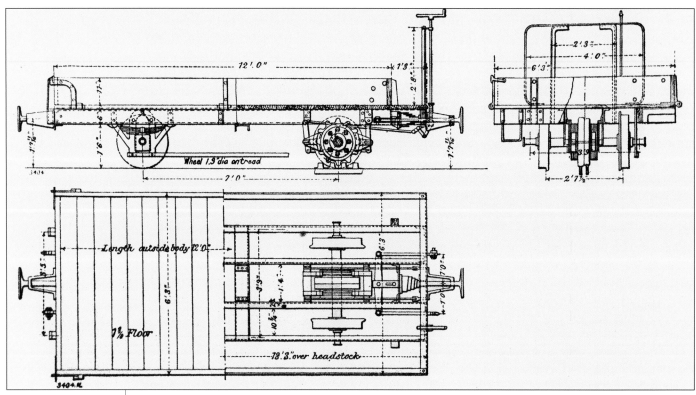

to those on the engines. The underframe is of light sections of channel steel. The two four-wheeled bogies are spaced 28ft centre to centre, the wheelbase of each bogie being 4ft; the wheels are of cast steel on steel axles.

On the rear bogie in each carriage is a double brake pinion, which is carried on a separate short axle in the centre of the bogie frame, between the two bearing axles, and to the outer sides of which

are bolted two grooved brake drums, on which four cast iron brake blocks operate. These blocks are applied by hand by the guard, from his compartment at the front end of the carriage, by means of a wheel. This brake arrangement is similar to the hand brakes on the locomotives. The claw, or gripper, is carried at the back of the rear bogie. The centre of gravity of the carriages has been kept as low as possible, in consequence of the strong and gusty winds experienced on the mountain. A carriage with its full complement of passengers is calculated to withstand a wind pressure of 36lb per sq ft. No couplings are ever used except to draw carriages out of the sheds.

The goods wagons are 12ft long and 6ft 3in wide, the sides being 11in deep. The under frames are of channel steel and the wheels and axles of steel; the distance from centre to centre of wheels is 7ft, and each wagon is constructed to carry 6 tons. A platform is provided for the conductor, with a hand or guard rail, to which the brake wheel is fixed. The wagon brake is similar in action to those on the carriages, but the pinion wheels and brake drums are attached direct to the rear axle.

The brakes, both on the carriages and wagons, are exceedingly powerful in action, completely controlling the carriage when applied on the steepest gradient. They are never applied except in case of emergency.

LOCOMOTIVES AND ROLLING STOCK

Locomotives and railcars

Number	Name	Wheel arrangement	Date built	Works number	Remarks
1	*L. A. D. A. S.*	0-4-2T Rack	1895	923	Joy valve gear. Single-sided rocking levers. Saturated boiler No 1,544. Named for Laura Alice Duff Assheton-Smith. Destroyed on 6 April 1896.
2	*Enid*	0-4-2T Rack	1895	924	Joy valve gear. Single-sided rocking levers. Saturated boiler No 1,545. Named for Enid Assheton-Smith who cut the first sod on 15 December 1894. Railway personnel pronounce the name *Ennid*. Rebuilt by Hunslet in 1958, allocated works number 58833. Work included straightening frame plates and replacing buffer beams and Davies & Metcalfe injectors. Whistle was also replaced and located on top of the dome. Oil fired 1971/2. Dark blue livery from 1998. Reboilered 1992, new firebox 2010.
3	*Wyddfa*	0-4-2T Rack	1895	925	Joy valve gear. Single-sided rocking levers. Saturated boiler. Rebuilt by Hunslet in 1960, allocated works number 58948. Work included replacing both injectors. 1988 the author was told that No 3 had been renamed *Yr Wyddfa* but photographic evidence reveals that this was not the case. In-house overhaul completed in 1996, when it was painted maroon. Reboilered 1995, new firebox 2010.
4	*Snowdon*	0-4-2T Rack	1896	988	Joy valve gear. Single-sided rocking levers. Saturated boiler. Rebuilt by Hunslet in 1963, allocated works number 59092. Work included fitting a new boiler. Rebuilt by Hunslet again in 1978. Brunswick green livery in 1990s. Reboilered 1995, new firebox 2010. Oil fired 1992-2001.
5	*Moel Siabod*	0-4-2T Rack	1896	989	Joy valve gear. Single-sided rocking levers. Saturated boiler. Rebuilt by Hunslet in 1959, allocated works number 58889. Work included straightening frame plates and replacing buffer beams. Chocolate brown livery applied in 1997 faded, repainted black in 2000. Out of service 2001-17.
6	*Padarn*	0-4-2T Rack	1922	2838	Walschaert's valve gear. Double-sided rocking levers. 220-240bhp. Superheated boiler. Named *Sir Harmood* until 1923. Black livery in 1997.
7	*Ralph*	0-4-2T Rack	1923	2869	Walschaert's valve gear. Double-sided rocking levers. Superheated boiler. 220-240bhp. Named *Aylwin* until 4 October 1978 when renamed *Ralph Sadler* after the SMR's late consulting civil engineer. Renamed *Ralph* 2 May 1987. Out of use since c1992. In store.

8	_Eryri_	0-4-2T Rack	1923	2870	Walschaert's valve gear. Double-sided rocking levers. Superheated boiler. 220-240bhp. Oil firing trial in 1971/2. Out of use since c1992. In store.
9	_Ninian_	0-4-0DH Rack	1986	9249	Rolls Royce C6 350R turbocharged engine rated at 320hp at 1,900rpm. 17½ tons in working order. Named after Ninian Rhys Davies, then chairman of the company, and in recognition of the Davies family's involvement with the SMR since 1922, on 2 May 1987. Re-engined 2011.
10	_Yeti_	0-4-0DH Rack	1986	9250	Rolls Royce C6 350R turbocharged engine rated at 320hp at 1,900rpm. 17½ tons in working order. Name chosen by Rhonda Golding, the winner of a BBC TV children's competition. Painted purple in the 1990s. Re-engined 2011.
11	_Peris_	0-4-0DH Rack	1991	9305/775	Ordered from Hunslet and built by Barclay; both companies allocated works numbers. Named after a local saint on 22 August 1992. Re-engined 2012.
12	_George_	0-4-0DH Rack	1992	9312	Named after George Thomas, Viscount Tonypandy, former speaker of the House of Commons, by Gwilym Jones MP on 21 June 1996. Mauve livery in the 1990s; green with yellow highlights in 1999. Re-engined 2012.
14	_Glaslyn_	Hybrid rack	2020	B4651/1	
15	_Moel Eilio_	Hybrid rack	2020	B4651/2	
21		Railcar	1995	1074	Out of service in 2001, stored off-rail in the car park from 2006. Scrapped 2010. Bogies in store.
22		Railcar	1995	1075	Out of service in 2003, stored off-rail in the car park from 2006. Scrapped 2010. Bogies in store.
23		Railcar	1995	1076	Out of service in 2003, stored off-rail in the car park from 2006. Scrapped 2010. Bogies in store.

There is no record of the original locomotive livery and none of the early writers mentioned it. Where the locomotive is visible in some of the early, late-nineteenth century, coloured postcards they are black. In 1933 E.R. Davies reported that a red line had been added. R.W. Kidner (see Bibliography for references to this section) contains the earliest reference to livery known, saying in 1937 that the locomotives were painted black; as he had visited the railway in 1935 this report has the benefit of being based on personal observation. Photographs are of little assistance because orthochromatic film would not normally distinguish the two colours, but evidence of lining can be seen in some 1930s photographs.

However, when enthusiast L.W. Perkins visited the railway in 1942, he photographed No 2 inside the shed, noting that it was out of service and painted and lined in green. As painting to this standard was unlikely to be carried out during wartime it must be assumed that it dated to the late 1930s. During the 1950s some locomotives had silver smokebox doors and a colour transparency of unknown date exists showing No 8 with its cab painted brown edged in black, its boiler barrel, smokebox and frames painted black, buffer beam red and chimney and smokebox door painted silver. The earliest dated colour photographs showing the locomotives in what became the standard green livery were taken in 1961.

During the 1990s Nigel Day, one of the drivers, started to decorate his loco, initially No 7 and then No 4, with various insignia, including some very ornate brass lamps. Feeling overlooked by the attention that Day's loco received, from 1996 the other drivers sought approval to decorate their locos too. Not having

No 2 in the shed on 17 June 1942. The photographer noted that it had been painted green. (L.W. Perkins)

No 7 at Llanberis in the 1950s, with its cab and tanks painted green and its smokebox door and chimney in silver.

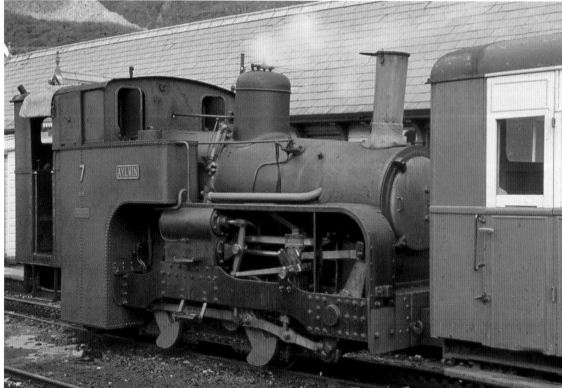

his metalworking skills, they settled for
painting the locos in different colours,
resulting in a multi-coloured fleet, although
No 6 retained the standard green, and only
two of the diesel locos were repainted. The
standard green livery was restored from
2001/2 although there are, at the time of
writing, variations in lining. A black livery
was applied to the diesel locomotives
following the entry into service of the
Garmendale carriages.

Derek Rogerson, the later general
manager, explained that the locomotives'
small fireboxes were designed to burn dry
steam coal. Traditionally the Ministry of
Fuel & Power defined this as being non-
caking, with 10 to 13.5% volatile matter
and an ash fusion temperature of more
than 1,300°C. Coal of this specification

is no longer mined in the UK and the
definition was widened to include coals
with 14 to 14.5% volatiles with some
caking properties and ash fusion above
1,200°C, a point at which the ash fusion
temperature becomes critical on the SMR
locomotives. The following information
illustrated the situation in 1988: Onllwyn
Colliery in South Wales provided the
best coal for the railway but switched
to anthracite. Deep Navigation coal was
then the first choice, followed by Daw
Mill. (Although Daw Mill was not a dry
steam coal, having volatiles above 30%,
it was non-caking and had an acceptable
ash fusion temperature). A combination
of the two coals was normally burnt in
the sequence, from Llanberis, first Deep
Navigation, then Daw Mill, and then Deep

No 7 as decorated by its driver, Nigel Day, in 1991.

Nigel Day and No 4 as decorated for the centenary, 6 April 1996.

No 2 looked good in blue. It was photographed crossing the bridge near Halfway, 4 May 1999.

No 6 in black, another of the staff liveries. 29 March 1997.

No 3 in its 21st Century standard livery, 1 April 2019.

The outdoor boiler shop in 1992. The two boilers show different construction techniques, riveted at the rear and welded in the foreground.

Navigation, the Deep Navigation thereby being used on the steepest sections and in the area of Llanberis itself, to reduce pollution. Primary and secondary air modifications were tried without success. British Coal fuel technologists investigated the railway's problems, concluding that they could only be overcome by redesigning the boilers. As an example of how critical it was for the railway to have the right fuel, the tale was told of the opencast coal burnt during the miners' strike; the fire on No 2 went out for no obvious reason and the locomotive had to be towed back to Llanberis where investigation found that the firebox tubeplate was filled with lava from the melted ash. In 2020 the railway obtained its coal from the Ffos y Fran opencast colliery in South Wales.

The SLM delivery notes for Nos 7 and 8 show that each locomotive was supplied with a comprehensive set of tools and equipment. In a packing case were: 5 paper rolls for speed recorders; 3 signal lamps with red and green discs; 2 chisels; 1 screwdriver; 2 punches; 3 files; 1 syringe; 8 water gauge glasses with 16 rubber rings; 3 box keys for lubricator; 6 spanners; and 3 water gauge lamps. A 10-ton winch was packed in the cab. In the coal bunker was packed: speed recorder; whistle; hammer; copper hammer; lead hammer; monkey wrench; 4 tube plugs for smoke tubes; 4 tube plugs for boiler tubes; 2 single spanners; 4 double spanners; spanner for axlebox wedge; 2 washout plug spanners; 1 brush; 1 slack shovel; 1 slack pricker; 1 grate scraper; 1 coal shovel; 1 tube cleaner; 1 box key for drain cock; and 1 water bucket. In a toolbox were five oil cans of different sizes and shapes.

When the diesel locomotives were designed, every consideration was given to interchangeability of common parts to aid integration with the steam fleet. Of the major mechanical components, it proved possible to use the same pinion ring and fixing but not the wheelsets. Pneumatic pump lubricators on timers replaced manual oiling.

Over the last seventy years the railway has become increasingly capable about the work that it carries out on the locomotives in house. This is No 4 stripped for overhaul. On the same date, 30 April 2010, No 3 was in a more advanced state behind it and No 2 was on the jacks alongside.

At Clogwyn on 4 May 1999, this view of No 12 in green with yellow highlights represents the staff contribution to the diesel fleet liveries.

Engine-hour meters in the cabs ensured regular maintenance. Carrying sufficient fuel for a day's work, in 1988 they used £3.20 of fuel per trip and had a four-minute Llanberis turnround, compared with an average of £51.00 and 30-minute turnround for steam. There were no hidden operating costs for the diesels, ash disposal being a particular bugbear of steam operating. Their engines were replaced in 2011 / 2.

To crew the diesels, the volunteers from existing footplatemen willing to undergo conversion training were offered a bonus for driving both types of locomotive. There was some initial reluctance but 'once a man qualified, getting him back on steam was like pulling teeth,' Derek Rogerson said, the clean enclosed working conditions being appreciated.

The railcars' clerestory roofs were intended to be reminiscent of traditional tramcars. They had triple-reduction gearboxes with single helical gear first and second stages and straight spurs on the final drive. The 1½-ton gear assembly incorporated the rack pinion drive and brake drum and the operating gear and electric drive motor. The electronic control equipment was supplied by Alstom. The downhill bogie carried an axle-mounted motor that incorporated the drive pinion. The uphill bogie has a brake pinion. Testing suggested that this would be inadequate on its own, leading to a prohibition on them operating singly. Within a year or two it became a regular occurrence for one of them to be out of service due to issues with their bogies, gearboxes or electronics. Several attempts were made to find a solution but the first was taken out of service in 2001 and the others in 2003. They were stored in the car park from 2006 and scrapped in 2010.

The Clayton locomotives were delivered without their passenger accommodation and testing was started without it being fitted. In January 2021 No 14 was returned to its maker to enable its software to be updated. The railway intends to have four hybrid locomotives and to retain two diesel locomotives to act as backups for the steam locomotives and for use on maintenance trains.

Carriages and wagons

The Lancaster Carriage & Wagon Company supplied six carriages and four drop-side, two-plank wagons to the SMR in 1896. The carriage returned to its maker for conversion to an open vehicle in 1897 was returned having been made

No 3 shunts No 12 while the latter was having its engine replaced in 2012. (SMR)

A line up contrasting
No 4, No 6 and
No 12 on 21 June
1996.

Nos 11 and 6 on shed
on 17 May 2018.

Components for the hybrid locomotives at the works of Clayton Equipment Ltd on 24 February 2020.

One of the Clayton locomotives on test as first delivered, looking rather odd without its passenger pod. (SMR)

Both of the hybrid locomotives outside the shed on 14 August 2020. No 14, left, has been fitted with its nameplates.

shorter, with five compartments, and with its roof removed. Another open, with four compartments, was obtained in 1900. Photographs showing them in service are uncommon; they were usually propelled in front of an ordinary carriage although one photograph shows a train using both. The older one had its body removed to carry water to the new summit building by 1938 and the other was probably withdrawn around the same time.

J.I.C. Boyd (see Bibliography) suggested that the 1911 minute approving a carriage being sent to Ince for repair concealed an order for a lightweight open carriage that could be run on Lancaster bogies in preference to a full-size carriage in the peak season. However, on 6 July 1911 Aitchison reported, 'Whilst in Wales [10-17 June] the carriage which had been repaired by Messrs Holme & King was returned,' which leaves no room for doubt. The reason for the repair is unknown but this might have been the first vehicle, if there was more than one so treated, to have the

panel glazed between the guard's coupé and the passenger compartment. It might also have been the first vehicle to have had its roof boards removed.

There has been some confusion about the number of carriages obtained in 1923. A report in the *Locomotive* states that there were three, Société Industrielle Suisse records, not seen by the author, apparently list four. In the earliest minuted reference to new carriages, 1 December 1922, Davies had 'suggested that the Swiss Locomotive Company might be invited to tender for the supply of two coaches,' and on 14 April 1923, 'It was reported that a formal contract had been entered into with the Swiss Locomotive Company for the construction of two new coaches,' which seems unequivocal. Photographs of No 9 loaded for delivery are dated 30 August 1923 although it and No 8 reached Llanberis too late to be used in the 1923 season. In common with the 1896 Lancaster stock, they had seating for 56 in seven compartments, with three more in the

At Clogwyn in 1927, a comparison of two Lancaster carriages with their roofboards removed and the company name written along the underframe, not long before the name was changed. The vehicle in the foreground has had the panel separating the coupé from the passenger compartment fully glazed. The difficulty in identifying the carriages, because their numbers were either not carried or could not be seen, makes it impossible to say if this one was unique. A picture on page 145 shows a carriage that not only has the coupé panel glazed but the two side panels too.

SIS carriage No 9 loaded for transporting to Llanberis on 30 August 1923. (SMR)

Carriages in the livery introduced in the 1950s. An underframe on the platform awaits attention.

guard's coupé. J.I.C. Boyd said that during the war these carriages were equipped with underfloor water tanks for supplying the summit and implied that they had been removed before 1980.

Stabled outside throughout the year the carriage bodies did not receive the maintenance they deserved. J.I.C. Boyd said that rebuilding was started on 'a small scale' before the war but gave no evidence and none has been found. A comprehensive programme that saw all the carriages fully enclosed and glazed was started in 1947. It took place in stages, probably in the light of experience and perhaps the passengers were more likely to complain than they had been. Firstly, the coupé was partially glazed, then the saloons were glazed in between the doors before, finally, the doors were made full height. Because the vehicle numbers are not visible in most photographs it is not possible to track the changes. It may be that some carriages went from being fully open to being fully enclosed in one move. Aerials were mounted above the front windscreens

from 1996. The guard's windows were equipped with a hand-worked windscreen wipers around 2000; No 10 had two wipers from new.

In common with the locomotives, the original carriage livery was not recorded. Given that the decorative motifs seen in photographs of the original carriages was unlikely ever to have been applied in Llanberis, the original paintwork does seem to have been remarkably long-lived. In 1933 Davies reported that four carriages had been repainted, red, grey, green and orange. R.W. Kidner, writing in 1937, said the carriage livery was red or grey. According to J.I.C. Boyd the 1923 carriages were painted red with white lining. A picture postcard posted in 1939 shows one of these carriages painted in a light colour without lining that might well be grey. The author guesses that the orange one was the first to be repainted.

J.I.C. Boyd said that the carriages were painted red in the 1930s, grey during the war and green in 1949. Brown and brown and off-white vehicles ran during the

1950s. By 1960 all had been painted 'cherry red and cream', a scheme that was retained with minor variations until the Garmendale carriages entered service in 2012/3.

Some photographs from the 1930s show the carriages with a roundel in the centre panel although none are sufficiently clear to reveal any detail. In the 1980s plastic stickers carrying the railway's name were affixed to the leading ends; some carriages also had these stickers on their sides.

Originally the carriages had their numbers painted on the front solebar. At least one of the Lancaster carriages had its number painted on the rear body, just above the buffer, but it is not known if this was as well as the number on the front or instead of it. In a similar manner, No 9 had its number painted to the right of its buffer.

Latterly, the original carriages had their fleet numbers painted on the back of the vehicles, at shoulder height, platform side

when loading at Llanberis. From the 1980s until circa 2001 they were painted on the front of the vehicle. When delivered, the 1923-built carriages had their numbers, 8 and 9, and the railway's name painted on their solebars, but this probably did not last beyond their first repaint. At some stage, perhaps during the 1950s rebuilding programme, the carriages were renumbered, the Lancaster carriages becoming Nos 2-5 and 8 and the 1923-built vehicles Nos 6 and 7.

The East Lancashire Coach Builders Ltd carriage was No 10, its maker's number GM1229. In 2013 it was adapted for use as a summit support vehicle (SSV). Retaining 16 of its 56 seats, it carries staff and goods to the summit, one of its doors being modified to accommodate commercial-grade wheelie bins and two underfloor 500 litre tanks added to carry fuel for Hafod Eryri's generators. The vehicle is painted in a plain green livery. The surplus

No 4 and carriage No 9 at Llanberis. There is some evidence of lining on the locomotive's tank. (York Radford)

The former carriage No 10 adapted to the role of summit support vehicle (SSV), capable of carrying personnel, stores, oil and industrial wheelie bins to and from the summit. It was seen being unloaded on 6 July 2014. The location of the oil tanks can be seen in the centre of the vehicle.

underframes and the out-of-service steam locomotives 5, 7 and 8 were placed in secure storage off-site.

The first four Garmendale carriages have their fleet numbers painted on the left of the front solebar. The two 'heritage' carriages, *Snowdon Lily* and *The Snowdon Mountain Goat*, are unnumbered. The steel body frames of these vehicles are trimmed with iroko, an African hardwood that references the appearance of the original carriages. Iroko was also used for the seats. As well as the underframes and bogies these carriages also make use of original door handles.

The Hunslet Engine Company supplied new carriage bogies in 1986. The design was improved in 2006 for the bogies used on carriage No 10 and the summit bogie wagon and again for the Garmendale stock. This batch was built by Hunslet's then owner, LH Group, at Barton under Needwood, near Burton-on-Trent.

In the workshop an ambulance bogie is used when a carriage bogie is removed

for maintenance. In 2009 the timber frame, clearly of some vintage, was replaced by a steel frame.

The Lancaster open carriage was converted to be a works car at the time the 1935 summit building was built, primarily for carrying water and other goods to the summit. Known as 'the truck' by staff, the earliest description and photographs of it are in Morris (see Bibliography); it was equipped with an enclosed caboose for personnel at its leading end, a 1-ton-capacity coal bunker and a demountable 400 gallon water tank. Initially the tank was stored at Llanberis during the winter. By 1964 (P. Ransome-Wallis) the personnel cabin had been rebuilt. For many years, this vehicle invariably formed the first train of the day, carrying blockmen, only one since the loops at Hebron and Halfway were automated, and summit personnel to their posts as well as the summit supplies. Oil replaced coal as the summit fuel following the 1982 refurbishment. The availability of the 2006-built Hunslet wagon to carry the

The interior of one of the Garmendale carriages, 16 November 2012.

The guard's control panel shows that the Garmendale carriages are quite sophisticated.

Delivery of the first of the heritage carriages, *The Snowdon Lily*, in May 2013. (SMR)

The interior of *The Snowdon Lily*.

The carriage ambulance bogie being renewed with a steel underframe, 22 May 2009.

No 6 and 'the truck' run alongside the Afon Hwch as they return from the summit with a wagonload of rubbish.

Seen from the summit works access road bridge over the Afon Hwch on 1 July 2012, the rebuilt truck with its new caboose and generator. A track was laid over the road bridge into the car park in 2020.

No 2 with two four-wheel wagons on 29 May 1967, when there was supposed to be only one surviving.

summit supplies in larger volumes allowed this vehicle to be rebuilt again, with a larger caboose and a mobile generator.

The other open carriage was also said to have been adapted for works use during the 1930s. J.I.C. Boyd said that he saw it in 1946 but was only able to sketch it; his description does not fit either of the photographs taken by O.J. Morris or P. Ransome-Wallis. Morris, presumably writing in 1950 and who travelled on and photographed a works train, did not mention seeing two similar vehicles so most likely it had been scrapped by then.

Although the four-wheeled wagons were used on construction trains, the SMR promoters also had expectation of freight traffic, providing sidings at Waterfall and Hebron. The traffic failed to materialise and now only one of the wagons survives. Only two had been useable by the early 1930s (J.I.C. Boyd) and the last one was derelict when O.J. Morris saw it in 1950, a statement he repeated in 1960. However, a photograph shows it in use, complete with brake, in 1956. By 1964 (P. Ransome-Wallis) it was 'used for many purposes'. It is not known when its brake was removed. Originally, the wagons were numbered in their own sequence.

To supply the summit building with fuel for its generators a bunded tank, seen here being loaded on 30 April 2010, was used, this procedure being superseded by the summit support vehicle (ex No 10) being fitted with underfloor oil tanks.

PROFIT, DIVIDENDS AND PASSENGERS 1895–2018

	Profit/Loss £	Dividend %	Passengers	Summit visits
1895	-	-		
1896	-	-	150 (est)	
1897	499	-		
1898	475	-		
1899	943	-		
1900	292	-		
1901	624	-		
1902	N/A	-		
1903	-615	-		
1904	-304	-		
1905	365	-		
1906	N/A	-		
1907	-97	-		
1908	-453	-		
1909	1,020	-		
1910	314	1		
1911	1,136	½		
1912	446	-		
1913	1,582	-		
1914	N/A	-		
1915	605	-		
1916	206	-		
1917	N/A	-		
1918	-958	-		
1919	4,624	-		
1920	4,649	-		
1921	3,935	-		
1922	5,342	-		
1923	2,967	-		
1924	3,256	-		
1925	5,397	-		
1926	5,512	-		

	Profit/Loss £	Dividend %	Passengers	Summit visits
1927	5,321	-		
1928	6,532	-		
1929	6,418	-		
1930	4,773	-		
1931	3,750*	-		
1932	5,624	-		
1933	6,474	5		
1934	5,141	5		
1935	5,664	5		
1936	5,633	5		
1937	6,263	5		
1938	6,469	5		
1939	4,955	-		
1940	-1,881	-		
1941	338	-		
1942	1,503	-		
1943	1,500	-		
1944	1,411	-		
1945	3,487	-		
1946	3,667	2½		
1947	4,572	2½		
1948	2,606	3		
1949	4,760	4½		
1950	4,342	4½		
1951	3,654	3		
1952	4,933	7		
1953	4,762	7		
1954	3,128	4		
1955	7,078	7		
1956	1,777	3		
1957	4,224	6		
1958	5,904	6		
1959	10,294	8		
1960	11,403	8		
1961	12,809	12		
1962	5,967	12		
1963	2,922	12		
1964				
1965				
1966				

	Profit/Loss £	Dividend %	Passengers	Summit visits
1967				
1968				
1969				
1970				
1971				
1972	22,285	12		
1973	21,485	14	92,280	
1974	18,879	5		
1975	13,653	9	99,695	
1976	19,753	9	99,695	
1977	20,773	9		
1978	22,183	10		
1979	-39,630	6		
1980	-37,246	-		
1981	7,747	-	68,525	
1982	4,009	-		
1983	75,180	4		
1984	104,948	6	86,541	
1985	78,719	-	76,539	
1986	11,615	-	85,204	
1987	34,791	-	88,933	
1988	13,764	-	97,578	
1989	98,560	-	120,826	
1990	73,388	-	122,172	
1991	-263,252	22.5		
1992	116,647	22.5		
1993	120,380	22.5		
1994	156,595	22.5		
1995	209,579	30	141,790	
1996	152,402	30	156,944	
1997	157,699	30	147,981	
1998	129,776	-	141,000	
1999	192,707	-		
2000	N/A	N/A		
2001	N/A	N/A		
2002	N/A	N/A		
2003	N/A	N/A		
2004	N/A	N/A	130,657	
2005	N/A	N/A	140,948	
2006	N/A	N/A	131,069	

	Profit/Loss £	Dividend %	Passengers	Summit visits
2007	N/A	N/A	126,732	
2008	N/A	N/A	123,703	
2009	N/A	N/A	157,570	
2010	N/A	N/A	142,199	
2011	N/A	N/A	143,244	
2012	N/A	N/A	131,413	
2013	N/A	N/A	110,378	
2014	N/A	N/A	131,144	445,890
2015	N/A	N/A	132,252	449,657
2016	N/A	N/A	117,077	465,000
2017	N/A	N/A	130,266	654,077
2018	N/A	N/A	140,000	

The loco shed on on 30 August 1936. It is not known when the building's left wing, it was not the full length of the building, was altered to accommodate a carriage, nor when it was extended - the location was not rail connected. The track layout shown probably dated from 1896; it was altered later to ease the curvature. (H.C. Casserley)

TIMETABLES 1898 AND 1901

Snowdon Mountain Tramroad.

TIME TABLE FOR JUNE.

Stations.	a.m.	a.m.	p.m. A	p.m.	p.m. B
Llanberis............dep.	7 30	10 15	12 45	2 10	3 45
* Waterfall .... „	7 36	10 21	12 53	2 16	3 51
Hebron.............. „	7 48	10 33	1 2	2 28	4 3
Halfway .... „	8 6	10 51	1 26	2 46	4 21
Clogwyn .... „	8 24	11 9	1 38	3 4	4 39
Summit (Y Wyddfa) ar.	8 42	11 27	1 56	3 22	4 56
	a.m.	p.m.	p.m.	p.m.	p.m.
Summit „ dep.	8 50	12 8	2 10	3 45	5 5
Clogwyn .... „	9 8	12 26	2 28	4 3	5 23
Halfway .... „	9 26	12 44	2 46	4 21	5 41
Hebron............. „	9 44	1 2	3 4	4 39	5 59
* Waterfall .... „	9 56	1 13	3 16	4 50	6 17
Llanberis...........arr.	10 2	1 19	3 22	4 56	6 23

Trains in columns marked A and B are specials, and run only when required.

* Passengers for Waterfall Station must inform the Guard.

No Sunday trains.

G. C. AITCHISON, General Manager.

June 1898

Snowdon Mountain Tramroad.

TIME TABLE FOR JULY, AUGUST, SEPTEMBER.

Stations.	a.m.	a.m.	A p.m.	p.m.	B p.m.
Llanberis............dep.	7 30	10 15	11 9	1 42	4 0
* Waterfall .... „	7 36	10 21	11 15	1 48	4 6
Hebron.............. „	7 48	10 33	11 24	1 57	4 18
Halfway .... „	8 6	10 51	11 39	2 12	†4 36
Clogwyn .... „	8 24	11 9	11 57	2 29	5 2
Summit (Y Wyddfa) ar.	8 42	11 22	12 15	2 47	5 20
	a.m.	p.m.	p.m.	p.m.	p.m
Summit „ dep.	8 50	11 39	12 39	3 23	5 30
Clogwyn ... . „	9 6	11 57	12 57	3 41	5 48
Halfway .... „	9 26	12 12	‡1 12	3 59	6 3
Hebron............. „	9 44	12 27	1 32	4 17	6 18
* Waterfall .... „	9 50	12 33	1 45	4 23	6 24
Llanberis...........arr.	10 2	12 42	1 54	4 35	6 33

* Passengers for Waterfall Station must inform the Guard. † Departs 4.47 p.m. ‡ Departs 1.24 p.m.

Train marked A runs in connection with L. & N.W. special excursion trains from Llandudno and coast stations. B—Saturdays excepted.

In addition to the above, special trains leave Llanberis at 12.10 p.m., 12.54 p.m., and 2.47 p.m., and these run only when required in consequence of large number of passengers.

G. C. AITCHISON, General Manager.

July-September 1898

Snowdon Mountain Tramroad.

TIME TABLE FOR OCTOBER.

L. & N.W. RAILWAY	a.m.		p.m.
Bangor .... .dep.	8 52	...	12 3
Carnarvon............... „	9 25	...	12 40
Llanberis .... arr.	9 56	...	1 11
SNOWDON MT. TRAM.			
Llanberis .... dep.	10 40	...	2 0
* Waterfall .... „	10 46	...	2 6
Hebron .... „	10 58	...	2 18
Halfway .... „	11 16	...	2 36
Clogwyn .... „	11 34	...	2 54
Snowdon Summit ...arr.	11 50	...	3 10
	p.m.		p.m.
Snowdon Summit ...dep.	12 8	...	3 28
Clogwyn .... „	12 24	...	3 44
Halfway ... . „	12 42	...	4 2
Hebron .... „	1 0	...	4 20
* Waterfall .... „	1 12	...	4 32
Llanberis .... arr.	1 18	...	4 38
L. & N.W. RAILWAY.			
Llanberis .... dep.	2 5	...	6 0
Carnarvon............... „	2 30	...	6 25
Bangor .... arr.	3 0	...	6 59

* Passengers for Waterfall Station must inform the Guard.

The running of these trains being subject to weather and other causes permitting, the Company retain the right of discontinuing any or all of them without further notice.

G. C. AITCHISON, General Manager.

October 1898

Snowdon Mountain Tramroad.

Working Time Table commencing April 6th, weather and other circumstances permitting.

Llanberis depart	10 40	2 16
Waterfall	10 45	2 22
Hebron	10 58	2 34
Half Way	11 16	2 52
Clogwyn	11 34	3 10
Snowdon Summit arrive....	11 52	3 28
Snowdon Summit depart ..	12 18	3 46
Clogwyn	12 36	4 4
Half Way	12 54	4 22
Hebron	1 12	4 40
Waterfall	1 20	4 48
Llanberis arrive	1 30	4 58

April 1901

Snowdon Mountain Tramroad.

Working Time Table for June
weather and other circumstances permitting.

			a.		a.
Llanberis, dep ...	7 30	1025	1245	2 10	3 30
Waterfall ...	7 36	1031	1253	2 16	3 36
Hebron ...	7 48	1043	1 2	2 28	3 45
Half-Way ...	8 6	11 1	1 20	2 46	4 0
Clogwyn ...	8 24	1119	1 38	3 4	4 18
Snowdon Summit, a	8 42	1137	1 56	3 22	4 36

			a.		a.
Snowdon Summit, dp.	8 50	12 8	2 10	4 0	4 46
Clogwyn ...	9 8	1226	2 28	4 18	5 4
Half-Way ...	9 26	1244	2 46	4 36	5 24
Hebron ...	9 44	1 2	3 4	4 52	5 39
Waterfall ...	9 56	1 13	3 12	5 0	5 47
Llanberis, arr. ...	10 2	1 19	3 18	5 7	5 53

a—These trains are only run when required, in consequence of large number of Passengers.

June 1901

Snowdon Mountain Tramroad

Working Time Table for July
weather and other circumstances permitting.

			a.	a.			a.
Llanberis, d,	7 30	1045	1210	1254	1 52	3 0	4 0
Waterfall ...	7 36	1050	1216	1 0	1 58	3 5	4 6
Hebron ...	7 48	11 0	1227	1 9	2 12	3 15	4 13
Half-Way ...	8 6	1115	1247	1 24	2 27	3 30	4 33
Clogwyn ...	8 24	1132	1 2	1 42	2 42	3 46	4 48
Snowdon S a	8 42	1150	1 18	2 0	3 0	4 4	5 6

			a.	a.			a.
Snowdon S d	8 50	1215	1 24	2 24	3 23	4 30	5 30
Clogwyn ...	9 6	1232	1 42	2 42	3 46	4 48	5 48
Half-Way ...	9 26	1247	1 57	2 57	4 1	5 5	6 6
Hebron ...	9 44	1 9	2 12	3 15	4 19	5 20	6 21
Waterfall ...	9 50	1 19	2 22	3 25	4 29	5 30	6 31
Llanberis, a	10 2	1 24	2 27	3 30	4 34	5 36	6 37

a—These trains are only run when required, in consequence of large number of Passengers.

July 1901

Snowdon Mountain Tramroad.

Working Time Table for September.
weather and other circumstances permitting.

			a.	a.			a.
Llanberis, d,	7 30	1045	1210	1254	1 52	3 0	4 0
Waterfall ...	7 36	1050	1216	1 0	1 58	3 5	4 6
Hebron ...	7 48	11 0	1227	1 9	2 12	3 15	4 13
Half-Way ...	8 6	1115	1247	1 24	2 27	3 30	4 33
Clogwyn ...	8 24	1132	1 2	1 42	2 42	3 46	4 48
Snowdon S a	8 42	1150	1 18	2 0	3 0	4 4	5 6

			a.	a.			a.
Snowdon S d	8 50	1215	1 24	2 24	3 23	4 30	5 30
Clogwyn ...	9 6	1232	1 42	2 42	3 46	4 48	5 48
Half-Way ...	9 26	1247	1 57	2 57	4 1	5 5	6 6
Hebron ...	9 44	1 9	2 12	3 15	4 19	5 20	6 21
Waterfall ...	9 50	1 19	2 22	3 25	4 29	5 30	6 31
Llanberis, a	10 2	1 24	2 27	3 30	4 34	5 36	6 37

a—These trains are only run when required, in consequence of large number of Passengers.

September 1901

Car park tickets for Llanberis and Aberglaslyn. The upper part of the Llanberis voucher is gummed, to be affixed to the vehicle. The lower portion had to be surrendered before the vehicle could be removed.

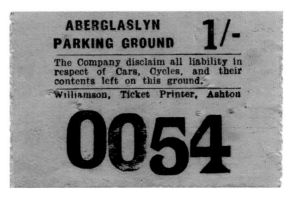

INCIDENTS REPORTED TO THE OFFICE OF THE RAIL REGULATOR 2002–2004

Date	Location	Details
22 July 2002	Clogwyn	Loco No 12, part of a doubler with No 9, left Clogwyn loop to make the descent to Llanberis and derailed on manual points. Blockman had issued written authority to proceed to the guard of No 12 before ensuring the points were in the correct position.
17 August 2002	Llanberis	Steam loco No 2 moved with its carriage from the arrivals platform to the coaling siding after it had unloaded passengers. The driver firstly having removed the interlock on the manual main line point placed the point to enter the siding the loco and carriages were then driven into the coal siding for refueling but the points were failed to returned back to the main line. The point remained set against the incoming main line and resulted in derailment.
24 July 2002	Llanberis	Steam loco No 3 being shunted to arrivals platform at Llanberis failed to stop sufficiently short of the buffers allowing the loco's raised rear canopy to come into contact with the shop viewing window. Two passengers in the shop received cuts from flying glass.
31 March 2004	Llanberis	Fire broke out on loco stabled overnight in loco shed. Footplate wooden floor destroyed and back timber of cab. Caused by flame blow back from beneath the fire box of No 3 sometime in the evening ignited wood planking on foot plate which set alight small amount of coal still left in the bunker.
22 September 2004	Hebron	Trailing bogie of carriage No 3 left the rails at the upper point at Hebron. As soon as incident had become apparent the engineering crew loaded up the rescue train with required tools and lifting equipment to get carriage back on track. The passengers were transferred to the rescue train and returned to Llanberis. When the carriage was returned to rails engineering crew were happy that the carriage was safe to return to Llanberis where it was inspected. On inspection the upper points mechanism was found to have caused the accident and the permanent way foreman identified the possible cause as an excess movement on a connecting bracket that could have allowed the points blades to open and pull the bogie off the track.

INCIDENTS REPORTED TO THE RAIL INCIDENT INVESTIGATION BRANCH 2006–19

Date	Details	Location
24 November 2005	Derailment of truck	Halfway
6 March 2006	Permanent way truck disengaged from rack	Llanberis
30 August 2006	Train collision with contractor vehicle	Llanberis
15 May 2007	Heritage train division at Hebron	Hebron
15 June 2007	Derailment of flatbed wagon between Llanberis and Hebron	Llanberis
18 March 2010	Derailment of a coach	Llanberis
14 April 2010	Derailment of heritage train	Llanberis
5 August 2011	Derailment of passenger train	Halfway
20 September 2013	Low speed derailment	Hebron
18 May 2014	Derailment	Halfway
6 September 2015	Collision	Halfway
10 July 2017	Derailment of locomotive at No. 2 points	Llanberis
19 June 2018	Derailment	Halfway
19 April 2019	Passenger train derailment	Clogwyn

PLANNING APPLICATIONS TO SNOWDONIA NATIONAL PARK AUTHORITY

NP3/12/34B	2 March 2001	24 July 2001	Installation of new septic tank to serve Snowdon summit café	Summit
NP3/12/34D	7 July 2003	21 January 2004	Redevelopment of and refurbishment of existing summit building with new café, shop and kitchen areas with amenities using existing retaining wall to the east and existing slab where possible, relocation of train platforms and tracks	Summit
NP3/15/181	3 July 2006	14 September 2006	Holding area for materials associated with re-building Snowdon summit visitor facility	Clogwyn
NP3/15/181A	7 March 2007	19 April 2007	Remove existing wooden telegraph pole type trackside signalling mast and install replacement aluminium mast	Clogwyn
NP3/15/181B	2 May 2007	9 July 2007	Siting of mobile catering unit while Snowdon summit café is being rebuilt *	Clogwyn
NP3/15/180A	11 November 2008	6 January 2009	Removal of Condition 2 of Planning Consent NP3/15/180 dated 10/04/2006 to allow permanent retention of temporary bridge	Llanberis
NP3/15/180B	14 June 2010	3 August 2010	Installation of a 12,000 litre diesel tank	Llanberis
NP3/15/180C	21 February 2014	31 March 2014	Installation of steel framed polytunnel *	Llanberis
NP3/15/AD180D	8 October 2014	18 November 2014	Application of advertisement consent to display one information panel	Llanberis
NP3/15/180F	18 August 2017	5 October 2017	Erection of single storey extension to provide new male/female and disabled toilet facilities	Llanberis
NP3/15/180H	23 September 2019	11 November 2019	Construction of staff car park *	Llanberis
NP3/15/180J	1 April 2020	1 May 2020	Change of use from theatre (Class D2) to exhibition space (Class D1) and external alterations	Llanberis

* application refused

GENERAL MANAGERS

Gowrie Colquhoun Aitchison 1895-1910
John Richard Owen 1910-34
David Henry Roberts 1934-41, plus seasonal cover during the war
Philip Harris Jackson 1946-50
Robert John Williams 1951-70
Claude Francis Jackson 1970-81
Derek Rogerson 1981-95
Tony Hopkins 1995-2001
Alan Kendall 2001-18

Snowdon guide Moses Williams established his temperance hut at Halfway in 1873, offering the weary visitor tea, coffee and ginger beer, 'fresh daily.' Opposition from the Vaynol estate caused him to withdraw a license application in 1875. In 1887 supper, bed and breakfast was offered for 2s. Williams died at his son's house in Waunfawr in 1899, aged 86.

BIBLIOGRAPHY

Abt, R.S., 'The Snowdon Mountain Tramroad', *The Locomotive*, 15 July 1931

Boyd, J.I.C., *Narrow Gauge Railways in North Caernarvonshire*, Oakwood Press, 1981

Fenton, R.S., *Cambrian Coasters – steam and motor coaster owners of North and West Wales*, World Ship Society, 1989

Freeman, Michael David, 'Early Tourists in Wales', *sublimewales.wordpress.com*

'Indicator', The Snowdon Mountain Tramroad, *Railway Magazine*, Vol 57, 1925

Johnson, Peter, 'By Rack to the Abode of Eagles - the Snowdon Mountain Railway', *Railway World*, March 1989

Johnson, Peter, *An Illustrated History of the Festiniog Railway*, Oxford Publishing Co, 2007

Johnson, Peter, *An Illustrated History of the Snowdon Mountain Railway*, Oxford Publishing Co, 2010

Johnson, Peter, *An Illustrated History of the Welsh Highland Railway*, Oxford Publishing Co, 2nd Edition 2009

Johnson, Peter, *Festiniog Railway: From Slate Railway to Heritage Operation 1921-2014*, Pen & Sword Transport, 2017

Johnson, Peter, *Festiniog Railway: The Spooner Era and After 1830-1920*, Pen & Sword Transport, 2017

Johnson, Peter, 'Henry Joseph Jack - a re-appraisal', *Festiniog Railway Heritage Group Journal*, No 126 Summer 2016

Johnson, Peter, 'In search of Sir John Henderson Stewart Bt', *Festiniog Railway Heritage Group Journal*, No 125 Spring 2016

Johnson, Peter, *Rebuilding the Welsh Highland Railway: Britain's longest heritage line*, Pen & Sword Transport, 2018

Johnson, Peter, The Davies family and its railway interests, *Festiniog Railway Heritage Group Journal*, No 109, Spring 2012

Jones, Norman, *Snowdon Mountain Railway Llanberis*, Foxline Publishing, 1998

Jones, Eric & Gwyn, David, *Dolgarrog - an industrial history*, Gwynedd Archives, 1989

[Keylock, John], Gowrie Colquhoun Aitchison – AMICE, FCIS, 1863-1928, *Welsh Highland Heritage*, No 8, June 2000

Morris, O.J., *Snowdon Mountain Railway*, Ian Allan, 1951, revised 1960

Partington, John, 'The Snowdon Mountain Railway', *Railway Magazine*, Vol 1, 1897

Pearson, F.K., *The Isle of Man Tramways*, David & Charles, 1970

Ransome-Wallis, P., *Snowdon Mountain Railway*, Ian Allan, 1964, revised 1967, 1969

Snowdon & Welsh Highland Holiday Book, Snowdon Mountain Tramroad & Hotels Co Ltd, 1923

Snowdon Mountain Railway Llanberis offer for subscription, Hichens, Harrison & Company, 1985

Snowdon – Snowdon Mountain Railway Souvenir Brochure, Snowdon Mountain Railway, [2003]

Turner, Keith, *The Snowdon Mountain Railway*, David & Charles, 1973

Turner, Keith, *The Snowdon Mountain Railway*, Tempus Publishing, 2001

INDEX

A PHOTGRAPHIC ADDENDUM

A portrait of No 4 outside the loco shed at Llanberis. Its chimney has gained an unusual cowl since it was delivered; see photograph on page 73.

A view of the summit with a trainload of newly arrived visitors in the inter-war years. Notable are the original station building with no render on its walls and details of the summit huts' construction, and the roofing felt partially torn away from one of them by the weather. (Photochrom)

An unusual view of Clogwyn circa 1930. In the background are Llanberis lake and the Dinorwic galleries and slate tips.

OWDON RLY. AT ROCKY VALLEY ABOVE LLANBERIS PASS.

A late 1930s view of a train passing the site of the later Rocky Valley Halt. (Photochrom)

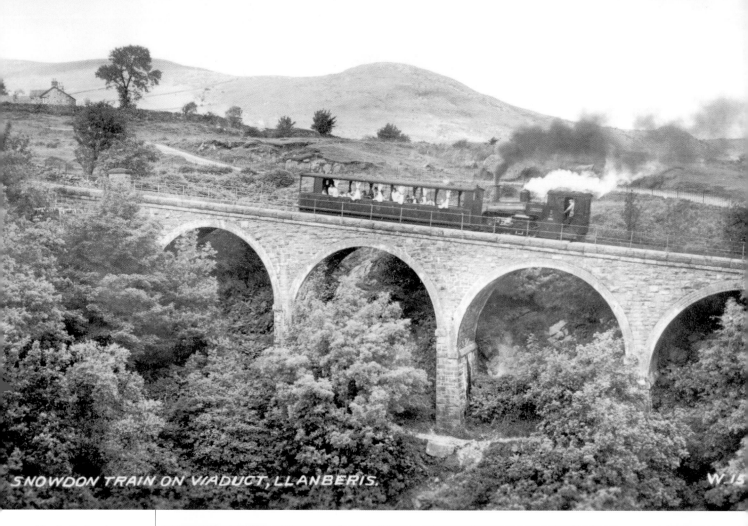

SNOWDON TRAIN ON VIADUCT, LLANBERIS.   W.15

No 6 climbs the upper viaduct with one of the Swiss carriages in 1939. (James Valentine)

Some time in the 1950s an American visitor found No 3 looking uncared for in brown livery, its chimney and smokebox door showing signs of overheating burning the paint off.

In contrast to the view of No3, in this July 1968 photograph No 2 looks well cared for apart from some paint damage on its dome. One of the council houses build on the former railway land at Ddol Isaf can be seen on the far side of the river.

No 7 at Clogwyn on 6 July 1975. The mast on the hut signifies the railway's adoption of radio control.

No 3 with a heritage steam service climbing towards the summit, seen from the heights of the Dinorwic slate quarries in September 2019. (Chris Parry)